D1569562

Masquerade

SCRIPTURALIZATION

DISCOURSE, FORMATION, POWER

Series Editor

Vincent L. Wimbush

This series aims to advance creative and provocative transdisciplinary thinking and conversation about, original research projects into, and wide dissemination of, the patho-, social-cultural-, and economic-political-logics and reverberations of mimetic practices, social relations, orientations that have been conceptualized by the independent scholarly research group called The Institute for Signifying Scriptures (ISS) (www.signifyingscriptures.org) and shorthanded by the term "scripturalization."

Titles in the series

Masquerade

Scripturalizing Modernities through Black Flesh

Edited by

Vincent L. Wimbush

LEXINGTON BOOKS/FORTRESS ACADEMIC
Lanham • Boulder • New York • London

Published by Lexington Books/Fortress Academic
Lexington Books is an imprint of The Rowman & Littlefield Publishing Group, Inc.
4501 Forbes Boulevard, Suite 200, Lanham, Maryland 20706
www.rowman.com

86-90 Paul Street, London EC2A 4NE, United Kingdom

British Library Cataloguing in Publication Information Available

Library of Congress Cataloging-in-Publication Data

Names: Wimbush, Vincent L., 1954– editor.
Title: Masquerade : scripturalizing modernities through Black flesh / edited by Vincent
    L. Wimbush ; foreword by Richard Manly Adams.
Description: Lanham : Lexington Books/Fortress Academic, [2023] | Series:
    Scripturalization: discourse, formation, power | Includes bibliographical references
    and index. | Summary: "This book focuses on the hyper-scripturalization (or
    the persistent degradation) of Black flesh, with the phenomenon of masquerade
    conceptualized as analytical wedge that makes a compelling case for seeing how our
    ongoing modern realities, with mixed and too often devastating consequences, are
    constructed"— Provided by publisher.
Identifiers: LCCN 2023014518 (print) | LCCN 2023014519 (ebook) | ISBN
    9781978715127 (cloth ; alk. paper) | ISBN 9781978715134 (epub)
Subjects: LCSH: Black race. | Black people—Social conditions. | Racism against Black
    people—History. | Slave narratives.
Classification: LCC HT1581 .M27 2023 (print) | LCC HT1581 (ebook) | DDC
    305.896—dc23/eng/20230417
LC record available at https://lccn.loc.gov/2023014518
LC ebook record available at https://lccn.loc.gov/2023014519

Contents

Foreword

Richard Manly Adams Jr.

I am often asked what will become of the role of an academic library given the ubiquity of the technologies in the digital world. The 2021 collaboration between Dr. Vincent L. Wimbush, the team of scholars he assembled, and the librarians of Pitts Theology Library (Emory University) which created an online exhibition and digital symposium that are documented and celebrated here, is an important answer to that question. Through this work, we celebrate the transition of libraries away from functioning merely as geographically-limited repositories and spaces, locations where the isolated scholarly enterprise would occur, accessible only to those with the privilege of the means to travel and the training to research. The collaboration reflected in these pages and in the online exhibition "Masquerade" and accompanying two-day symposium in November 2021 shows what libraries are becoming: catalysts for conversation, portals inviting diverse patrons to discover resources and insights that may be spread across the globe.[1]

Most tend to define a library by its physical collections. And the physical holdings of Pitts Theology Library certainly were essential to this project, centered, of course, on the library's holdings of Equiano's *Interesting Narrative*.[2] Many of Pitts's and Emory's holdings have been digitized and are presented in the online exhibition and serve as points of reflection in these essays. But the library's contribution to this project is far greater than digitizing its books. Instead, the library provided a platform for conversation between texts, images, scholars, and the general public. By drawing upon the library's technical expertise, the research capacity of the librarians, and tools like Pitts's Digital Collections and Exhibitions site, Dr. Wimbush has found a way to teach and shape learners in a new way. By integrating the visual arts, archival records, and audio-visual recordings, with the printed page, Dr. Wimbush's digital exhibition, entitled "Masquerade: Scripturalizing

Modernities through Black Flesh," engages the senses in ways the printed page cannot, creating an affective experience that does not merely argue a point as one might in a lecture or books. The effect is to invite a viewer to reach his or her own conclusions about how worlds, be they that of an eighteenth century formerly enslaved person or of those living in America today, are constructs, systems put together over time by individuals and organizations, and that all of us, though some in ways very different than others, continue to put on the masquerade, to play certain games to fit in, to have our voices heard, and in many cases, to survive.

This scholarship is a model of the conversations libraries are uniquely positioned to foster. The exhibition is the product of Dr. Wimbush's vision and the hard work and creativity of colleagues at Pitts, including Ann McShane (digitization), Brinna Michael (metadata), Spencer Roberts (digital systems), Anne Marie McLean (graphic design), and Jamie Bostick (communications, marketing, and logistics). Wimbush masterfully uses the visual elements made possible through digitization and the magic of the internet to create an exhibition that lays bare the games that have been and continue to be played and guides visitors to look around and consider anew how the world works, and the librarians have preserved this work and made it accessible for years to come. I am thankful to have been a part of this collaboration; I am hopeful that generations will continue to learn from it through these essays and the open-access online content; and I am proud to promote this example of scholarship as a model for libraries in the digital age.

NOTES

1. The digital exhibition is available at http://pitts.tl/masquerade. On that site, visitors will also find archived versions of all presentations from the two-day symposium.

2. Among other holdings, Pitts Theology Library holds an early Dutch translation of the narrative (see https://search.libraries.emory.edu/catalog/9937349058102486). The text of Equiano's work is available in an open-access format from Project Gutenberg: https://www.gutenberg.org/files/15399/15399-h/15399-h.htm.

Acknowledgments

I should like to express my appreciation to all those who supported and facilitated the Emory University Candler School of Theology Exhibition and Symposium that are the basis for the essays in this volume.

Although the theme, focus, and organization of the Exhibition were my decisions, Dr. Richard M. Adams Jr., director of the Pitts Library, proposed the idea of the Exhibition, to be based around my scholarly interests. He and his staff (Ann McShane, Brinna Michael, Anne Marie McLean, and Jamie Bostick) provided from beginning to end the professional and technical support to make the project a successful one.

The participants in the Symposium proved to be professional, creative, and stimulating interlocutors all. I am grateful for the opportunity to work again with some of them, for the first time with some others. Their revised Symposium contributions are included as essays in this book.

I remain grateful to Roddy for her love and support and smart and inspirational counsel.

Introduction

"Everything about Me Was Magic": The Black-Fleshed and the Making and Management of Modernities[1]

Vincent L. Wimbush

The project that has facilitated this book I prefer to call—if not the *non-*, perhaps, more accurately—the *meta-*, "Exhibition." It is most certainly a complex, contrapuntal project insofar as it does not have simple aims; it does not propose, for example, simply to showcase the traditional and dominant cultural-political order's treasures—to be sure, ancient Greek and Roman/ Mediterranean, and so forth—with Emory University as synecdoche (for the historical imperial/European-North Americanist/colonial/U.S. nationalist/ elite cultural-academic-institutional site or theatre). What would normally or historically obtain for such a situation is the showcasing/curation of manuscripts, printed books, images, but also other objects, indeed—going far back but also not so far at all from our own time (after European and other imperial-colonial campaigns)—even including, it is chilling to mention, the flesh, sometimes dead, other times alive, of the "discovered" or invented (human) Others. Many items among such "discovered," or "found," or invented Others were stolen, certainly restrained and conscripted, then impaneled/boxed/fixed, then exhibited as such. Different objects were historically and normally exhibited for the purpose of advancing the interests and representations of the stable order dominant, the imperial-colonial-cum-nationalist agenda of showcasing, hence, nervously internalizing and naturalizing a stable story or ideology and its politics. Such efforts in the service of naturalization of stability on the part of political and social-cultural regimes have in the presentation of their "found" objects or symbols through the projects of curation or museumization/monumentalization (all part of what I have preferred to call for moderns scripturalization) or other types of performativity at court or in the public or private high cultural institutions established and fixed the "reality"/"unity."

I am in making this argument thinking of and with the fascinating theoretical work of social and cultural theorist Tony Bennett (and others) on modern museums and other cultural institutions that engage in the work of finding or fabricating objects and entities for the sake of "governance of the social." With sensitivity to the need on the part of museums and related institutions of *Weltkultur* (including the university, with their libraries and academic discourses, of course) to reorient themselves—away from the work of merely displaying objects "'as if' they were texts," "readable as ideologies"—Bennett followed another critic, Alfred Gell, with his concern for the "action-centred" approach to art as "a system of action, intended to change the world rather than to encode symbolic propositions about it." More specifically, Bennett argued for the shift to the "practical mediatory role of art objects in the social process," with attention to the "distributed relations between classes, or castes, or state groups, or communities." It is very clear that such a shift demands attention to the processes by which objects come to be "enfranchised" or and fabricated and made displayable—and with what interests and psycho-social dynamics and effects.[2]

What I would claim we have in the virtual/digitized contrapuntal/meta-Exhibition and the related Symposium (Masquerade) of which this book is a revision of a sort (arrangements for which were a concession to our situation in relation to the worldwide Covid virus) is intended to be and to do something different from the traditional positing of a stable "text" of a slice of presumed *Weltkultur*; it is something more akin to Bennett's and Gell's ideas: so we offer in this book counterpoint(s) to the canonical show-and-tell as a message about the workings of power and control. The Exhibition to which this essay and the essays below respond was intended to open a window not simply onto some different historically hidden or undervalued items or objects or registrations and behind all such under- or badly theorized peoples. Although that is indeed the case in comparison to what is the focus of the usual library exhibitions as *stagings*, with the intentional arrangements of different types of objects and representations, the aim of the Exhibition is to offer provocative, even disturbing, significations—of half-views, veil/ing/s—what I call "masquerade"/maskings—of multiple, conflicting sources, objects, alter-representations, of the instability if not the impossibility of story-telling, of refusals, denials, of signify*in(g)*[3] on the center/the canonical, always appearing (in some form or medium/a, mode) as the *scriptural*, the hyper-mediatized, in culture. It is a wide-open window onto multiple and layered stories—onto brokenness, humiliations, degradations, chaos, slavery, violence; but also, onto flight, resistance, intentionally alternative orientations, occasional instances/islands of refreshment, joy, all short of redemption. It is, in sum, *a window onto the construction, naturalization, maintenance, defense, disruption, and destabilization of modernities*—those social-cultural and political-economic arrangements, performances and practices, politics, (s)creeds, ideologies, mediatizations that we (are made to) differently experience, inhabit, undergo, and negotiate, in different types of bodies, in different but overlapping times, and by which we differently and complexly identify ourselves and relate to others.

The essays collected here represent the play of a variety of themes and analytical problems and challenges. No claim is here made about exhaustion of the play. There was no attempt to make essayists represent a particular discipline or field or thematic entry point. What was requested and expected among essayists—a willingness to play, with (psycho-social-cultural) play.

The "masquerade"—the "play-element"[4] "in" culture captures the paradox of the rather serious implications for our thinking and ramifications for the orientations and psycho-politics and dynamics that bring on and maintain modernities. Just as in general and as a matter of official (dis)course the Exhibition itself is, I claim, metonymic of the masquerade, of the claims about modernities normally assumed to be controlled and represented by those whom we now call "white men" (always and everywhere, with few exceptions, the curators), so the term "masquerade" is here used as broad if not universal framing concept for social-cultural play and production and capacious and provocative social and cultural theorizing and analysis of such. "Masquerade" does not in the most basic (archaic) terms and should not even now signify only or narrowly moralizing or duplicity of some sort; from its archaic European uses—Spanish, *mascara*; French *mascarada*; Italian *maschera*—we are already thereby located in some places within modernities. The word signifies complexity, the necessarily layered and indirect ways that humans and other living creatures communicate with one another and negotiate their shared space, including the psycho-social and political environments. The masquerade is quite natural in almost all social situations—among almost all earthly creatures, for a variety of interests. In other types of fraught situations among humans—systems of slavery, serfdom, caste—it may be imposed or accepted as necessary for survival.[5]

What proves to be striking, disturbing, and unavoidable in excavating modernities—with or without masquerade in mind—is the persistence and ubiquity of difference, complexly and disturbingly refracted as "race," racializations, racialisms, and racisms. And since the eras of (European experiences of) "First Contact" (if not before) connected always to the black-fleshed as phantasm (eventually as fixed "text"/"scripture"), to blackness, made(-up) to be and to produce and reflect a certain construal or hierarchi-calization of "reality."[6] The production of the racialized world that are moder-nities involves facilitating the translating/mediatizing, mirroring, ordering, identity-construction, boundary-maintenance, and orienting operations and dynamics—what I call *"scriptural-izing"* (as play)—all necessary for the varied developments and refractions.

All too evident as a charged phenomenon in the aftermath of the dynamics of first contacts that becomes the permanent enslavement of black-fleshed peoples, "race," following, not preceding, racialization/racism[7] becomes if not the originary, certainly, the most persistent, consequential impetus behind and production/iteration of masquerade in the making of the modernities. "Race" has come to define or frame the modern regimes (what I call "scrip-turalization") and the twists and turns, the dynamics (what I call "scriptura-lectics") of modernities. (The term as I use it here is not a simple reference to the less geographically sweeping local/regional/cultic-tribal premodern or ancient situations often in mind with the use of the term. It is here rather a ref-erence to the situations that emerged after "contact" beyond the local.) Within such regimes "race," as effected or performed by masquerading (scripturaliz-ing) practices and gestures, and as situations and interests, fears and fantasies have required—has been, and continues to be, obsessively focused on *black flesh* or in terms of *blackface(-ing)*. Thus, modernities, I argue, cannot be honestly grasped without deep excavation of the historical and continuing complex phenomenon of scripturalization, including the scripturalizing and scripturalectics, of black flesh/face as means by which control is effected after "contact." Many different representations of the modern may be identi-fied, to be sure, but none can be deeply excavated or analyzed apart from attention to what is done with black flesh—and blackness as the results of its scripturalization. There is simply too much history that goes unanalyzed apart from consideration of it.

The opening of the wide window onto the phenomenon of scripturalization/-izing of black flesh/blackface is facilitated in the somewhat (intentionally) destabilizing "meta-Exhibition." In the latter there is no stable regime or stable regime message represented—except to be signified *on*. There are no canonical-archival sources that showcase and define and delimit in simple terms the state or the dominant cultural order, its project or its argument or orientation. On the contrary, in this non-Exhibition the dominant or sym-bolic order is de-centered, noncanonically positioned. This destabilization is effected through playful (viz., my decidedly *un*-disciplinary) and layered focus, as a kind of gateway to—and, in turn, making use of as specific site in the gateway—one of the earliest and best known and complex of the early Anglophone Black Atlantic narratives.

Poignantly entitled *The Interesting Narrative of the Life of Olaudah Equiano, or Gustavus Vassa, The African. Written by Himself,* first published in 1789, this performance of self-narration on the part of a male ex-slave in the context of Anglophone maritime culture and related slave-holding cultures was something of a best-seller during the author's lifetime. Its sales reflected and consolidated the author's notoriety as one of the most widely known end-of-the-eighteenth century English-speaking Black Atlantic figures. His narrative as window shines blinkered moments onto and provokes thinking about issues and problems about the constructed-ness of modernities, including his own mimetic practices pertaining to, and subjectivities and politics allowed if not compelled by, such modernities. His all too revealing and all too elusive/masking story, including his thinking through and determining how he would be visually represented in what is the frontispiece—intended, for the most part, for self-styled abolitionist subscribers/readers of his time (not, as many interpreters still assume, for contemporary and later Black readers)—is layered and begs consideration of what in my view has in interpretation been placed into interpretive frames too narrow, flat, and superficial.[8] He was engaging in masquerade of whiteness.

The Interesting Narrative, as the writer had hoped it would be, is indeed of (compelling) "interest" in many respects to (would-be white) moderns. This "interest" registers because the work offers, even forces itself upon the reader as, a freighted and provocative touchstone for discussion of and thinking about a wide range of topics, not least that having to do with the complex intertwining of modern subjectivations and racialization, especially, although not exclusively, subjectivations of the black-fleshed. Equiano/Vassa (the double-named author) tries to help the reader understand how and why he and with what ramifications the world which he was forced to negotiate appeared to turn around the subjection and humiliation of black-fleshed peoples. And, of course, it included an accounting of how over time and through very painful experiences and exploits the writer became a complex type of subject ("Black"; "Negro"; "African," "almost Englishman," "christian" . . . ; not any more, if ever, simply Igbo).

These phenomena and dynamics are through the writer's story or gaze necessarily, unavoidably, to be seen in terms of basic masking, as play and mimetics, as the invention and fraught exercise of the patho-psycho-socio-logical imagination, with the writer's complex subjectivation as disturbing challenge to all "moderns" regarding simple default notions of a certain story line—regarding identity, culture, nation, ideology, politics. The narrative is also of profound interest because it opens a window—of critical imagination, akin to what I understand Saidiya Hartmann to mean with her concept of "critical fabulation"[9]—onto disturbing issues and questions and developments over time. It supplies from the perspective of a "stranger"—one who both on account of significations of his black flesh and his own "excess" of mimeticized awareness[10]—nodal points for theorizing and analyzing the pertinent issues and problems and developments having to do with finding a self and with social-cultural formation. Thus, Equiano's/Vassa's story provides the larger focus of conceptualization—regarding self-making and psycho-social-cultural formation, as well as the conceptual divisions and developments and dynamics to see/think through[11] in this "strange" Exhibition, using the "interesting" story of a "stranger" as springboard.

With the language "[E]verything about me was magic" as the overarching framing epigraph for the Exhibition (as well as the first part of the title of this lecture), the story of Equiano/Vassa as the story of the construction of modernities, their subjectivations and psycho-politics is opened and unfurled. Magic, masquerade, masking—with these categories and the phenomena they point to we are invited with the Exhibition and Symposium now reflected in this collection of essays to think hard about hard things.[12] *The Interesting Narrative* inspires us to think in terms of the critical *stages* (not periods, not necessarily universal, not necessarily in strict historical order, but poignant all) in relationship to—reflected in; assumed by; looking beyond—what it is as masquerade. (It will be useful to take note of my use of expressions from Equiano's/Vassa's narrative on which to hang various stages.)

Stage I—"We [Eboes] are . . . a nation of dancers, musicians, poets. . . ." These words Equiano/Vassa wrote in his narrative—from his lively imagination, his memory, from stories told him, from book sources, or from all these sources—about the tribal peoples about whom he dreams, with whom he identifies, by which he (re)names himself. This short reference in his narrative (with some elaboration in terms of textures of tribal ways) I take as springboard to allow the Exhibition to stretch forward toward displays of examples—mostly from western Africa—of the basic representations of the play-element or masquerade (often viewed as frenzied or ritualized gestures and referenced by outsiders as "magic," by insiders as something far more complex). These representations have from the beginning to this day marked human (if not, as I indicated above, some scientists try to teach us, all sentient beings') formation and ongoing sociality. The literal colorful mask of human beings makes the dramatic point—that complex social life entails masking, the cult of masking, ritual masquerade for the sake of basic communication and structuring of and orientation to the world. Note here the work of G. Harley, *Masks as Agents of Social Control in Northeast Liberia*. The frontispiece to the book, also included here, is basic representation: a small personal mask—*me*—of an important man (*zo*) (almost always a man) in the community through whom all things are believed to be kept in balance. (More about this work below.)[13]

The traditions behind the mask image are quite fascinating. But I must with this reference here leave it to readers according to interest to follow leads and links for more information, including recordings of traditions of sounds and movements of the peoples of what is today called Sierra Leone.[14]

The basic yet complex phenomenon as imaged here is universal; it is found in real or contemporary time and throughout history. It is, contra Huizinga's book title, not really a matter of reflecting the *separate* "play-element" "*in*" culture; rather, it suggests culture *as* play. This play, as we follow the lead of the "interesting" narrative written by the late eighteenth century "stranger" finding himself among differently-fleshed or white-fleshed peoples (as some understood themselves), is refracted into different forms of psycho-politics reflecting in turn different geographical and psychic spaces and times and situations having to do with epistemic authority and control—about who knows things; about what is worth knowing; and who can know what is worth knowing. All such to make and keep things and persons in balance, in place, and under control. Thus, the other sections that follow:

Stage II—"The White men had some spell or magic." These words reflect Equiano's/Vassa's summing up of (his hunches about and experiences of) the white men's source of power and authority in the world. Within and beyond his narrative they point us to the long history of modern-world European colonial and before such other imperial dominant regimes and their control of bodies and of forms of representation and mediatization. In the modern world this control has especially (although not exclusively) involved writing and the printing and distribution of books (and related objects). As well as or as part of the advancement of "scientific exploration," or classification, categorization. This is the import of Francis Bacon's cover page of his *Instauratio Magna* (1620), prominently situated in the Exhibition, featuring the ships going beyond the ancient Mediterranean world's Pillar of Hercules.

In that going beyond there is much poignancy and multiple levels of irony in the fact that among the "discoveries"/"contacts" that to some extent had been made but were soon to be made with poignancy and with enormous repercussions—black-fleshed peoples (to be conscripted). To be sure, such peoples would become a great source of wealth, a site on which the wandering/adventurous destabilized self (soon to become white) would be made, but collectively they were also due to unrestrained and unacknowledged violence to become—as Thomas Jefferson would later sum it up with all the anxiety and fear that defined the era—a "wolf by the ears."[15]

It is the fetishization of what is "discovered" by Bacon's folks that Equiano/Vassa deftly identifies and characterizes for the reader that is so very

Frontispiece. Small personal mask, *mä,* of an important man, *zo.*

G. Harley, *Masks as Agents*, 1950, frontispiece.

Francis Bacon, Title Page, *Novum Organum*, 1620, Instauratio Magna.
Source: Biodiversity Heritage Library

disturbing. This situation also makes clear the psycho-political and violent uses—captured perfectly in the ancient cum European-world trope *translatio studii et imperii* ("transfer of knowledge and power")[16]—of flesh and bodies, books and related objects and instruments that are part of a larger culturalist masquerade that can be more poignantly described and analyzed as "scripturalization." The latter is my preferred term to capture white men's semiosphere or epistemic regime for the mediatization of knowledge.

A profound imaging of how things looked or were arranged in Bacon's age and beyond and were poised to develop can be seen in the anonymous image of the 1575 inauguration of the University of Leiden, with all the assumed important discourses and their representatives festooned/masked (as university discourses) in procession.

The position of what was deemed *Sacra Scriptura*—first (#3) among all the important fields/discourses and, I maintain, then and even now, metonymic of modern western discourse—should not be lost on anyone. The entire enterprise—of the making of the western university and its practices and discourses—should be understood always to have had to do with, indeed, to turn around, the scriptural, or scripturalization.[17]

Stage III—"The book remained silent." This stage casts a light onto the disturbing nature of the violence that "white men's magic" in the form of the regime of the fetish of the scriptural (scripturalization) is made to do. Traditionally analyzed in terms of the "talking book" trope by which Black Atlantic figures of the eighteenth and nineteenth centuries—mostly slaves or ex-slaves—recognized the "magic," the special power, of white men's books and announced their desperation and anxiety over at first not being able to read these books, in this Exhibition the concluding part (in re: silence) of the traditional expression as found in *The Interesting Narrative* is understood

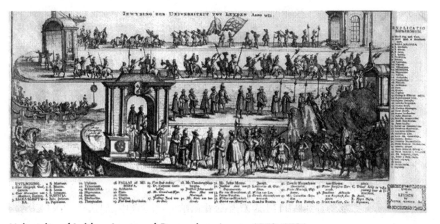

University of Leiden, Inaugural Procession, Anon., 1779–1781.

to function differently: notwithstanding the fact that some Black Atlantic individuals (within the narrative and beyond) learned to read the book, the silence persisted. The silence I argue here signifies a blocking—keeping black-fleshed persons from seeing/being seen, from hearing/being heard on their own terms, through their own agency, being represented as human and experiencing their full humanity. Various expressive practices and ideologies in the maintenance of such silence are masquerade and so become the chaotic impetus behind the production of modernities as we know them. See as one fascinating example of this phenomenon the painting of the so-called Seven Years' War/French-Indian Wars (in chilling complex even cringe-worthy relationship to which, by the way, the newly renamed Gustavas Vassa was made to "serve," as aide to British naval officer Michael Henry Pascal on duty in the same war). At any rate, in the painting one notes how the colored "Native" body that is figured in the center is used as a kind of hieroglyphics, signifying complex impulses and emotions/anxieties having to do with the making of the modern world in relation to the presence of flesh white and black, in total silence, of course.[18]

The same point about the use of nonwhite bodies I should like to make in relation to the development reflected by another famous and fraught, even eerie, representation—of T. D. Rice as "Jim Crow" at the Bowery Theatre in New York City in 1833. Actual, black-skinned persons in New York City and elsewhere notwithstanding, all the noises and images and gestures that define minstrelsy or blackface traditions render such persons silent (and invisible).

I agree wholeheartedly with critics such as Eric Lott[19]—love and theft, indeed—who sees in the dynamics registered in the painting the anxiety that the black body provokes, even as it is clearly part of a now infamous and disturbing (borderline or) white class-specific masquerade. It is a must-see/must-dwell-on representation of what we should name as anti-black-flesh anxiety and its programs and protocols of anti-black racism. This involves among other practices taking on and taking over the body and sounds of the black-fleshed. The latter cannot be seen or heard.

Stage IV—"The Ethiopian was willing to be saved by Jesus Christ." This stage turns to efforts on the part of black-fleshed peoples to "make do with the (white men's) fetish." In *The Interesting Narrative* this includes religious conversion, to be sure. In fact, it meant for Equiano/Vassa several experiments in conversion to white men's religious ways and arrangements (most of which were new and still being worked out). But the reader-critic engaged in transdisciplinary excavation can hardly fail to take note of the fact that in Equiano's/Vassa's life story the religious conversion is metonymic of the larger ongoing attempt on the part of this black-fleshed person to be "saved" within/into white men's world. To be positioned to survive and negotiate

Thomas D. Rice performing at The American Theatre, The Bowery, New York City, 1833.
Source: National Portrait Gallery; Owner, New York Historical Society

this world. The fall into theological/doctrinal differences and conflicts is too much obfuscation. These attempts to "convert" on the part of many if not most in the Black Atlantic worlds constituted a layered and complex history—of representations, resistance, flight, accommodation, survival. These attempts are all masquerade, all mimetics all the time, in every public space, at any rate. No source regarding the experience of the black-fleshed person "being saved" can or should be taken seriously as it denies this phenomenon. Religious conversion must no longer be taken flatly or as something obvious and simple. Because it takes place in the world that all experience in time and space the business of "conversion" must be interpreted as part of the dynamics of negotiation of the dominant. The most important points to take into consideration—that "conversion" is here meant to convey the whole complex of efforts to navigate, if not totally to come to terms with, the violent dominant world. These efforts are found in every domain or context and in every period of history, including our own. Our own period seen in critical historical perspective might reflect to our horror the most thoroughgoing efforts at integration and the most naïve views about what has taken place, that is, that to which we have converted ourselves—in language, "religion," dress, comportment, ideology, and so forth. All of it—as Equiano/Vassa's story of experimentation shows—is masquerade of some sort.[20]

Stage V—"[T]he Scriptures became an unsealed book [of] . . . things . . . that . . . can never be told." This stage helps us to recognize sedimented and ongoing complexity—specifically, the challenges pertaining to the need both to (continue to) mask and unmask, indeed, to identify and negotiate layers of masks that define the trauma of black-fleshed existence. Equiano's/Vassa's story complexly registers both the sentiments and the gestures and with them suggests ways of continuing to be enslaved and to escape from enslavement. This story may be viewed not only as registration of the impossibilities in the situation for unmasking and relating the complete story of experiences, but paradoxically also the imperative of doing so. The imperative, as the double-naming of authorship and other narratological indicia suggest, is also carried out through masking or masquerade. But this masking is of a different sort and for a different purpose. On this side of the trauma of the Middle Passage and all that has followed throughout the West but especially in what has become the United States, the masquerade/masking may go on, but now must entail more—including more self-reflexivity and theorizing work. Examples of critical experiments of different sorts in such play are put in focus in the Masquerade Exhibition. Of course, there is so much more to be mined.

Again, I make the point that there is from my perspective as curator and critic no redemption assumed to be on the horizon—racialization produced by scripturalization and scripturalization supercharged by racialization cannot now be unread or undone; there remains for all only constant struggle for and the maintenance of sharp-edged self-reflexivity. Only when this is the case can we begin to address the injury done. Perhaps, the most appropriate conclusion to draw from this project is that nothing can or ever should be concluded—at least not simply or straightforwardly, or without being disturbed, or without "seeing through" racialization in order to honestly face the chaos and violence, as well as the possibilities ahead. The examples that can be highlighted and analyzed are numerous and enormously complicated, begging to be analyzed with sustained attention and sensitivity.[21]

There are in this book and in the Exhibition on which the book is based implications for thinking about thinking about and acting in the worlds we made and inhabit. I should like now to attempt to draw some of the strings together, so to speak, to try in sum to be suggestive and provocative about possible implications for further consideration. All such issues will turn around the framing phenomenon or dynamic as a historical and analytical concept for the theme and problematic of this book—Masquerade. I suggest this concept throws light on the making of the modern as racialization of the human. Much more excavation work is required in order to get anywhere near the bottom of what Equiano's/Vassa's performance and references to performance suggest. Analysis of the type I have in mind would continue to make critical use of the likes of the ethnological work of George W. Harley, who was referenced above. That is, with all necessary corrections, qualifications, and updates, to be sure. His extended essays that became part of the Papers of the Peabody Museum of Archaeology and Ethnology, which appeared in book form entitled *Masks as Agents of Social Control in Northeast Liberia*, focused on the Poro peoples, should be required reading for anyone interested in the type of work I am here calling for.

Harley is important I should like to stress here because of his focus on function—the function of the "cult of masks" he had in evidence. From observation of dynamics of social relations, it became clear to him that "controlling the people" (vii), not so much in sinister terms, but in terms of realizing a sort of "equilibrium" of society, was the fundamental interest and issue. This equilibrium was maintained through "ancestor worship." And the ancestors were worshipped, or better, heard, translated, through "visible manifestations . . . by the necessity of using the masks as practical implements to guarantee the smooth working of a system of government founded on stricter adherence to custom" (vii). "[E]ssential power," Harley goes on to argue, "was thought of as emanating from the ancestral spirits" (42). The various officers or agents— *zos, ges,* "doctors," and so forth, all males (viii) (another matter that needs further exploration, surely)—exercised the functions necessary for control of the society in different domains:

> [The] mask and its keeper were . . . inseparably united in spirit by mutual responsibility to the people on the one hand and to the ancestors on the other, both by custom and by tradition . . . The sense of their responsibility . . . was kept alive by the unknown mysteries of sickness and calamity . . . Masks, whether they were human or half animal could . . . represent ancestral spirits . . . the belief that they possessed the essential soul-substance. . . . [Each keeper was assumed to be] *en rapport* with the spirit of the mask and subconsciously was inspired by his concept of what the mask represented. (42–43)

What is described can be understood as basic to social control. Basic because no one could possibly name precisely or face directly the unfathomable/ unspeakable that was life experience. Mask(-ing) is shorthand for the necessary obliqueness, the indirectness, that we use to name the hard to name and grasp. Criticism aplenty can be levelled against this assumption and arrangement. It can be argued to be all too convenient for power-tripping. It is universal in terms of occurring in every locality. It was universal precisely insofar as it was experienced as local reach. As with all masking cults, it facilitated the illusion of all things—to channel Chinua Achebe—being held together and not falling apart. This is one type or level of mask-ing.

It is with the "advancement" of the scriptural—of the written (at least in terms somewhat close to what we know)—and its claims to and reflection of translocality, if not universal reach, that we see another mask (or layer of play) is put on. At this level of psycho-social development the mask of the fixed script, especially with the invention of the printing machine, reflective of extensive reach and power—military, economic, epistemic, and so forth—of the European colonial world, reveals not only expansiveness and differ-ence geographical and social-cultural, but the assumption and proclamation that all such is manageable, under (colonial/imperial) control. It facilitated the illusion/fantasy of (white) men's magic of empire, turning around what Linda Colley in her book by the same title calls "the gun, the ship, and the pen."[22]

With all its potential and excitement, the expansiveness of the scriptural proved to be stressful and challenging. Contact with Others, whether from 1619 or earlier times, from the point of view of European imperialists' expansionist exploits, brought difference sharply in view, to the point that the scriptural needed to be deployed not simply for inventorying and classifying spoils of domination but now for ideologization as part of maintenance of the regime. That is, for the sake of control, including the fixity of the difference discovered and named. This meant that another mask was needed—to be placed and fixed on black-fleshed bodies and other nonwhite bodies in order to facilitate management of the psycho-politics and economics of difference. (The different dynamics and turns in such management challenges I remind you I call "scripturalectics."[23]) This means essentially making classification or taxonomies clear and fixed, but also manipulable, like "soft wax" (*sem-blable á une cire mole*) as provocatively suggested by Abbé Demanet in his *Nouvelle Histoire de l'Afrique francoise* (1767).[24] Here the fantasy of race (refracting racialization and racisms)—most especially of black-fleshed bod-ies being a sign of the *nec plus ultra*, of the radical limit (and bottom rung), of all things—was required.[25] Black flesh could not possibly be left to be what it was—simple difference; it had to be made readable, had to be made into a "text" that could be controlled, heavily signified. Herein was found the way "forward"—to make black-ness a supercharged/hypersignified "reality" and in every respect the lack and the limit. Thus, black flesh becomes a "text" made up/"read"/"writ up." (The violence of it all is clear, as Lévi-Strauss meets Sojourner Truth.)[26]

The dynamics discussed above suggest that black-fleshed peoples needed for survival (not thriving or redemption) to be at least *triply* masked. This was of course an extra burden. But the surprising and inspiring survival of such folk means that their tactics, their orientation, play, gestures, soundings—all should be watched and studied carefully by all. In their very survival there may be opportunities for all if not to throw off all the masks, at least to "see through"[27] their experiences and gestures, to gain heightened self-awareness of the masquerade that defines all human foibles and strivings in the world after Contact with difference.

What we might make of or do about the situation that is, as Blue Magic sang about the "sideshow," or as the Stylistics sang about "people mak[ing] the world go 'round"? Might we, as several writers and activists such as Harriet Tubman and Richard Wright challenged and showed us, at moments and in particular places, to go "underground"? Or would we pledge, like the rural-based blues-gospel singer Blind Willie Johnson of the early twentieth century and the mid- to late-twentieth-century Atlanta-area folk revivalist song-stylist C. J. Johnson sang, to be always in the mode of running, always singing/thinking "I'm gon' run"/"You better run"? These and so many forms of expressivity reflecting mimetics and resistance remain to be thought about more seriously.[28]

Now in particular regarding the scholar and scholarship, given the "context"—virtual and otherwise—in which the Masquerade Exhibition project takes place, the means through we seek to disseminate discussion and thinking about it, and the persons who are part of the discussion. Whatever our immediate context, it is incumbent upon us to ask again and more honestly whether and in what ways the scholar or scholarship facilitates not merely museumization or curation as the not so benign medium of communication, but also actually advances the psycho-social-economic-political game, the masquerade that is the arrangements of the larger world that we know and share. What was/is now the scholar's role in the ideologization of the politics of, and in general orientation to, the colonial-empire-turned-nation? This project about masquerade shows just how significant a part was played by writing turned into recording/classification turned into interpretation/scholarship as part of the management of empire and its civilization. It shows also how disturbed or shaken up if not dismantled and reoriented scholarship—traditional, canon-setting scholarship—should be. This book and the project behind are opportunities to raise the issue; but I leave this as challenge for professional scholars and thoughtful persons of all types to begin or continue more honestly and persistently to fathom.

It is impossible for me, given my academic field and especially my original subfield specialization—put most broadly and technically in terms of participation in a certain construal of the operations and politics of philology and history (that some call by the traditional nonsensical name "biblical studies")—to ignore in this situation the role and offices of the new modern professional bureaucrats, following in the footsteps of the old court scholar, with his—always with few exceptions until the near present moment *his*—service in the management of empire, empire orientation and stability, culture, politics, economics. "*Mis*reading" of the field insofar as I am oriented to the critical signifying (on) scriptures project provokes me to consider old issues and assumptions differently and a new different set of issues altogether.[29]

Put more pointedly, and as a reflection of the kinds of conversations had and facilitated by the Institute for Signifying Scriptures (ISS), we are confronted in the Exhibition and Symposium on Masquerade with what I prefer to call the psycho-politics of the "scriptural."[30] The latter term is for me fraught shorthand for all that which in the world is naturalized and taken for granted. There is, as our daily headlines remind us, especially regarding the institutions and operations of these scholar-bureaucrats (who call themselves exegetes), some fraying around the edges in terms of reputation and authority, with some recent instability and disturbances, some pointed questioning or criticism. This is due to recognition among enough of us—in humanistic studies and research, at least—that we are in many respects in the "endgame" in terms of being the consistent source of authority for what is real or important.

Clearly, what is desperately needed is reform and reorientation—away from toxic colonial era discursive regimes and mimetic exegetical practices and politics—assuming, for example, that a simple history or story can any more be told (in a book or as part of a curated exhibition), as though there is any such thing as a simple stable subject to tell such a story. This is the challenge offered by *The Interesting Narrative* as a complex, binomially-authored story. Equiano/Vassa told too much truth—about identity formation—including black identities; they are, he shows us, masks worn this way or that way. Real change away from the masquerade that is this or that modernity in all its iterations must entail a turn away from such notions to: ex-centric thinking and practices, including the un-veiling, taking off or as many layers of the masks as possible; or, perhaps, not so much simply doing away with masking altogether, but going forward with a new orientation. This means going forward with the creation and emplotment of masking games in which sharp persistent even if disturbing and painful self-reflexivity is allowed and encouraged, self-reflexivity in which as many as are able may play with passion and creative force toward addressing what matters or is always at stake—brokenness of spirit, of bodies, slippage of categories, of systems, of identity, as a type of poignant tragedy not as romance of resistance overcoming, as C. L. R. James is interpreted as having come to re-read in his classic *Black Jacobins*, the story of Toussaint L'Ouverture and the Black revolution that shook and still shakes European/white colonial empires.[31] This focus, instead of the poisonous and burdensome scheme of multilayered masquerade-ing—otherwise aptly even if disturbingly called slavery that projects onto the flesh-specific dysselected the burden of representation that facilitates identity-making and ordering of the world—is sorely needed. Thus, black made into a hyper-signification, made to be all too fixed and too soft, like wax made available to be manipulated, a mask too layered and thick, is not the prescription needed.

Literary critic Houston Baker got it exactly right when he observed that masking is minstrelsy, and that the minstrel mask is a

> space of habitation not only for repressed spirits of sexuality, ludic play, id satisfaction, castration anxiety, and a mirror stage of development, but also for that deep-seated denial of the indisputable humanity of inhabitants of and descendants from the continent of Africa. And it is . . . the mastery of the [white-men's-invented] minstrel mask by blacks that constitutes a primary move in Afro-American discursive modernism.[32]

Furthermore, I agree with Baker that the work of masquerade—ancient tribal in origins and likely nearly universal but accepted, but now, especially after Europeans' "first contact" experiences still ongoing even if denied—is a kind of "possession" that profoundly and differently grips and effects all and so must be analyzed with utmost sensitivity and self-reflexivity. This possession, Baker brilliantly argues,

> operates both in the spirit work of voodoo and in the dread slave and voodoo economics perpetuated by the West. What is involved in possession, in either case, is supplementarity—the immediately mediating appearance, as spectre or shadow, of a second and secondary "self." In specifically diasporic terms, "being possessed" (as slave, but also BEING POSSESSED) is more than a nec-essary doubling or inscribed "otherness" of the *con-scripted* (those who come, as necessity, with writing). . . . [T]he possessed are governed not simply by *script* but also by productive conditions that render their entire play a *tripling*.[33]

I had hope that the disciplinarily ex-centric Exhibition and Symposium behind this collection of essays would provoke readers to see issues along these lines—the lines of what I call in complementarity to and in analytical steps going beyond Baker (although it is admittedly hard to go beyond his notion of "tripling"). Yet I maintain that it is the *script*-ural that, as psycho-social-cultural (necessarily including racialized) dynamics, as psycho-social-cultural politics, disturbing and exploding old disciplinary orientations and practices, that offers conceptual and analytical advances. This is because the scriptural is the site, the crux, of the problem, the deep hole into which we have fallen, the slavery to which we submit. We are all in the modern West, certainly—differently positioned, of course—projections and effects of, and mostly occluded/dim- or un-witting players within the realm of the scriptural.

Here is the challenge to you who have come close, you who now read these words, to prove my hope was not groundless—not only to see things this way, but to commit to work with others to open wider many more windows beyond Equiano/Vassa. There is so much work—about our consequential including deadly play—within and beyond the academy, yet to be done. Who among us taking note of what we have all over the world undergone during the last few years will disagree? Who reading our headlines as they register the fear and anxiety among all peoples about identity (de)formation, too often offloaded onto historically dominant peoples, would not agree that more attention to issues named here is needed? Who in our age of mediatization and its persistent and cruel disinformation practices cannot understand that we desperately need deeper and more honest probing of conscientization? Does the chaos among us across the world including scripturalized modernities and especially in the scriptural formation that is the United States suggest the historical masquerade of dominants is running its course? What else can we expect to ensue from the big historical masquerade recognized, outed, and examined, except, on the part of the most anxious and insecure (white males, especially, and all those who identify with them, aspire to be like them), appeal in the form of histrionics, of course, to the "Big Lie," as though to project onto others the (really big) masquerade (race/racialism)? Who can now fail to see how the current local school boards controversies over what children are to read (CRT, anyone?) is anything other than an updating of this phenomenon of politics of the scriptural? Is there more fear and anxiety and rage because the old masquerade no longer can be counted on (always) to work—witness the turning blue of the state of Georgia in 2020, in the presidential and senatorial campaigns, for example—or because there are now more counter-masquerades? In a time in which we have been literally forced (for the sake of trying to save ourselves and others from catastrophic illness and death) to mask ourselves, forced to stage a university library Exhibition as a "virtual" event—with all such, how can we refuse to think again about how masking in so many other respects, including illusions and delusion about the flesh, has worked in the world that we inhabit? Do the historically disprivileged suffer more or suffer less from the mimetics required for participation in the old historical masquerade of dominants? Is Equiano/Vassa today more or less part of the modernity he fought to integrate himself into? Absent persistent and aggressive interpretation (of self and/in the world as critical conscientization as critical scripturalizing)—gross and crass domestication ensues.[34]

These are some questions that beg our attention and consideration, leading me back to the terms and plane on which Frantz Fanon understood and powerfully argued about these matters. In his performance that is his narrative writing, production/printing and selling—defying and unsettling the gravity of traditional scriptural authority and identity—was Equiano anticipating "forms" of Fanon(ism)?[35] As he ends his haunting *Black Skin, White Masks*, was Fanon channeling Equiano/Vassa, when he asserted *le negre n'est pas*

("The Negro is not") ("[a]ny more than [is] the white man")?[36] As a means of drawing matters to a close, I must make Equiano and Vassa (through Fanon and Morrison) engage each other, and thereby provoke us all onward into ever more difficult thinking and conversation about important matters.

I remind readers that Toni Morrison, especially in the hard lesson she conveys in story form that is *Beloved* is the story that many local majority white school boards around the country as I write these words are so fearful of because it makes the children faint. It is the story that renders the traumatic experience of the black *female* as the synecdochical dirtied, haunted, and haunting figure who both cannot be denied ("passed" [over]) and also cannot be really related ("passed" on, in terms of scripturalization). This female figure is such only, possibly, through reading (to try to match Morrison's "reading" reflected in her writing) that is hyper-sensitive, hyper-reflexive, transgressive, courageous, and persistent—always "next" to, or in the company of, another or others of her kind. She is masqueraded; she is herself a particular type of passing.

The October 24, 2021, Sunday *New York Times Magazine* featured a piece called "There's No Room for Escape"[37] that could not be more poignant here in the context of the end of my argument, precisely about complicating even Morrison's notion of "passing"/ "passing on." The piece focused on the recent Netflix film produced by Rebecca Hall (a "white" female who is herself racially destabilized and haunted) that is based on the 1929 Harlem Renaissance-era novel by the same name by Nella Larson.[38] The Netflix film and Larsen's novel provoke us to continue to make Morrison's notion of "pass[ing]" even more haunting and disturbing (but only if we are brave), fruitful of sharp critical analytics. *The New York Times Magazine* writer had already invited us into this work as she points out that the phenomenon of passing—of characters seeing each other "face to face, skin to skin," the one "occluding, the other hidden"—makes all of us more "aware" of the way our "perception is positioned and constructed." The more Larsen's characters transgress "boundaries" of race and class the more they "expose the falseness of the racial categories" upheld by all and the "psychic afterlife of racial trauma—the quiet holes pressed into the psyche by self-denial." One Twitter user provoked by the film production and commenting on Larsen's era made the important point that "passing did not necessarily mean persuading others that you were white, only persuading them that you were 'not-Black.'" Again, and finally, it is the black-fleshed individual in western modernities who historically and even now necessarily "resists assimilation into both whiteness and the middle ground of the mixed." Herein lies the scriptural; here is the regime of scripturalization: To be black-fleshed in western modernities is to be (made to be) eminently "readable"—indeed, the phenomenon of "passing" makes very clear that in terms of being read "there's no room for escape."

This notwithstanding the fact that since the first contacts that were creative of and created by (the impetuses of) modernities there are in reality "as many racial identities as there are racial stories." I agree with *Magazine* writer Alexandra Kleeman who, with honesty and sensitivity, admits her own mixed or transgressive background and the destabilization that it evokes toward what she calls the "fulfilling work." I should rather prefer to stress what is the compelling work ahead, that should entail among other things, "dwell[ing] in these stories [of racial passing] rather [than] their categorization."

Indeed. Was not Equiano/Vassa in and through his binomially-authored work passing? Of course! Equiano was passing as Vassa, Vassa as Equiano. This should for all of us be henceforth a challenge to read our social relations and their arrangements and hierarchies as passing; and the passing as "farce,"[39] as masquerade that is part of the big masquerade that defines modernities.

Again, the essays that follow represent creative play with different arguments and provocations (from this essay and from the Emory University Pitts Library Masquerade Exhibition in relation to which this essay was conceptualized and written, and beyond). Like blues and jazz and spiritual notes that are responses to what Houston Baker argued to be ongoing "soundings" in (intellectual) marronage, these essays require no capsulation from me or anyone else, as though representing some sort of canonical discourse.[40] There is here no standard beginning and end point for joining the play, the sensitivities herein to different social historical contexts and movements and developments notwithstanding. Even as they represent the beginning of the next level of hard discussions about matters having to do with masquerade, with play, with social construction, the essays should be approached not as stand-alone end-of-discussion pieces, but as parts of ongoing discussions— with the Exhibition as key baseline provocative project or argument, and with Equiano/Vassa and his wonderfully compelling and playful narrative as starter. Along with this introductory essay, the essays beckon and provoke others to join the discussion. It makes sense for readers, like the essayists themselves, to refer again and again to the Exhibition as well as this Introduction. Then to the essays that follow—and then back again, in different orders. Disturbing and unsettling as they may be, the essays below, examples of (disciplinarily) transgressive discourse, should help readers find in the different arguments and analyses opportunities for jumping into, tightly holding on, and then engaging earnestly with a most important conceit for our times. The conceit I have in mind here was developed and modeled before and differently from Nietzsche and his company of European males who were privileged because they were self-possessed, including being possessors of their own bodies. In other situations, within and constituting modernities, some who were/are still among the (psycho-socially-politically) "dead," such as Equiano/Vassa, made grasping of this conceit compelling and decisive, a matter of life and death. This was the conceit that all is masquerade. Henceforth, what matters most—discerning the types of psychic, political-economic, social relations and dynamics that characterize the masquerade and making repeated efforts to position oneself to some limited advantage thereto in relationship.

NOTES

1. The larger project of which this Introductory essay and the essays that follow are a part of a larger critical disciplinarily transgressive-political project.

Readers are here invited to visit the (digitized) Exhibition I curated in 2021, at the invitation of Dr. Robert Bo Adams, for Pitts Library, Candler School of Theology, Emory University, entitled "Masquerade: Scripturalizing Modernities Through Black Flesh." In order to learn from, challenge, and be challenged and provoked by, this project, readers are required to visit and engage the Exhibition. Due to the challenges of the Covid virus, the Exhibition was not experienced as goes the usual. First, it was from the beginning completely digitized. Go to http://pitts.tl/masquerade. Second, the essays that follow represent revision of presentations made as part of the Symposium (November 3–4, 2021) related to the Exhibition. Third, there is not even the pretense of offering something exotic, never seen, or that may be considered obscure, not seen by many. What makes this project compelling—its somewhat (disciplinarily/field) transgressive conceits about modern formations.

I should like to offer readers at the outset two helpful aids not so much for the sake of insuring agreement with me about all points, but for the sake of facilitating the quality, coherence, and urgency of the project and the quality and terms of engagement.

First, this very pointed challenge that I should like to put in the boldest, starkest possible terms: if after this essay has been read and you as reader conclude that this project is all about old standing categories: Black folks; or race; or religion (and scriptures in relationship to narrow traditional terms); and possible ranges of responses to such, you've missed the point; you should read again until you come near a point of understanding, not agreeing with me—you may want to agree with one of Joseph Conrad's characters in *Heart of Darkness*, shouting "The horror! The horror!"—but understanding that what this essay and the essays that follow are about have to do with nothing short of challenging a different order of and orientation to thinking; with the disruption or destabilization, if not explosion, of standing categories and social-cultural practices, including, but not limited to academic ones—all such that shape and define our world.

Second, assistance, in the form of epigraphs (here four in number)—short, provocative expressions that capture and serve as helpful nodes of translation of many if not all the major points of a book or essay or other type of presentation. I have felt the need to include more than the usual number and types of epigraphs. The number and nature of the arguments below may make clearer what I think I'm up to. You should keep in mind one if not all the epigraphs I offer here when at points there is too much pressing on you as reader at once and things seem bewildering or disturbing. One or more may help with the framing of issues.

2. See Tony Bennett, "Civic Laboratories: Museums, Cultural Objecthood and the Governance of the Social," *Cultural Studies* 19(5), 521–547; and A. Gell, *Art and Agency: An Anthropological Theory* (New York: Oxford University Press, 1998).

3. See his *Signifying Monkey: A Theory of African American Literary Criticism* (New York: Oxford University Press, 1988).

4. J. Huizinga, *Homo Ludens: A Study of the Play-Element in Culture*, 1955. But now see also: Toni Morrison, *Playing in the Dark: Whiteness and the Literary Imagination* (New York: Vintage Books, 1993); and Michael Taussig, *Mimesis and Alterity: A Particular History of the Senses* (New York: Routledge, 1993)

5. Beyond Huizinga, see the persuasive arguments in Robert N. Bellah's *Religion in Human Evolution: From the Paleolithic to the Axial Age* (Cambridge, MA: The Belknap Press of Harvard University Press, 2011), s.v. mammals: play; play: mammals and birds, and so forth.

6. This argument needs here to be forcefully made—other types of enfleshed and engendered persons, have been, to be sure, historically and still are so instrumentalized and subjugated. About the truth of this reality there can be no denial. Intersectionality of oppression and violence is real. Competition over whose flesh has been more degraded is not useful. I maintain and invite serious thinking among all about how and to what extent the black-fleshed might and should serve as fraught synecdoche for the construction of modernities. I direct your attention to the provocative discussion if not the same conclusion reached in Anne McClintock's *Imperial Leather: Race, Gender, and Sexuality in the Colonial Contest* (New York: Routledge, 1995).

7. So we must learn from M. Merleau-Ponty, *Phenomenology of Perception* (New York: Routledge, [1945] 2013), among others.

8. The author was not simply one of the earliest *black* black men—for Black peoples; nor was he simply white folks' *white* black man. His story confounds, destabilizes, and renders problematic almost our current frozen categories of identity. No matter the demographics of initial groups of readers, that Black-fleshed peoples have had a stake, a special claim, in the work is of course quite clear. This begs even more consideration or study—about interpretation and identification and cultural ownership, among many other issues.

9. See her "Venus in Two Acts," *Small Axe* 12 (2) (2008); also, *Wayward Lives, Beautiful Experiments* (New York: W.W. Norton & Company, 2019).

10. On this matter of "excess," see M. Taussig, *Mimesis, passim.*

11. See W. J. Mitchell, *Seeing through Race* (Cambridge, MA: Harvard University Press, 2012), as inspiration for this way of phrasing the analytic challenge and the opportunity.

12. From this point onward I aim only to summarize what is unfolded in the Exhibition through focus on a few examples, some included in the Exhibition, some others not.

13. G. Harley, *Masks as Agents of Social Control in Northeast Liberia* (Cambridge, MA: Peabody Museum of American Archaeology and Ethnology, 1950.).

14. https://re-entanglements.net/sierra-leone-masquerades/.

15. Thomas Jefferson used the ancient world expression in correspondence on more than one occasion. See John C. Miller, *The Wolf by the Ears: Thomas Jefferson and Slavery* (rev. ed.; Charlottesville, VA: University of Virginia Press, 1991).

16. *See* Eric Cheyfitz, *Poetics of Imperialism: Translation and Colonization from* The Tempest *to* Tarzan (New York: Oxford University Press, 1991), *passim*; and Leonard Tennenhouse, *The Importance of Feeling English: American Literature and the British Diaspora, 1750–1850* (Princeton, NJ: Princeton University Press, 2007), 13–14, for useful background information and perspective.

17. Thus, I draw your attention to the continuing hold of the book/discourse regime/mediatization—in other forms. See for example a *New Yorker* cartoon registering intimidating books: https://www.newyorker.com/magazine/2021/08/02/facebooks-broken-vows.

18. Jason Farago, "Close Read" series: "Myth of North America" 2020 *New York Times* piece: https://www.nytimes.com/interactive/2020/11/25/arts/benjamin-west-general-wolfe.html; https://extragoodshit.phlap.net/wp-content/uploads/2020/11/The-Myth-of-North-America-in-One-Painting.html. I owe inspiration for my continuing interest in this genre of visual "text" to be interpreted to ISS member and colleague Katrina Van Heest. Part of her ("Scripturalizing Here and There") contribution to the 2021 ISS meeting was an examination of the image.

19. See his *Love and Theft: Blackface Minstrelsy and the American Working Class* (New York: Oxford University Press, 1993). I hope that I am not the only one who sees a rather unnerving connection between the anxious crowd surrounding Rice/Jim Crow and the frightening crowd that on January 6, 2021, chased the Black officer upstairs and through corridors in the U.S. capitol.

20. See Walter F. Pitts Jr., *Old Ship of Zion: The Afro-Baptist Ritual in the African Diaspora* (New York: Oxford University Press, 1993); K. W. Benston, *Performing Blackness: Enactments of African-American Modernism* (New York: Routledge, 2000); and Gena Dagel Caponi, ed., *Signifyin(g), Santifyin', & Slam Dunking: A Reader in African American Expressive Culture* (Amherst: University of Massachusetts Press, 1999), among many others, for aid in investigation into issues having to do with performance and/as masquerade.

A few examples (from a narrow slice of the narrowly religious domain) that register with respect to only one set of the myriad thematics to be explored, I turn the reader to one such that I have been struck by—the theme or trope of running, or escape (from what are the obvious challenges in the world that the black-fleshed face). Moments or situations or expressivities are abundant. These might include the likes of: Blind Willie Johnson, "I'm Gonna Run to the City of Refuge" (1928), and the updating for another differently-situated generation (mostly urban, mid- to late twentieth century) in C. J. Johnson's "You Better Run"; Gospel song composer/arranger Thomas A. Dorsey's "The Lord Will Make a Way Somehow," and "The Old Ship of Zion" in the early to mid-twentieth century (made even more compelling by the performances of these songs by Mother Willie Mae Ford Smith, well into the twentieth century and into the twenty-first). Among so many others. And, of course, there were the famous artists that made these and other arrangements so compelling. The documentary film

Say Amen, Somebody (2019) is worth another consideration in light of arguments made here.

21. A few examples that have "struck" me—the lyrics of rapper Busta Rhymes' in "Glory of God," that was part of an album signifying on Handel's *Messiah*. His transmutation of sentiment from

"Glory of God" to "feel[in'] the glory"—

[I]t's about time to feel the Glory of God from the inna,

Another winna . . . "

is stunning as signifying arts, and very much worth focused critical attention of the sort I think is being modeled in this book. See/hear "Glory to God," in *Handel's Messiah: A Soulful Celebration* (1992).

Also worth attention is singer/songwriter Chantae Cann's song "Reason to Live" (*Sol Empowered*, 2017). Her focus on convincing a listener with a certain history of being "writ up" (Sojourner Truth) that he or she has

"got a reason to live,

there's no need to question your existence"

is very powerful. And what she leaves this certain type of listener with is a challenge that (as it channels Morrison and so many others) cannot be more haunting:

"Remember, Remember, Remember,

Remember, Remember, Remember"

22. See Linda Colley, *The Gun, the Ship, and the Pen: Warfare, Constitutions, and the Making of the Modern World* (New York: Liveright, 2021).

23. See my *Scripturalectics: The Management of Meaning* (New York: Oxford University Press, 2017).

24. See Christopher Miller, *Blank Darkness* (Chicago: University of Chicago Press, 1986), 48–49, for more discussion of Demanet's use of such language..

25. Sylvia Wynter, "1492: A New World View," in *Race, Discourse, and the Origin of the Americas*, ed. Vera Lawrence Hyatt and Rex Nettleford (Washington, DC: Smithsonian Institution, 1995), 21–22, 36–38, 43. This "discovery" of the already there that was experienced by the Others as violence, I remind the reader, was the disturbing outcome of the European exploration—going beyond the traditional boundaries—that Francis Bacon crowed about and which was imaged as the frontispiece of his book. It was also placed at the beginning of this Exhibition.

26. Here Lévi-Strauss in my mind meets and is tutored by Sojourner Truth. The former (in *Tristes Tropiques* [New York: Atheneum, 1973 (1955)]) was channeling the already stated truth that the latter figure knew and registered in her profound words (necessarily handed down/"passed" on in less stable ways).

27. Again Mitchell, *Seeing through Race, passim*.

28. Note the 1928 Blind Willie Johnson ("Blues") production of "I'm Gonna Run to the City of Refuge," in *The Complete Blind Willie Johnson*, Sony Music Entertainment, Inc., 1993. And Rev. Dr. C. J. Johnson's decades-later rendition of the song ("You Better Run") for nostalgia-minded urban dwellers from the countrysides, in *Wade in the Water: African American Congregational Singing.* Smithsonian Folkways Recording, Volume II (1994). Go to folkways.si.edu/wade-in-the-water-vol-2-african-american-congregational-singing/african-american-music-gospel-sacred/album/smithsonian.

29. By the late nineteenth century, the professionalization or academicization of scholars, including the establishment of academy-site or related learned societies, alongside other professional societies, had gained much momentum, with consequences for standardization and apologetics of dominance. These regimes tightly controlled practices and ideas. Given what many thought was at stake in this situation (including the present, especially with the tightness of the job market and the anxieties provoked) there is little room from *mis*readings or *mis*translations. It is enough in this book to stress that the work of academic scholarship and all related colonial-empire professional protocols and research, with their obsessions over classification, invest in and promote canons, canonization/orthodoxy, with attendant museumization/archives which complexly function as mostly unrecognized and unexamined forms of violence. See as example of courageous possibilities for *mis*readings the orientation of and the models of Saidiya Hartman, "Venus in Two Acts," *Small Axe* 12(2) (June 2008), 1–14; and *Wayward Lives, Beautiful Experiments* (New York: W. W. Norton, 2020). Also, go to https://www.thenation.com/article/archive/saidiya-hartmans-astounding-history-of-the-forgotten-sexual-modernists-in-20th-century-black-life/ for sharp analysis of Hartmann's work.

30. This term the reader must know by now is by me understood in the broadest term; in fact, if you are still thinking only of the religious domain in relation to the scriptural you have, as I warned above, missed the larger points made in this Exhibition. In re: ISS, its history and programs and projects, including its work to render problematic the conceit and concept of "scriptures" in culture, go to www.signifyingscriptures.org.

31. David Marriott, *Conscripts of Modernity* (Durham, NC: Duke University Press, 2004).

32. Houston A. Baker Jr., *Modernism and the Harlem Renaissance* (Chicago: University of Chicago Press, 1987), 17.

33. Houston A. Baker Jr., *Modernism and the Harlem Renaissance* (Chicago: University of Chicago Press, 1987), 53.

34. Take note of an image of OE/GV in the contemporary world—by James Marshall Kerry, London Bridge painting, owned by Tate Americas Foundation. Go to https://www.tate.org.uk/art/artworks/marshall-untitled-london-bridge-l04083; https://www.tate.org.uk/tate-etc/issue-44-autumn-2018/kerry-james-marshall-untitled-london-bridge-mark-godfrey.

I am provoked to ask: how is Equiano/Vassa here recalled? As one who showed us that all is play and that scriptural pretensions are just that, all masquerade albeit violent and deadly? Or is he viewed here as an oddity now firmly imbedded in the culture, as Stanley Diamond put it, a "conscript of civilization" (Stanley Diamond, *In Search of the Primitive: A Critique of Civilization* [New Brunswick, NJ: Transaction Books, 1974]), only in crass terms now simply to be played with?

35. See Reiland Rabaka, *Forms of Fanonism: Frantz Fanon's Critical Theory and the Dialectics of Decolonization* (Lanham, MD: Lexington Books, 2010) for provocative arguments in re: five forms of Fanonism.

36. Franz Fanon, *Black Skin, White Masks* (New York: Grove Press, [1952] 1967).

37. https://www.nytimes.com/2021/10/20/magazine/rebecca-hall-passing.html ?searchResultPosition=1.

38. Nella Larsen, *Passing* (New York: Penguin Classics, [1929] 2003).

39. https://www.nytimes.com/2021/03/02/t-magazine/passing-nella-larsen-brit -bennett.html.

40. Houston Baker, *Modernism and the Harlem Renaissance*, xviii; 76–79.

BIBLIOGRAPHY

Baker, Houston A., Jr. *Modernism and the Harlem Renaissance*. Chicago: University of Chicago Press, 1987.

Bellah, Robert N. *Religion in Human Evolution: From the Paleolithic to the Axial Age*. Cambridge, MA: The Belknap Press of Harvard University Press, 2011.

Bennett, Tony. "Civic Laboratories: Museums, Cultural Objecthood and the Governance of the Social." *Cultural Studies* 19, no. 5 (2006): 521–547.

Benston, K. W. *Performing Blackness: Enactments of African-American Modernism*. New York: Routledge, 2000.

Cann, Chantae. "Reason to Live." Song. Album *Sol Empowered*. INDIES. 2017.

Caponi, Gena Dagel, ed. *Signifyin(g), Santifyin', & Slam Dunking: A Reader in African American Expressive Culture*. Amherst: University of Massachusetts Press, 1999.

Cheyfitz, Eric. *Poetics of Imperialism: Translation and Colonization from* The Tempest *to Tarzan*. New York: Oxford University Press, 1991.

Colley, Linda. *The Gun, the Ship, and the Pen: Warfare, Constitutions, and the Making of the Modern World*. New York: Liveright, 2021.

Diamond, Stanley. *In Search of the Primitive: A Critique of Civilization*. New Brunswick, NJ: Transaction Books, 1974.

Fanon, Franz. *Black Skin, White Masks*. New York: Grove Press, [1952] 1967.

Farago, Jason. "Close Read" series: "Myth of North America" 2020 *New York Times* piece: https://www.nytimes.com/interactive/2020/11/25/arts/benjamin-west -general-wolfe.html; https://extragoodshit.phlap.net/wp-content/uploads/2020/11/ The-Myth-of-North-America-in-One-Painting.html.

Gates, Henry Louis. *Signifying Monkey: A Theory of African American Literary Criticism*. New York: Oxford University Press, 1988.

Gell, A. *Art and Agency: An Anthropological Theory*. New York: Oxford University Press, 1998.

Hartman, Saidiya Hartman. "Venus in Two Acts." *Small Axe* No. 26, Vol. 12(2) (June 2008): 1–14.

———. *Wayward Lives, Beautiful Experiments.* New York: W. W. Norton, 2020. https://www.thenation.com/article/archive/saidiya-hartmans-astounding-history-of -the-forgotten-sexual-modernists-in-20th-century-black-life/

Huizinga, J. *Homo Ludens: A Study of the Play-Element in Culture.* Boston: Beacon Press, 1955.

Johnson, Blind Willie. "I'm Gonna Run to the City of Refuge." Song. 1928, in *The Complete Blind Willie Johnson*, Sony Music Entertainment, Inc., 1993.

Johnson, C. J. Rev. "You Better Run." *Wade in the Water: African American Congregational Singing.* Smithsonian Folkways Recording, Volume II (1994). folkways.si.edu/wade-in-the-water-vol-2-african-american-congregational-singing/african-american-music-gospel-sacred/album/smithsonian.

Larsen, Nella. *Passing.* New York: Penguin Classics, [1929] 2003. https://www .nytimes.com/2021/03/02/t-magazine/passing-nella-larsen-brit-bennett.html

Lévi-Strauss, C. *Tristes Tropiques.* New York: Atheneum, [1955] 1973.

Lott, Eric. *Love and Theft: Blackface Minstrelsy and the American Working Class.* Oxford University Press, 1993.

Marriott, David. *Conscripts of Modernity.* Durham, North Carolina: Duke University Press, 2004.

Marshall, Kerry James. Untitled (London Bridge), 2017. https://www.tate.org.uk/art/ artworks/marshall-untitled-london-bridge-l04083; https://www.tate.org.uk/tate-etc/ issue-44-autumn-2018/kerry-james-marshall-untitled-london-bridge-mark-godfrey

McClintock, Anne. *Imperial Leather: Race, Gender, and Sexuality in the Colonial Contest.* New York: Routledge, 1995.

Merleau-Ponty, M. *Phenomenology of Perception.* New York: Routledge, [1945] 2013.

Miller, Christopher. *Blank Darkness.* Chicago: University of Chicago Press, 1986.

Miller, John C. *The Wolf by the Ears: Thomas Jefferson and Slavery.* Rev. ed. Charlottesville, VA: University of Virginia Press, 1991.

Miller, Norman, et al., producers. *Handel's Messiah: A Soulful Celebration. Album.* Alliance, 1992.

Mitchell, W. J. *Seeing through Race.* Cambridge, MA: Harvard University Press, 2012.

Morrison, Toni. *Playing in the Dark: Whiteness and the Literary Imagination.* New York: Vintage Books, 1993.

Pitts, Walter F., Jr. *Old Ship of Zion: The Afro-Baptist Ritual in the African Diaspora.* New York: Oxford University Press, 1993.

Rabaka, Reiland. *Forms of Fanonism: Frantz Fanon's Critical Theory and the Dialectics of Decolonization.* Lanham, MD: Lexington Books, 2010.

Taussig, Michael. *Mimesis and Alterity: A Particular History of the Senses.* New York: Routledge, 1993.

Tennenhouse, Leonard. *The Importance of Feeling English: American Literature and the British Diaspora, 1750–1850.* Princeton, NJ: Princeton University Press, 2007.

Wimbush, Vincent L. *Scripturalectics: The Management of Meaning.* New York: Oxford University Press, 2017.

Wynter, Sylvia. "1492: A New World View," in *Race, Discourse, and the Origin of the Americas,* ed. Vera Lawrence Hyatt and Rex Nettleford. Washington, DC: Smithsonian Institution, 1995.

Chapter 1

Scripturalectics and Masquerading Flesh

Shay Welch

In the introduction to this book, Vincent Wimbush curates an exposition of the role of psycho-politics in processes of scripturalization as those emergent of practices—metaphysical and metaphorical—of masquerade and veiling. To do so, he buttresses his distinguishing analysis of storied life of freed slave Gustavus Vassa with an attendant feast of artifacts that signify the role of black flesh in the production and maintenance of hierarchical racializations in modernity. Specifically, he invites us to think deeply about whether, and how, black flesh operates as a metonymy for modernity as such qua identity.

Wimbush's project takes aim at the notion of naturalized race and its role in grounding and building modernity. Such practices of socio-political construction function in part through the ability of ideas to take root and spread into ideology. Distinctive, though, is the extent to which certain notions or conceptions operate as deep text; a text unlike any other in its power to command and direct. For modernity, a fundamental text, if not *the* fundamental text, has been—and continues to be—the Holy scripture(s) of the Enlightenment. Domination is as central to scripture as it is to modernity, in part, because of, and not consequent of, the workings of domination as the very structure for, and motivation behind, scripture. Consequently, all notions that feed and foster practices of domination find their way into scripture and proceed to more brilliantly illuminate the mission of modernity, and to more finely carve out its thirsty, creeping trajectory. In effect, when inventive mechanisms for command and control are made known to the virtual scribes of modernity, they become scripture when enacted as psycho-social-political doctrine.

DIALECTICAL SCRIPTURALECTICS

But what does it mean for an idea to become *scripture*? When conceived of as a constructing process, scripture scripturalizes. The "scripture" becomes scripture and thus comes to frame the very core of individual and institutional life. And because the ideology that anchors the idea is—without metaphor—the text for living, the idea becomes enfolded into the scripture as scripture. Scripture, as such, is the framing mechanism of the machine of modernity. When this machine consumes and refabricates ideology as scripture, it scripturalizes the ideas within. And when members of society act from this scripture, they, too, scripturalize through their affirming actions and adherence to the socio-political apparatus. *To scripturalize* is to fabricate the very frame and its mechanisms itself through socio-cultural-historical dynamics.

Scripturalizing, then, is a very specific dialectical procedure. Ethico-political-economic-psycho-social-arrangements manifest via the individual and the institution in a web-like, interweaving dynamic. Ideologies that articulate these all-consuming frameworks inform the lives of individuals. Individuals shaped by ideologies then enact these frames in their social relationships. Then the force and nature of interpersonal relationships passes via exchange through the community, seeping its way into the walls and the halls of socio-political institutions. Then the institutions shore up, validate, and cement the emergent epistemologies over time until individuals inevitably affirm institutions permeated through with ideology. What makes such processes of social construction specifically dialectical is the web-like, iterative nature of the dynamics. For this reason, the ongoing introduction of relations and institutions can enter in to, and be traced through, any part of the discursive reiterating/reiterations.

What makes the scripturalizing of modernity a distinctive mode of politico-historical dialectics is its faithfulness to intuitional and individual dynamics of domination vis-à-vis scripture. And one essential ingredient for the scripture of modernity is black flesh. Black flesh didn't accidentally become racialized; black flesh needed to be racialized. For it was—and remains—necessary for black flesh to be naturalized into Blackness. Blackness carried/carries modernity forward on its back. In any conception of socio-political historical dialectics, one can imagine being able to reach in at some point and unravel a thread of ideology and the iterating process would persist in its sweeping vacillations. Almost as if a direct signifier for domination, race cannot be so plucked from the psycho-social frames and epistemologies of modernity. Race cannot be unwritten or unread—it cannot be erased from the text that is scripture. To do so would collapse modernity as a whole, which is why attempts to do so have been met with violence. To remove race is to remove the most visible and viable validation of, and for, ethico-political domination. If race is a metonym for domination, then it must be so for modernity.

A specific point Wimbush makes that I want to think more deeply about is his reference to flesh and racial signification. He says:

> Black flesh could not possibly be left to be what it was—simple difference; it had to be made readable, had to be made into a "text" that could be controlled, heavily signified. Herein was found the way "forward"—to make black-ness a supercharged/hypersignified "reality" and in every respect the lack and the limit. Thus, black flesh becomes a "text" made up/"read"/"writ up." (Introduction, 15)

This claim accounts for the metaphysical construction of race from a realist perspective. The realism about constructivism position holds that race is socially constructed but real in the deepest sense. That is, race was invented as an idea, as is all facets of ideologies in ongoing dialectics. Then race and the processes of racialization—the scripturalization of racialization—was attributed to bodies qua material substratum, and thereby solidified. Race qua domination became codified through social practice and discourse to such an extent that the ontological realness of race could no longer be fiction or fantasy. The swift transition of race from idea to ideology, carried along and through and on by bodies of difference, become very, very real—real in material politics, material science, material morality, and material deprivation. This is precisely why the dialectics of the Enlightenment are so distinct from most, if not all, others. The dialectics of modernity make practices of racialization that transmute the notion to the material conceptually and mechanically necessary. The structuring of an entire society on practices of domination that encoded flesh makes race as metonym for modernity totalizing—it makes it scripture.

This process of ideological dialectics appears to be somewhat linear until we take historical processes into account. Over time and over place, conceptions of race have been actualized—and reactualized—in guises that remain entrenched in the scriptural purpose of/for race. For each new realization relies upon narratives of race and racialized pasts to move forward into futurities. As ideologies change/d, as the Enlightenment moved into something more sinister and then out again, race has had to be rewritten to function as a core anchor for modernity. This is one of the ways in which the Enlightenment remains to be regarded as a model for ideological and material psycho-social progress. When attitudes change, particularly with respect to race, the economic-political institutions must reach back into earlier constructions and adapt them into new manifestations suitable to the times. In most instances, race has been constructed in ways that make white flesh comfortable with the uses of black flesh to preserve a white sense of innocence or moral validation. Race is typically constructed in ways that make white-fleshed bodies feel as if the evils of sin executed onto black flesh is needed because of how such flesh is written and read. Black flesh can move from deserving, to needing saving, to needing rescue, to needing blindness. All dialectical reformulations of race have served both the economic prosperity or material comfort of white flesh. And this is always done through a scripturalization that dips into the explicit attitudes of the immediate past, enfolding them into more progressive actualizations of the present until they are buried inside; yet they shine through. This is how the distinctive operation of scripturalization feeds itself. It creates horror to exalt the Enlightenment and transmutes it into a sort of helplessness to romanticize the Enlightenment's "inherent" urge toward perfection.

STAGES OF SCRIPTURALIZATION

A second idea Wimbush extends that merits philosophical reflection is how we can see within the evolution of masking-as-survival a masking-to-play. Regarding the relationship between veiling and survival, he eloquently explains:

> The "masquerade"—the "play-element"[1] "in" culture captures the paradox of the rather serious implications for our thinking and ramifications for the orientations and psycho-politics and dynamics that bring on and maintain modernities. . . . The masquerade is quite natural in almost all social situations—among almost all earthly creatures, for a variety of interests. In other types of fraught situations among humans—systems of slavery, serfdom, caste—it may be imposed or accepted as necessary for survival[2] . . . These attempts to "convert" [to Christianity] on the part of many if not most in the Black Atlantic worlds constituted a layered and complex history—of representations, resistance, flight, accommodation, survival. (Introduction, 3, 12)

One may be initially shaken by a claim that survival and play have anything at all in common. However, play, here, is not necessarily taken to mean jubilance. What it means in these specific kinds on contexts is more a notion of what, in the area of embodied cognitive psychology, is termed "pretend play" or play "as if."[3] Play is taken to be a highly skilled mode of imagination that helps one conceive otherwise. When one is set to operate in survival mode through conditions of trauma and desperation, they must mask. Merely existing in any psycho-political milieu exacts a bit of pretend play from everyone. But social participation involves participating under a light veiling necessary for cooperation; conventional playing "as if" is akin to "playing nice." But for those who are held under the cooperative structure and must find ways to gasp air, a more dire contrivance of pretend play is necessary in order to not perish—physically or spiritually. The veil, the mask, of the masquerade of misfortune and despair is a play-element that dictates individual psycho-social cloaking of the mind and soul. In this way, survival and play are united through practices of persistent imaginings of otherwise-subsistence.

But Wimbush harks to something quite significant in the masquerade. This is the evolution of masking. While racialized others exist below the scriptures, they are made through practices of scripturalization. Accordingly, they are carried through—though never directing—the evolution of scripturalectics, along with everyone else, though differently. I recognize here four stages of scripturalectics. This means that the practices of pretend play needed for survival will mutate over time and place. And even, in some times and places, real moments of masking-as-play rather than masking-to-play. When looking at the progressing alterations of race, racialization, and practices of masking within the scripturalectics of modernity, I find four distinct phases of masquerading.

The first stage relates to the initial foisting of the mask qua hyper-signification onto black flesh—a coercive infliction of masquerade. This is the process of social construction in which black flesh becomes naturalized through a multitude of intersecting practices of scripturalizing and psycho-political dynamics. While processes of scripturalectics are intended to elevate white flesh over all other flesh, this process cannot be concretized without the participation of those upon whom scripturalizing is being enacted. For a product of social construction to be naturalized, all must come to accept the order that is being established in some manner. For this reason, and over much time, a second stage emerges. This stage is one fleshed out by Frantz Fanon (Fanon 2008); this is the stage of psychological internalization for the purpose of generating psychological oppression on behalf of/ within those who have been racialized hierarchically.[4] Psychological oppression is a phenomena whereby oppressed others internalize beliefs about their supposed flaws from the dominant narrative and police themselves accordingly, without need for intervention by those who have constructed the narratives about those flaws (Bartky 2001). For many cultures, masking in dance and in ritual is seen as an ontologically real transformation into the spirit of the persona of, within, upon the mask. To bear the mask is to internalize and bear the spirit within and upon oneself. Much the same can be said about the internalization of the scripturalizing of black flesh within modernity. Here, individuals internalize the scriptures and tropes about their flesh and regard them more as character flaws rather than as signals of systemic repression. This is how psychological internalization engenders psychological oppression. Psychological oppression is the mechanism that motivates recognition. Calls for recognition manifest in the way of assimilation—in a mask that is a bargaining with the scripture of modernity for acceptance despite one's flaws on the promise of moving to overcome those flaws. Unfortunately, and inevitably, mask manifestation drives individually perceived psychosis and neurosis.

But neurosis is a mask that scrapes, which leads to the third stage of recognition of assimilative ill-fit and the potential of removal. The third stage functions exists as an in-between stage, within which many are transitioning in-to and out-of naturalizing scriptures. The eventual recognition of ill-fit by those who have been racialized within the dominant narrative and socio-economic-political system engenders a process of demystification. Subsequently, those who are hyper-signified under and within the scriptures of modernity thrust themselves as active challengers into the scripturalectics. But this interception and intervention is more than physical struggle for psychological liberation— it is a moral struggle. Many virtue ethicists have argued that the virtues of the oppressed are burdened (Tessman 2005). That is, what makes for a necessary character under conditions of oppression are not the same character traits that lead to flourishing, or living the good life. Many oppressed individuals who seek liberation from the scriptualizations of the naturalization of race must cultivate the burdened virtues of anger, resilience, solitude, and detachment to existence and resist under materially, psychologically, and spiritually violent conditions. Thus, in this way, the stage is one of a re-whittling of the mask itself and a rejection of "recognition" politics. This transition stage is a masking game of transition—one that Wimbush gestures toward. The cultivation of the burdened virtues is, as he explains:

[a] . . . sharp persistent even if disturbing and painful self-reflexivity . . . toward addressing what matters or is always at stake—brokenness of spirit, of bodies, slippage of categories, of systems, of identity, as a type of poignant tragedy not as romance of resistance overcoming. (Introduction, 17)

The fourth stage is one we're transitioning into today. This is a new masquerade of the kind of passion and creative forces Wimbush prescribes. It is a presentation and revolution of the re-formed mask. Wimbush states:

But the surprising and inspiring survival of such folk means that their tactics, their orientation, play, gestures, soundings—all should be watched and studied carefully by all. *In their very survival there may be opportunities for all if not to throw off all the masks, at least to "see through" their experiences and gestures, to gain heightened self-awareness of the masquerade that defines all human foibles and strivings in the world after Contact with difference.* (15–16; italics added)

This new unveiling of a veil lies in and through the power of performance arts and social media, which offer new and creative public participatory apertures.[5] From this reformation born of creativity is a moral renewal from an epistemic liberation grounded in the ability to "see through" to "see into" to "see differently." These public modes of performance by the racialized are the masking games anew. These performative practices are not an embracing of the mask that was indicative of the move toward recognition. They are a vehicle through which the oppressed can embrace difference differentiated. This is a stage of scripturalectics as descriptualization through rescripturalization. Social media and public art seems to be allowing folx to pursue social justice through praxis of epistemic justice that close the hermeneutical gaps forced open and locked down for so long by the sheer for of the scripturalization of naturalized black flesh in modernity. Thusly, we can identify the four staged scripturalectics of masquerade: *Rejection, Resignation, Refusal, and Resignification.*

SCRIPTURALIZING COLONIZING

The scripturalization of race was, in part, engendered for the purposes of justifying and materially maintaining colonialist-capitalist ventures. The metaphysical magnitude of this constructed reality is fascinating, if only in a macabre sense. It is fascinating for nothing more than its curious self-undermining process, which is what, astoundingly, ensures its stability. The scripturalization of race is self-undermining insofar as the dialectically embedded conventions for scripturalizing rely on variations and *contradictions* in its recursive processes. Through the racializing flesh of a different color to that of flesh by a different name, colonial powers—and especially the well-compensated philosophers—found a means to paint a body with more than difference. This additional layer of ideology of sin and defectiveness constituted, as Wimbush says, a hyper-signification insofar as the racialized body says more, politically and morally speaking, than a non-racialized body. And all racialized bodies are hyper-signified through the same scripturalizing and for the same scripture. This brings me to the interesting and curious component: in order to justify the various colonial and slave practices and imperial investments, the ideology of sin and defectiveness was applied consistently but inversely across all flesh but white flesh. Universalism, that moral cornerstone of the Enlightenment, meant that flesh was scripturalized equally. But the principle of universalism has always been a bit quirky. In the scripturalization of race, universality demands difference to naturalize difference for domination.

The scripturalization used to justify slavery was the idea of persisting blackness that is definitively *undilutable*. In order to assure the maintenance of slaves and an increase in their numbers, the ontological realness of blackness had to be defined according to a one-drop rule, such that any miscegenation between black flesh and the flesh of any other racialized or non-racialized body yielded more black flesh. However, modernity is signified most mightily for its spread of the word; this spread of the word, of the text, of the scripture was made possible through the colonization of other places and bodies. White men set out to save bodies fleshed differently; they carried the burden of saving the world through saving souls. But they could not do this alone. While the white man carried the word, black flesh carried its literal weight. In the Americas, to save the soul of the land and the people, they scripturalized red bodies, as fast as possible, into white flesh. There could be no progress alongside sin. In order to ensure the complete eradication of Native North American indigenous bodies—the "Indian"—the scripturalectics of sin and defectiveness stipulated that any miscegenation with red fleshed bodies, except with black fleshed bodies, would begin the process of progress by eradicating the existence of the "Indian."

Economically and politically, the need for land was the priority. They needed somewhere for the slaves to put down and build up scripture. To get this land—land that slaves would have to work to actualize the mission of modernity—they had to clear the land of sin first. This necessitated a discrete kind of genocide—one of dissolution, or, at least, disappearance, through a hundred-drop rule. The scripture of the hundred-drop rule dictated that any introduction of differently and non-racialized flesh rubbed off on—and so rubbed out—red flesh. Ironically, as I mentioned previously, the scripturalization of hyper-signified racialized flesh to establish modernity as such requires, paradoxically, opposing, scripturalectics. The way to heal the sin of red flesh was to make it white. Not only was this necessary to gaining land—for what saved/white soul would deny another saved/white soul the blessing of the anointed land that belonged, intrinsically, to saved/white souls—but it was also necessary to making space for black bodies to develop this land.

One example that can unveil the masquerade of racial scripturalectics is the 1770 painting by Benjamin West "The Death of General Wolfe" that Wimbush highlights. Wimbush explains:

> At any rate . . . one notes how the colored "Native" body that is figured in the center is used as a kind of hieroglyphics, signifying complex impulses and emotions/anxieties having to do with the making of the modern world in relation to the presence of flesh white and black, in total silence, of course.[6] (11)

The Native body is hieroglyphic qua the "Indian." The "Indian" is interesting in so far as it is a forever frozen moment in the scripturalectics. The "Indian" signified many things but two chief attributes of this idea are the taming of a wild land and a taming of a wild man. The "Indian," as depicted here, is a permanent romanticization of the white mind that is another metonymy for modernity. The "Indian" symbolizes the sheer persuasive force of the Enlightenment. The white man was able to go into this new land, teach the "Indian" of his sins, and rescue his soul. In return, the "Indian" befriended the white man, taking him around and showing him wild secrets of savage land and savage war. The "Indian," who disappeared as fast as he was found, will always be remembered . . . as a guide . . . as a good friend . . . as an especially *noble* kind of savage. And the "Indians" who were not so noble, well, they had to be dispensed with; it was for their own good—they were rabid. And this is one of the most confounding impulses and racialized anxieties of colonization. The "Indian" was savage but appeared to be savable. When saved, the "Indian" transubstantiated into what is beloved and represented what is wise. But then the "Indian" went missing. While all the "Indians," sadly and mysteriously, went extinct, burdensome red flesh remained. And red flesh needed to be moved when it could not be fully removed, for space was needed for new and more black flesh. This process itself was a pivotal movement and moving-silence exacted by the insatiable demands of modernity.

Wimbush astutely tells us that racialization cannot be undone. This, again, is why modernity vis-à-vis scripturalization, is a scripturalectic rather than a mere dialectic. Everything modernity is built upon, literally, required the most nonsensical dialectical. That there seemed to be no reason to it points to the "reason" that grounds modernity. For the invisibility of consistency or patterning, the unfound meaning that made it all so seemingly unfounded, was the tool that constructed race into reality. It is true that no analysis of modernity can be proffered without acknowledging and privileging the role of race and black flesh in its empire. But more than that, there could be no modernity without a scripturalization of race. From Hobbes to Kant, philosophers and scientists ensured that any understanding of universality and fraternity, of discovery, progress, and science, could not exist apart from naturalized race. The entire understanding of Enlightenment in which modernity was couched demanded that difference be made into dominance.

PERFORMATIVITIES OF BLACK FLESH

I found Wimbush's reflections enacted in Stage III to be especially interesting. Wimbush titles this stage "The book remained silent" to account for the ways in which white men "fetishized" books in, and for the purpose of, scripturalectics. He rightly depicts the perspective of the time as one that attributed unbound and godly power to books. The power of books can be understood as unbound in many respects. But one that is most germane to my purpose here is the unboundedness of their creation. Books were written from biased and uninformed information for the very purpose of creating practices of scripturalizing that would consecrate their vision of the Enlightenment. There were no true constraints to which a scholar or scientist had to bow, outside of the sovereign or the church; there were no limits they set upon themselves on their journey to modernity beyond their own rendered dictates of "reason." Books were godlike in that they defined reality. And, further, books carried the intentions behind the scripturalectics far and wide. In this way, books can be seen as being omnipotent, omniscient, and omnipresent. It makes sense that white men would worship the word and racialized others see scripture as magic. The anxiety that black folx experienced as a result of being forbidden from the word would have been palpable and poisonous.

Wimbush further explicates that this severance entrenched a deep kind of silence—not only silencing but a literal ontology of silence. He explains:

> The silence I argue here signifies a blocking—keeping black-fleshed persons from seeing/being seen, from hearing/being heard on their own terms, through their own agency, being represented as human and experiencing their full humanity. (11)

This incisive assessment provides an original lens through which to understand and examine the afropessimist claim that black flesh was naturalized specifically as flesh by white men to preclude their participation from the Enlightenment conception of the human, and thus to ensure that anti-blackness could anchor the passages of modernity into all modes of futurity.

The original slant is the articulation of the role of epistemic silencing via a kind of literary violence to engender a literal social death. The wording of silence and the silencing through wording brought an end to black folx's power to know themselves or their oppressors. They were told of their deservingness for violence. It was known because it was written that their suitability at being inherently suitable came from the mouth of God—it was written in scripture. The Bible justified the "scripturalization of white violence on black flesh." Books, in this sense, had the power to erase and repurpose human existence. The social death magicked away humanity and left behind mere flesh. Books, then, manipulated more than just narrative and socio-political practices. Books enacted scripturalizations of being-ontology through the control of psycho-political belief formation itself.

Another way through which the fetishization of the written word drove ontological social death through epistemological silencing was through the literal demonization of traditional indigenous forms of knowing. Many indigenous worldviews contain performative epistemologies that enact the world (Welch 2019). Many African cultures posit this general feature, as indicated by the significance of the role of masking and masquerade in social practice.

Additionally, many cultures were/are oral and shared knowledge through sharing narrative. Both masking and narrative are performative modes of creating and participating in knowledge. When the white man naturalized black flesh into being a black (non)being, he had to terminate and invalidate all possibilities for epistemological masquerade to fuel the deprivation of black humanity. The scripturalectics of racialization engendered the elimination of masking-as-knowing, leaving only enough remnants of the knowledge of masquerade to allow for the masking-as-play-as-survival.

CONCLUSION

Wimbush rightly tells us that racialization cannot be undone. Racialization is one of the foundational components of modernity vis-à-vis scripturalization; and to attempt to pull its thread from the dialectic would be to unravel much of what the Enlightenment dictates—particularly with respect to reason. For this reason, Wimbush advises that we must learn to deal with the "reality," consequences, implications, and institutions that have emerges from the scripturalizing of racial construction practices. What remains to be done in the absence of a power to eliminate race is to develop a critical mode of self-reflexivity to address subsequent injuries (see Introduction, p. 13). This approach reminds me of one that is used within many Indigenous psycho-political perspectives. This approach aims to remind the people that, even in the face of continued epistemic, psychological, and ethico-political violence, one must continue to recognize the sacredness in everything (Cajete 2000). The colonial practices that aim to destroy any worldview that counters the scriptures of modernity cannot, however, destroy the true ontological nature of the world. By continuing to find the sacredness in the world, one may find a way to see the sacredness in themselves. This manner of self-reflexivity does not overcome or erase continued colonialism, but it does open spaces for epistemic resistance and the recognition that such resistance can but used to create futurities outside of the scriptures of modernity.

A particularly significant avenue for constructing creative futurities of otherwise being is performance. A return to performance as a way of knowing is a turning away from the scripture itself. Performance is the domain of the narrative and, as such, performs as an act of refusal—of modernity and its word. One way of enacting refusal is a return to the performance of masquerade qua masking-as-play. These sorts of masquerades, these "as if" performances, enact the world through ontological practices of worlding. When one participates in enactments of worlding, one is able to create otherwise places and spaces for knowing and being. With respect to masking, Wimbush states:

Mask(-ing) is shorthand for the necessary obliqueness, the indirectness, that we use to name the hard to name and grasp. (Introduction, 14)

In the context of the African cultural practices that he is gesturing towards, this is accurate. But it is also accurate in another way. When thinking about the role of masking-as-masquerade-as-resistance, the performance of masking can perform as a deeply resistant veiling. And the veiling here has the capacity to veil those who are racialized from the psycho-political internalizations of the scripture of modernity.

With respect to addressing the injuries of racialization, Wimbush further tells us:

Perhaps, the most appropriate conclusion to draw from this project is that nothing can or ever should be concluded—at least not simply or straightforwardly, or without being disturbed, or without "seeing through" racialization in order to honestly face the chaos and violence, as well as the possibilities ahead. (13)

Performing masquerades and enacting new worlds "as if" is not an illusory or fantastical idea. Narrative has no other starting point than that one in front of you. Narrative demands that before any story can be told, before any worlding can take place, one must have a beginning from which to even begin to "see through." In the reality of modernity, the starting point of any narrative must be the violence inherent in its scriptures. But, as he prudently pronounces, by facing this chaos, we orient ourselves in such a way as to see-through in order to see-beyond. Performative practices of epistemic, embodied, fully fleshed self-reflexivity can motivate new practices of veiling ourselves through performances of worlding through rewording through re-fleshing. While we cannot undo modernity, and while we cannot interject into the recursive processes of scripturalization, we can perform futurities of otherwise knowing and freshly fleshed being. And these fleshed performative futurities are what is seen-beyond; they are masquerades of resistance.

NOTES

1. Wimbush's Introduction note #4.
2. Wimbush's Introduction note #5.
3. See: Gallagher, Shaun and Robb Lindgren, "Enactive Metaphors: Learning Through Full-Body Engagement," *Educational Psychological Review* 27 (2015): 391–404; Gallagher, Shaun and Micah Allen, "Active Inference, Enactivism, and the Hermeneutics of Social Cognition." *Synthese* 195 (2018): 2627–2648; Gallagher, Shaun and Zuzanna Rucińska, "Prospecting Performance: Rehearsal and the Nature of Imagination," *Synthese*, 2021: 1–19.

4. For an interesting take on Fanon's analysis from a Native perspective, see: Coulthard 2014.

5. See also: Welch 2019.

6. Wimbush's Introduction note #18.

BIBLIOGRAPHY

Bartky, Sandra. *Femininity and Domination: Studies in the Phenomenology of Oppression*. New York: Routledge, 2001.

Cajete, Gregory. *Native Science: Natural Laws of Interdependence*. Santa Fe: Clear Light Publishers, 2000.

Coulthard, Glen Sean. *Red Skin, White Masks: Rejecting the Colonial Politics of Recognition*. Minneapolis: University of Minnesota Press, 2014.

Fanon, Frantz. *Black Skin, White Masks*. New York: Grove Press, 2008.

Gallagher, Shaun and Micah Allen. "Active Inference, Enactivism, and the Hermeneutics of Social Cognition." *Synthese* 195 (2018): 2627–2648.

Gallagher, Shaun and Robb Lindgren. "Enactive Metaphors: Learning through Full-Body Engagement." *Educational Psychological Review* 27 (2015): 391–404.

Gallagher, Shaun, Lauren Reinerman-Jones, Bruce Janz, Patricia Bockelman, and Jörg Trempler. *A Neurophenomenology of Awe and Wonder: Towards a Non-Reductionist Cognitive Science*. New York: Palgrave Macmillan, 2015.

Gallagher, Shaun and Zuzanna Rucińska. "Prospecting Performance: Rehearsal and the Nature of Imagination." *Synthese*, 2021: 1–19.

Gallagher, Shaun and Dan Zahavi. *The Phenomenological Mind*. New York: Routledge, 2012.

Tessman, Lisa. *Burdened Virtues: Virtue Ethics for Liberatory Struggles*. Oxford: Oxford University Press, 2005.

Welch, Shay. *Existential Eroticism: A Feminist Approach to Women's Oppression-Perpetuating Choices*. Lanham, MD: Lexington Books, 2015.

———. *The Phenomenology of a Performative Knowledge System: Dancing with Native American Epistemology*. New York: Palgrave Macmillan 2019.

Chapter 2

Under the Sign of "The African"

Masquerade and Identity Formation and Deployment in Equiano . . . Vassa's Interesting Narrative/*Memoir*

Carolyn M. Jones Medine

African religious traditions are masquerade traditions, on the continent and in the diaspora. Jean M. Borgatti writes of the Okpella (Ukpilla) who hold the Olimi masking festival to honor the ancestors and to purify the community.[1] Douglas Curran documents the Nayau, a secret men's masquerade association which is the "primary spiritual practice of the [rural] Chewa people of Malawi."[2] In the masquerade, the ancestors and animal spirits come to reconcile mankind with the spirit world. This ritual adds contemporary figures, addressing important community developments, like AIDS, and political developments, multiplying the number of masked orisha to 200 figures in the ritual so far. *Mardi Gras New Orleans* says that Mardi Gras masks originated in ritual celebration and that "New Orleans has been celebrating Mardi Gras for hundreds of years and is the largest masked party in North America."[3]

We see a more heart-rending use of the mask in the poetry of Paul Laurence Dunbar (1872–1906) and Maya Angelou (1928–2014), who intertextually repeats Dunbar's poem, "We Wear the Mask" and continues it, like the Nayau add figures to their masquerade. Their poems illustrate the mask as resistance and protection. The mask, for both, "grins and lies," hiding the true face," as Black folks, as Angelou puts it "smile and mouth the myriad subtleties.[4] Angelou's poem, "The Mask," about a maid she observed riding on the bus who smiles as a form of survival and resistance,[5] hiding deep sorry and anger. The mask is necessary when the "child I work for calls me girl" and as she contemplates the "submission" of Black fathers, their "living on the edge of death," that let future Black folk stay alive:

> They laugh to conceal their crying.
> They shuffle through their dreams
> They stepped n' fetched a country
> And wrote the blues in screams.[6]

Masking has been a strategy of resistance and survival, from putting on an individual mask to hide one's true feelings, as in Angelou's poem, to masquerading indigenous practices in religion as Christianity. In this work, I want to look at the figure with whom Vincent Wimbush frames his *Masquerade* exhibit, Gustavus Vassa, who writes his narrative in both the name he was given by an owner, Vassa, *and* in his African name, Olaudah Equiano—both of which, I suggest, are his masquerade under the mask of "The African." This paper is not an analysis of the narrative, but an analysis of Equiano's deployment of his African mask, of his masquerade. I suggest that Equiano, who was called Vassa in all his official documents,[7] deploys his double identity in a strategic essentialist way; hence I will call him "Equiano . . . Vassa."

I am using the ellipsis to engage his name, in the way that Charles H. Long uses the ellipsis in his work. As I have written, in Long's work the ellipsis suggests "an interruption of the perfect form," signaling a change in the structure of thought itself," opening the potential to narrate "otherwise than," letting us, as Jacques Derrida puts it, exit from closure.[8] For Long, "the ellipsis marks and is a gap that may suggest a hiatus, the opening of a space for refiguring identity itself,"[9] a space for counter-memory.[10] Such a site of difference that may be remapped only from traces, but those may open up another epistemology, pointing to another viable mode of being in the world.[11]

Equiano . . . Vassa strategically deploys "The African." Gayatri Spivak, in "Subaltern Studies: Deconstructing Historiography," argues that a disruption or functional change in a sign-system, performs the task of elaboration,[12] challenging hegemonic essentialisms, with their dualistic tendencies to create hierarchies. A perspective "from below" can deploy in a pragmatic mode, "a strategic use of positivist essentialism in a scrupulously visible political interest"—for rights, for example, as Vassa . . . Equiano does in abolitionist work.[13] Such a deployment of essence can be risky, as we see when Equiano . . . Vassa deploys Igbo or African identity, but it also can open up discourses. Gustavus Vassa's identity as Olaudah Equiano gives him authority: he is born in Africa, survives the Middle Passage and earns freedom. He, thereby, deploys both his identity as Vassa, an ex-slave, who purchased his freedom, becoming a self-made gentleman who gains what Helen Rhee, Melanie Harris and I call "approximate whiteness," and his identity as Equiano, an African.

This double identity—one which might seem unimaginable to an eighteenth-century audience—produces cognitive dissonance. It "knots," as Jaros puts it, the metropole in which Vassa is a success with the "the extra-colonial space of the African interior," to support his abolitionist work, to give voice to African slaves.[14] He occupies, with his double name, both margin and center,[15] and, I would argue, in the ellipsis, reveals the complexity—that which he can and cannot say in his narrative and that which he does say and which he avoids saying, all of which is startling and "interesting."

This marks him, as Sylvester Johnson reminds us, as more than just complex.[16] He is eliding, bringing together as well as suppressing and altering some dimension of his identities. In Wimbush's installation, *Masquerade*, we sail with Equiano . . . Vassa in this crisscrossing, cutting across, the Black Atlantic, two continents, and multiple places, including the Arctic. How to theorize this figure is difficult. Many critics turn to Victor Turner, rites of passage, and the *limen* to analyze this figure who is slave and slave master; African Igbo and genuine Christian convert and missionary; Black and British; African prince and Black Salt, a midshipman—an officer, though a low-ranking one, serving a young Horatio Nelson; and one who resists colonial representations of Africa and of Blackness yet, sometimes, engages in them. He was transnational before we used the word, and cosmopolitan. Along with Turner's *limen*, I also suggest contact zones[17]—for, Equiano . . . Vassa is, indeed looking with his "imperial eyes," as British gentleman as well as his subjected, Black, ex-slave eyes as he is producing "'the rest of the world'" for European [and American] readerships," even as he, on the receiving end of these kinds of constructions, claims, revises, rejects, and transcends them.[18] As one who is transcultural, he engages us in contemplating the complex reality of home in the multiplicity characterizing diaspora. With these ideas in mind, I walk through the exhibit, responding to the triptych— what I am going to call "Masks: Black," "Adaptations: New World Masks," and "Equiano . . . Vassa." Then, I want to speak of Black Salt—Black British Sailors and their impact on Black freedom.

MASKS: BLACK

Equiano . . . Vassa is eleven, he tells us, when he is taken. He may have been younger. The slave ship is his rite of passage. He is so young when taken captive that he has to use other sources— books like that of slave ship doctor, Alexander Falconbridge—to supplement his memory.[19] He tells us that, in his life in Africa, he spends most of his time with his mother and sister. He had not, it seems, been through rites of passage to manhood, any "initiation into the world of the incarnate being," called "masquerade."[20] Raphael Chijioke

Njoku's important book, *West African Masking Traditions and Diaspora Masquerade Carnivals: History, Memory, and Transnationalism*, explores the importance of masking and masquerade, which he describes as a device of narratology and as "one of the most potent survival devices in the Americas," as Bantu-African slaves reenacted what they could of their traditions in the Americas."[21] Njoku uses "Bantu" as an indigenous theoretical concept, not an identity, to describe the movement of a people that "subjected African culture to a process of intense and dramatic refinements and harmonization," that was extended to the Americas developing a persistence of culture.[22]

The masquerade, the theatrical art form, which included music and move-ment, of performing the mask embodies "the essence of African civilization," Njoku argues, translating meaning.[23] The mask, which does not so much conceal as make real, tells us we are under masquerade—a time, for example, that an ancestor enters and initiates a *limen*. The masquerade carried many functions in Bantu culture, from sacred representation of cosmology and religion, to secular maintenance of the social order, as masked figures "aided governments as an arm of law enforcement, supported justice administra-tion, compelled social conformity, and fought crimes in order to maintain balance."[24] Masquerade signals exercise of identity in other way, as well, as we saw in the Nayau secret societies.[25] Masquerade is the hierophany mani-festating[26] in a human action in which the sacred and secular meet, in which the human is *and/with/experiencing* the gods and ancestors: "the embodiment of . . . tradition and a guarantee of continuity" in a tradition unique "because of its ability to walk, talk, and dance; express emotions and drama or create humor; fight, carry out justice, and even predict the future."[27]

Young Equiano does not fully experience African masquerade. He is one of many Igbo children in the slave trade—including infants. He recovers it in memory, but also, likely, in his encounters with Igbo in the New World. Marcus Rediker tells us that Equiano . . . Vassa was born in a "time of crisis: when drought and famine created the collapse of the Nri civilization, opening it to plunder by Aro traders," who kidnapped Equiano . . . Vassa and his sis-ter.[28] As Njoku shows us, everywhere the Igbo were enslaved, the masquerade persisted. In the British West Indies, in the Dutch Virgin Islands, in Congo Square and in Mardi Gras and Mardi Gras Indians in New Orleans, in the Caribbean Jonkunnu,[29] in the Bamboula, and, even in slave revolts[30]—in all the forms in which Africans recreated community and resisted and mobilized outside of the colonial structures that controlled them. Masquerading "gave the Africans a platform on which they registered their feelings on diverse sociopolitical issues affecting their lives," in a "contested arena of space, politics, social change, and mythmaking," performed in the black body, in what Njoku calls a "somatogenic" mode, showing the human body as a site of narrative.[31]

As Henry Chadwick suggests, in a provocative footnote concerning Augustine of Hippo's mother, a woman—and, by extension, a slave or anyone without power—had only the body through which to answer for offenses:[32]

> The inferior status of the slave was enforced in antiquity by subjection to corporal punishment, the prime distinction between a slave and a free person being the fact that a slave "has to answer for his offenses with his body." (Demosthenes 22.25; cf. 21.72)

Hence, the body *is* the site of performance, both positive and negative. This capacity—indeed, necessity—of the body to carry, enact, and rewrite narrative, to open performative "mode[s] of dialogue"[33] around social issues is what Equiano . . . Vassa demonstrates in his narrative and, I suggest, in his choice of naming himself "The African." How much he remembered about masquerade might be debatable, but he probably remembered the spectacle and came to remember more as he encountered masquerade in the Americas.

ADAPTATION: NEW WORLD MASKS

Masquerade was a performance mode that both African slaves and White enslavers, in the European trade, had experienced. Masquerade in the New World drew on multicultural origins, as Njoku tells us,[34] from the masks used by Egyptians as early as 3000 BCE; to masks in the Roman Catholic Carnival of Venice, beginning in the twelfth century; to eighteenth-century British masquerades which, though the upper-class control mostly still held, sold tickets open to lower classes, making a challenge to social order and opening spaces of potential. Indeed, the costume of the masquerade—for example, the domino, was a symbol of crossing, "from the realm of what 'was' into the realm of what 'might be.'"[35] Masquerade offers the freedom to imagine "a perfected human community free of the ravages of difference and alienation."[36]

In the New World, the Spanish, Portuguese, and French, beginning in the fifteenth century, brought the Roman Catholic religious *carnaval* ("farewell to flesh or meat"), the Shrove (Carnival) Tuesday celebration, which was adapted from pagan festivals, into the New World where it intersected with the African masquerade Njoku describes. Song, music, costume and dance are part of all these forms.[37] Celebrated in Catholic centers that were diasporic sites, *carnaval* is a mixed form, with many of its elements—like percussive rhythms and dancing styles that come from the Yoruba[38]—now traced back to Africa, creating, and I struggle for the right word, a layered, intersectional celebration.[39]

Indeed, this event is complex. Ayodeji Ogunnaike, for example, argues that "mere masking" is not going on in such religious expressions; this is not hybridity or syncretism, Ogunnaike argues, but the creation of an inter-religious theology through a sort of double masking that is made in contact and out of the ongoing fluid and dynamic practice Africans brought to the New World.[40] The orisha is not "hidden" behind a mask, as Roger Bastide's influential theory argues; the practice around the saint and the orisha does not indicate that one is "true or real and the other false or insincere" in the practice of devotees.[41] This suggests, Ogunnaike argues, continuity in Yoruba traditions in the New World, "understood and enacted as the merging of forms of worshipping and interacting with the same cosmological domains."[42] And, if we think about Achille Mbembe's assertion that in Africa, "Christianity in practice was turned upside down, undone, and then outfitted in masks . . . all without being stripped of its core concept"[43]—and, I would argue earlier than the colonial period and the slave trade—we see a multiple scripturalizing of African slaves re-Africanizing a Christianity they already had Africanized.

All these came together in the British West Indies that Equiano . . . Vassa entered, where Igbo slaves, by the force of their numbers, influenced music, dance, and masquerade and where "slaves not only influenced each other interculturally but [also] transformed the culture and lifestyle of their mas-ters as well.[44] Here, I would argue that we what Charles H. Long calls the "oppressive element in the religion of the oppressed,"[45] as the slave commu-nity reaches back to the mythic, overlapping and injecting an Igbo cosmology into New World adaptations. In these, the slave recreates the god under a new sign, in a modern masquerade, that the oppressor participates in, chang-ing his consciousness. In masquerade and in the slave narrative, the logic of the slave, Black Reason, Black knowledge,[46] indigenous theory, meets Enlightenment Reason, new forms of freedom.

We could use Paul Gilroy's negative dialectic of conviviality, or multicul-tural coexistence to examine this, his theory about dwelling with difference in a "fragile" planetary humanism. In these interactions, many taking place in times of masquerade, like *carnaval*, people interact with one another in ways that they may not in the hierarchialized "day-to-day." Racism does not disap-pear, but "forms of comprehension and communication" can emerge to pro-duce "everyday virtues" or "convivial capabilities" that enrich life.[47] It may seem that nothing changes, but from the slave, as Ralph Ellison's Invisible Man puts it, sounds a voice who asks the master, "Who knows but that, on the lower frequencies, I speak for you?"[48]

EQUIANO . . . VASSA

As a sailor, Equiano . . . Vassa moves in, to the center, to the metropole, and out, imaginatively back to Africa: he loves London, but can one be there and not go mad? Are you just black skin in a white mask?[49] The center is, Conrad says, a "whited sepulchre."[50] To live its logic is to be immune to terror, Equiano . . . Vassa tells us, naming what Slavoj Žižek argues quoting Derrida on the madness of the *cogito*: "Whether I am mad or not, *Cogito sum* . . . even if the totality of the world does not exist, even if nonmeaning has invaded the totality of the world, up to and including the very contents of my thought, I still think, I am while I think."[51] Madness, then, is maintained in "an all-encompassing world-view,"[52] like that of colonialism, masquerading under rationality. Even Equiano . . . Vassa, a slave in this madness, "grew a stranger to terror of every kind, and was, in that respect, at least, almost an Englishman."[53] Almost is important, and we will return to it. The further we move from Africa, in the narrative, the more contingent and brutal life becomes; cruelty increases the more we experience Enlightenment authoritative madness, as Wimbush shows us in his exhibit, in the white masks—the covers of books—are masquerades that suggest *this* knowledge in the magic of the book is the only authoritative knowledge.

Enlightenment masks—white books—assert power through Orientalizing ideologies that establish epistemic hegemony. From the "epistemologies of Kant and Descartes" to "the ethical economies of Adam Smith and Karl Marx," and under the many other masks of Enlightenment rationality, there seems to be, as Long puts it, no "soul stuff."[54] Unlike the masquerade of the African masks, in white masks, no divine beings appear.

Enlightenment reason, assuming that it is, as Long reminds us, the "complete language of humankind," categorizes and twice creates those "unreasonable" ones, who undergo its creativity.[55] They are twice created from the human oriented in time and space, masquerade, into objects, units of energy, at the hands, under the scalpels, through the discourse, by the torture, by being multiply murdered under the mask of the mad *cogito* whose brutal curiosity needs to know at any cost. Doubleness, Du Bois's double consciousness, becomes a mark of sanity: not to be double, we might argue, in modernity, is to be mad. As Toni Morrison puts it, the double consciousness is a strategy.[56] Theologians, anthropologists, physicians, priests and preachers, and scientists participate in and further this madness. The rational language of books masks a delight in dismemberment, and ultimately dismembers the dismemberer. Leah Kalmanson argues that the Modernist self cannot center; therefore, it engages in ongoing and increasingly extreme repetition (think of the brutality of slave punishments) that leads nowhere. Its suspension of the subject at an uncrossable border [is] both exhausting and disempowering. In conflating nothingness with the limit of a certain type of phenomenological interiority, death becomes a stand-in for all manner of trans-egoic experiences.[57]

Nietzsche calls this "objective man" a "tool" and a mirror,[58] with no end in himself, submitting to everything, in a mad banality of evil, which may be at the core of Western *cogito* that has ideologically supported the "terror of history."[59]

Equiano . . . Vassa exhibits double consciousness and the saneness of double identity. He lived, we know, as Vassa. Equiano, I suggest, is his masquerade, as well as the reality of the life he was forced to lead. Vincent Carretta, in his "Questioning the Identity of Olaudah Equiano, or Gustavus Vassa, the African," finds evidence that suggests that Equiano may not have been born in Africa. Looking at Equiano's baptismal record, for example, he finds that it lists Equiano's birthplace as "Carolina" and argues that he used his African name and the epithet "the African" only after his memoir was published.[60] Therefore, his "first-hand" accounts of Africa and the Middle Passage, which made it important in abolitionist work, might be seen as invented or as suspect, even as they allowed Equiano . . . Vassa to fashion himself as a person and political actor.

As James Sweet suggests, Equiano's shifting identity reflects captive life. At the center of the question of authenticity, Sweet argues, lies "important questions about continuity and survivals, the fixity or malleability of African identity in an ever-changing and pluralistic Atlantic world," the "process of African acculturation."[61] Deploying an Atlantic analytic leads us to emphasize "the multitude of overlapping cultural circuits and their influences on the individuals who move through them," who experienced situational identities in which African-ness was "a filter of perception in the accumulation of new ideas and ways of being, a crucial compass in negotiating how the new might be put to use in . . . unfamiliar and volatile environments, leaving Africans to construct identities in discontinuity."[62] Normalizing European labels and categories, generated in particular official contexts, such as those of a ship's log, might be seen as a form of Enlightenment categorization.

Equiano . . . Vassa, deploying his double identity, no doubt, was aware of the ways in which his narrative would be utilized and how he wanted to use it, as an abolitionist and a capitalist. Just as the masquerade needs the body to animate it, so, to be useful, did slave narratives, which needed multiple bodies, that of the slave, the abolitionist, and the body politic, all of which were animated by conventions, to make and to introduce difference.[63]

Like the masquerade, these narratives occupied an interstitial space— between the African and the American, the public and the private, the self and the other, slavery and freedom, and autobiography and persuasive rhetoric or ideological "weapon." They were, in a sense, a type, giving the narratives, James Olney argues, "overwhelming *sameness*."[64] Yet, as John Sekora puts it, the mask belied difference; each narrative contained a unique "black message . . . sealed within a white envelope"[65] made of "white-authored evidence and analysis."[66] This envelope made the slave narrative questionable. For example, Georgia's Ulrich B. Phillips (1877–1934), *the* dominant voice in assessing slavery in the twentieth century, did not see the narratives as reliable historical testimony. His racist, *American Negro Slavery* (1918), still shapes how some view slavery today,[67] as it pictured slavery as paternal. The envelope made Phillips assess the nineteenth-century American slave narratives as "inauthentic and biased."[68]

Equiano . . . Vassa consciously undercuts this reading, complicating the genre. He called his narrative, for example, a memoir—and, indeed, his life was not typical of most slaves or of most people of his time.[69] More than half of his work is about his life as a free man.[70] Like Frederick Douglass's narrative, his was a bestseller—Douglass's work actually supplanted Equiano . . . Vassa's, causing it to go out of print until Arna Bontemps brought it back in the 1960s.[71] In the genre of memoir, the story is more important than historically accuracy. Memoirs are dialogic and invitational, and they exhibit a personal style.[72] A memoir writer creates a lens, a way of seeing it, directing our attention: for example, Equiano . . . Vassa tells us it is "interesting." Equiano . . . Vassa, writing memoir, is at play in British (he is not and can never be English, which is ethnic—remember the "Almost"), playing on all the available genres to draw in as many readers as he can: spiritual autobiography, captivity narrative, travel and adventure story, economic treatise, and apologia.[73]

Equiano . . . Vassa is too big for the envelope (he has been called the "Black Benjamin Franklin"[74]), and, when he is wedged in, he tears it. For example, although Equiano . . . Vassa's story helped shape the anti-slavery movement, some in the movement worried that he was too atypical.[75] He, certainly, acquires and masters the white magic of texts—even using the Bible to do magic himself, but, more than that, he puts his spell in the book. Having mastered the white magic, the technologies of reading and writing,[76] he addresses us directly, as reader, drawing us into his narrative to witness; fearing to bore us; and even asking God to give us right understanding of his aims. He looks directly at us from the frontispiece of his narrative, human being to human being. In addition, he travelled throughout Britain, selling his book, drawing white money. In many ways, he reminds me more of Sojourner Truth than Douglass. Truth, too, was a traveler who took control of her story, and she sold the shade, photographs of herself and her narrative, to sustain the substance—though she did not, like Equiano, end up wealthy.

His mask allows Equiano . . . Vassa to criticize Western norms through their own terms, to cast Europe as a "'primitive' slaveholding culture in a global context" with the Igbo as their more civilized and peaceful oppositional "Other."[77] Even as he recognizes the problematic ways in which Christianity would have made Equiano . . . Vassa view Blackness, including placing Africa as an ahistorical place in a racialized geography, Sylvester Johnson sees Equiano . . . Vassa's making a claim of a Jewish origin narrative for Africa, turning biblical authority on Europe and scripturalizing as he remaps Africans "onto the cartography of history . . . as a visible empire." Doing so, he attempts to invent "a biblical Africa to overturn Christian colonial ideas [typical in the eighteenth century, which did not accept an African origin for human beings] that denied Africans a place in the historical world."[78] Johnson sees Equiano . . . Vassa's attempt as a "start," as establishing a foothold within the "terrain of humanizing representations,"[79] as making a step in helping his audience to see African religions as something other than evil, even if he had to mask them with Abrahamic origins—"*biblical*, if not *Christian*"—to do so.[80]

As we noted, the farther we move from Africa, in the narrative, the more contingent and brutal life becomes. Equiano . . . Vassa turns the binary hierarchy on its head: Africa, in the narrative, is the civilized, while the West is the primitive. The white slaveholders' "scramble" for newly arrived slaves, for example, is chaotic and wild.[81] The cruel treatment of slaves, during and after the Middle Passage, and particularly the sexual exploitation of slave women, was, to use Mary Wollstonecraft's phrase, enough to "make the blood run its course."[82]

Equiano . . . Vassa problematizes Whiteness. White people are cruel, unpredictable, and crazy. The sailors, the white men, toss him around, and he sees them as bad spirits who intend to kill him.[83] Their brutality—they are savage[84]—knows no bounds: one sailor dies from a flogging. They flog Equiano . . . Vassa for refusing to eat.[85] He believes they are cannibals who will eat him, and indeed, black bodies *will* be consumed in the plantation machine in New World, sold into the "deadly work of making sugar in Barbados."[86] As Marcus Rediker puts it, "white people" becomes "synonymous with mysterious and oppressive terror."[87] Equiano . . . Vassa finds them cruel,[88] engaged in illicit and titillating jouissance in which they get to enjoy what Derek Hook calls "the thrill of hate."[89]

BLACK SALT

And in it all stands the Black Salt. Equiano becomes/adds the identity of Vassa on the sea and the ships. Marcus Rediker, in an interview, says sailors and pirates were poor people, who moved around: "they are transnational, at the intersection of multiple authorities and multiple economic systems, which they themselves feed and give expression to."[90] In his "history from below," Rediker seeks to learn how people freed themselves, and the sea, far from being a "place without a place," is for Rediker a "real place where history is made,"[91] a site where freedom is negotiated. On the ships, he argues, there emerged a unique set of class relations based on the reality that "they trusted their lives to each other on a daily basis."[92] In addition, life on the sea is a "culture of opposition," based on the reality that a deep-sea ship captain held nearly unchecked authority; sailors, therefore, had to resist *together* to survive.[93] Rediker gives an example including Equiano . . . Vassa. When some sailors wanted to re-enslave him, others, including white sailors protested because he was their "brother tar."[94] In addition, Equiano . . . Vassa also witnessed slave resistance on the ships.[95] We can see that Equiano . . . Vassa's seafaring career shaped him in ways that "scholars of the terracentric," to use Rediker's word, may not be able to see.[96]

Rediker also points out that Equiano . . . Vassa came from a place in Africa which was marked by a relative equality and autonomy. The Igbo were fiercely independent: "They would long be known for the proverb, '*Igbo enwegh eze*,' which means, 'the Igbo have no king.'"[97] Chinua Achebe comments on the Igbo "proclivity for adaptation," which has led to their success—and notoriety—in postcolonial Nigeria.[98] These qualities are ones Equiano . . . Vassa brought onto the ships on which he served.

When Equiano . . . Vassa is first on the slave ship, he thinks it moves and stops by magic, but he masters this white man's magic, the magic of the seafaring world, learning it bit by bit. Since he was so young, Rediker reminds us, he had relative freedom on the slave ship, and his "own strategy of resistance was to learn all he could from the sailors about how the ship worked. This would, in the long run, prove to be his path to liberation."[99] On his third voyage, he begins to speak English, and his white friend, a slave-owning American, fifteen-year-old Richard Baker, who, out of some shared distress, becomes Equiano . . . Vassa's friend and instructor, [helps] him adjust to the Euro-American world.[100] In addition, Equiano . . . Vassa strove to communicate with other African peoples from different tribes on his own slave voyage and, no doubt, as a sailor, which probably aided him in his career. This contact also gave him an alternative family—"shipmates"[101] with whom he went through common suffering and out of which African American culture was born.

On the sea, as a sailor in the Royal Navy, from 1755–1762, Equiano . . . Vassa experienced relative equality. Vincent Carretta writes that Equiano . . . Vassa found an almost "utopian microcosmic alternative to the slavery-infested greater world," and one reviewer suggests that "on these ships he saw a model

for relationships between Europeans and Africans."[102] The liminality of the
sea offers, it seems, a site for self-exploration and creation out of "controlling and shifting identities." Indeed, among the first six slave autobiographies
published in English before 1800 were those by sailors, who, in the maritime
trade had access to the whole African Diaspora.[103] On the ship, Equiano . . .
Vassa, as Matthew Brown puts it, "masters" other voices as he learns to
master the ship[104]—indeed, he did command a ship on which his commander
died. He gains mobility, which plantation slaves lack, that lets him see the
variety of roles black people are forced into and play in slavery.

   Though Equiano . . . Vassa does not himself speak directly of it, we can
guess that these sailors carried and transmitted knowledge that aided in slave
resistance as well as in abolition—Brown calls this the "Sailor's Telegraph,"
a "network of information that flowed through free black and enslaved
sailors" in the diaspora, acting as a conduit between slave and free.[105] This
is not to say that Equiano . . . Vassa did not experience the fear of being
re-enslaved—he feared impressment—and the difficulties of racism. Still, in
Equiano . . . Vassa's time, Black sailors found the rules of the ship, like the
rules of the street in *carnaval*/masquerade, unexpectedly free.[106] Using this
limen, he masquerades doubly as Black slave and British gentleman; sailor
and abolitionist; powder boy and commander—gathers doubleness into identity as a human being in a diasporic mode, in which, I contend, the edges
show and are sharp. (These identities are not smoothly "mixed," a word we,
in the south often use to describe biracial people; the elements still show,
even as they exist together.) As Equiano's childhood fear, astonishment, and
wonder become Vassa's knowledge and capability, his mastery gives him the
tools to set himself—and, ultimately, others—free.

CONCLUSIONS: THE CONFOUNDING
VARIABLE:[107] THE AFRICAN

I chose to use the ellipsis in relation to Equiano . . . Vassa's identity because
we think we know what links those two identities, what words—like hybrid,
mixed, syncretic, etc.—we need to use to fill in the absence, the space. We
think we understand what the context is for an identity like his, and how
one dimension of his life is related to or determines the shape and efficacy
of another. Equiano . . . Vassa's masquerade, I think, makes us see what we
do not know. Indeed, the spaces between his names—Equiano, which he
reclaimed after thirty-five years of his life and the name Gustavus Vassa,
given to him by Captain Michael Henry Pascal—were filled by the names
Michael and Jacob, which he preferred to Gustavus. Gustavus Vassa was
the name by which he would call himself only after being beaten for not

answering to it. We do not know if he ever, truly, fully answers to it even as he uses it. In the title of his narrative, he is primarily Olaudah Equiano, with Gustavus Vassa as the "or." The way the title is constructed is (intentionally?) disorienting; both names seem to signify "The African." Both are, as Rediker suggests, compromised: "He . . . lost his original name to violence and gained a new one in the same way."[108] He moves, strategically, between these identities.

Sylvester Johnson offers a positive reading of Vincent Caretta's cautious assertion that Equiano . . . Vassa invented an African home and identity and confirms that we may not know how to read such a figure. Johnson argues that Equiano . . . Vassa is not a hero, tragic or otherwise. Instead, Equiano . . . Vassa is a complex human being, embedded in his time, and adapting to and resisting it. Johnson writes that even if Carretta is right, Equiano . . . Vassa resisted erasure and natal social death. He

> was pioneering not only because he asserted that Africa was historical but also because he deployed a native African identity in his autobiographical act of self-representation. When he did so, he succeeded in negating the social death through natal alienation that attends the institution of slavery. Despite the fact that slavery has functioned throughout human history to dissolve the ancestral linkages of slaves, Equiano has for centuries existed in the minds and memory of his readers not as Equiano the Negro or black American (read as ethnically rootless) but as Equiano the African, a member of the Igbo nation.[109]

Equiano . . . Vassa is remembered, historically, as Equiano, who wrote himself and the Igbo into history. As Njoku writes, Equiano . . . Vassa carries out, in his "powerful modernist dialogue," the project and goals of the masquerade which is to examine "the somatogenic abilities—the conscious and unconscious capacities of the human body as a site of narrative,"[110] as a site of making that addresses current needs:

> The fact is that he used what he committed to memory, or rather what he chose to remember, to advocate change in his eighteenth-century world. This was the prerogative need of "the present" in his time.[111]

Everyone knew and knows that under the masks of masquerade, there are people *and* also that the gods are walking among us, at the same time. The masquerade, like all human constructions, has its fault lines and through lines. As the current African maskers with whom we began demonstrate, masquerade upholds as well as challenges social norms. Njoku writes that wherever masquerades are "the narrative of identity and remembering that masquerades espoused has always been a contested arena of space, politics, social change, and mythmaking."[112] Equiano . . . Vassa's masquerade is the same. It shows him working between cultures, searching for belonging, for home, in the culture to which he was taken by force in order to attain freedom, both for himself and for his enslaved brothers and sisters, whose origin, whose natal home, Africa, he aligns with virtue.

In the end, I do not think it matters where he was born. I concur with Marcus Rediker, in *The Slave Ship*, as he argues that Equiano . . . Vassa is a profound figure either way: he either was an Igbo who told the truth as he remembered it or he was the "oral historian," who gathered memories from Africans who had made the Middle Passage and recorded them for posterity, becoming the "'voice of the voiceless.'"[113]

What matters is what Equiano . . . Vassa did with what he had at hand and how he recognized the pressure of the moment. He may not always show his "true" face, or speak in his "true" voice, or tell us his "true" name—indeed, the reality of diaspora is that his life and being are multiple, and locating what is "true," including notions of home, origin, race, and legitimacy,[114] is always problematized by experience, by contingency, and by, as Toni Morrison says, the reality that Western civilization imagines race in its constructed hierarchies to manage it as barbarism.[115] Therefore, in Equiano . . . Vassa's testimony, even as he utilizes some of the traditional elements of the slave narrative, to testify in order to free his people, the memoir voice of the lone free man speaks in tension with it.

Even as ex-slave *and* British gentleman, he is the African, masquerading. I think that we see Equiano . . . Vassa deconstructing, signifying, engaging in masquerade for his own and his people's good. He masquerades under identities forced on him and under one he, whether in recovery or in invention, chooses, Olaudah Equiano: The African. Under this sign, he gathers his lived experiences, makes a claim, and turns that claim loose on Western forms. He is African and *almost* an Englishman[116]—Remember the "almost": he never can be an ethnic Englishman; therefore, his identity always carries limitations, interruptions, and unsettling excesses; arrivals and deferments. As The African, with Ibo ingenuity, he makes and practices identities, asserting full humanity in a diasporic mode that talks back to the mad *cogito* of the West. As Equiano's childhood fear, astonishment, and wonder become Vassa's knowledge and capability, his mastery, ultimately, he gathers the tools to name himself so as to set himself—and, ultimately, others—free.

NOTES

1. Jean Borgatti, "Okpella Masking Traditions," *African Arts* 9.4 (1976): 24–33, 90–91.

2. Douglas Curran, "Masks and Ritual," *African Arts* 32.3 (Autumn 1999): 68–77. I recommend this article for the photographs. https://www.jstor.org/stable/pdf/3337711 .pdf?refreqid=excelsior%3A08eb19422d165d77ad2ae648bd31f403&ab_segments=0 %2FSYC-6427%2Ftest&origin=.

3. Mardi Gras New Orleans, "Mardi Gras Masks," https://www.mardigrasneworleans .com/history/traditions/mardi-gras-masks.

4.Maya Angelou, "The Mask," and Paul Laurence Dunbar, "We Wear the Mask," Poetry Foundation, https://www.poetryfoundation.org/poems/44203/we-wear-the -mask. Dunbar's poem reads "mouth with myriad subtleties."

5. Maya Angelou, "We Wear the Mask," https://www.youtube.com/watch?v= _HLol9InMlc.

6. Maya Angelou, "The Mask," https://www.facinghistory.org/resource-library/ mask-maya-angelou.

7. Peter Jaros, "Good Names: Olaudah Equiano or Gustavas Vassa," *The Eighteenth Century* 54.1 (Spring 2013), 1.

8. Charles H. Long, *Ellipsis: The Collected Writings of Charles H. Long: Ellipsis* (New York: Bloomsbury Academic, 2019), 8. Quoted in Carolyn M. Jones Medine, "Ellipsis: The Deconstructive Practice in the Work of Charles H. Long," *American Religion* 2.2 (Spring 2021), 9–10, 14.

9. Medine, 14.

10. Ibid., 15.

11. Ibid., 23.

12. Gayatri Spivak, "Subaltern Studies: Deconstructing Historiography, Crisis and Change," in Spivak, *In Other Worlds: Essays in Cultural Politics* (New York: Methuen), 198.

13. Elizabeth Eide, "Strategic Essentialism," *Wiley Blackwell Encyclopedia of Gender and Sexuality Studies* (Hoboken, NJ: John Wiley and Sons, 2016), 1.

14. Jaros, 14.

15. See, for example, Samantha Manchester Earley, "Writing from the Center or the Margins? Olaudah Equiano's Writing Life Reassessed," *African Studies Review* 46.3 (December 2003): 1–16.

16. Sylvester A. Johnson, "Colonialism, Biblical World-Making, and Temporalities in Olaudah Equiano's Interesting Narrative," *Church History* 77.4 (December 2008), 1022ff.

17. Mary Louise Pratt, "Arts of the Contact Zone," *Profession* (1991): 33–40. Pratt defines contact zones as "Social spaces where cultures meet, clash, and grapple with each other, often in contexts of highly asymmetrical relations of power, such as colonialism, slavery, or their aftermaths as they are lived out in many parts of the world today." (34)

18. Mary Louise Pratt, *Imperial Eyes: Travel Writing and Transculturation* (New York: Routledge, 1992), 4. Indeed, Equiano . . . Vassa sometimes exercises his "imperial eyes" as a British gentleman and sometimes his subjected eyes, as ex-slave, as he travels.

19. Alexander Falconbridge, *Account of the Slave Trade on the Coast of Africa* (London: J. Phillips, 1788). The full-text is available free on GoogleBooks.

20. Felix U. Egwuda-Ugbeda and Obiorah Ekwueme, "The Wheel of Life in African Worldview and Its Sustenance Through Performances," *Interdisciplinary Academic Essays* 8 (January 2016), 12.

21. Raphael Chijioke Njoku, *West African Masking Traditions and Diaspora Masquerade Carnivals: History, Memory, and Transnationalism* (Rochester, NY: University of Rochester Press, 2020), xiii, 1.

22. Ibid., 6–7.

23. Ibid., 10.

24. Ibid., 21.

25. Ibid., 88.

26. Mircea Eliade, *The Sacred and the Profane: The Nature of Religion*, trans. Willard R. Trask (New York: Harvest Books, 1987), 11.

27. Njoku, 37.

28. Marcus Rediker, *The Slave Ship: A Human History* (New York: Penguin Books, 2008), 78–79.

29. Sylvia Wynter, in her work was interested in the Jonknnu as a "cultural site which registers the various strata of cultural encounters, adaptations, and reinventions attendant on the indigenization of African in the New World." See Norval Edwards, "'Talking About a Little Culture': Sylvia Wynter's Early Essays," *Journal of West Indian Literature* 10.1/2 (November 2001): 12–38.

30. Njoku, 112, 115, 117ff., 127, 135, 137. Njoku argues that the slaves were trying to recreate sociopolitical structures and roles, but with minimal success because of the colonial structure (133).

31. Ibid., 194–195.

32. Augustine, *Confessions*, trans. Henry Chadwick (New York: Oxford, 1991), 169; fn. 24.

33. Njoku, 186.

34. Ibid., chapter 1: "On Origins of Masking."

35. Terry Castle, *Masquerade and Civilization: The Carnivalesque in Eighteenth-Century English Culture and Fiction* (Stanford: Stanford University Press, 1986), 78. The carnival, Castle argues, combined English folk tradition with continental influences.

36. Ibid., 198. Some reviewers take issue with Castle's reading of the masquerade as a social phenomenon. See, for example, William B. Warner, *MLN: Comparative Literature* 103.5 (December 1988); 1144–1147.

37. Michael LaRose, "History of the Caribbean Carnival," *Charleston Clarifest* (23 January 2015), https://charlestoncarifest.com/information/history-of-the-caribbean-carnival/.

38. "The African Roots of Carnival," http://ayibamagazine.com/african-roots-carnival/.

39. See Carl Lindahl, "Bakhtin's Carnival Laughter and the Cajun Mardi Gras," *Folklore* 107 (1996): 57–70. Lindahl lists Bakhtin's list of carnivals: German *Fastnacht*, French *Mardi Gras*, Spanish *Carnaval*, and Italian *Carnevale* (58).

40. Ayodeji Ogunnaike, "What's Really Behind the Mask: A Reexamination of Syncretism in Brazilian Candomblé," *Journal of Africana Studies* 8.1 (November 2020), 147, 155.

41. Ibid., 164.

42. Ibid., 166.

43. Achille Mbembe, *Critique of Black Reason*, trans. Laurent DuBois (Durham: Duke University Press, 2017), 101.

44. Njoku, 112.

45. Charles H. Long, *Significations: Signs, Symbols, and Images in the Interpretation of Religion* (Aurora, CO: The Davies Group, 1995). Previously published by Fortress Press, 1986. See chapter 10.

46. Mbembe, 10.

47. Les Beck, "Afterword: Giving Multiculture a Name," in *Studying Diversity, Migration, and Urban Multiculture: Convivial Tools for Research and Practice*, ed. Mette Louise Berg and Magdalena Nowicka (London: UCL Press, 2019), 193–194.

48. Ralph Ellison, *Invisible Man* (New York: Vintage Books, 1995), 581.

49. For a reading of Equiano . . . Vassa's white mask, how he used it to assimilate and negotiate his status in a white world, see Ronald Paul, "'I Whitened My Face, That They Might Not Know Me,' Race and Identity in Olaudah Equiano's Slave Narrative," *Journal of Black Studies* 39.6 (July 2009): 848–864. Paul sees Equiano's narrative as showing us the Black experience of racism as Equiano exercises an Ronald Paul, "'I Whitened My Face, That They Might Not Know Me,' Race and Identity in Olaudah Equiano's Slave Narrative," *Journal of Black Studies* 39.6 (July 2009) alienated identity and social disguise under the white gaze. Whitening himself, he moves as closely to whiteness as he can, even veiling violent excesses against black slaves, but this identity, Paul argues, is unstable. Even marrying a white woman, Paul argues, as a sign of "migration upward through the hierarchy of color" (860). His white mask, Paul suggests, is the image of a "failed quest for authentic identity" (862) and could be torn away at any time by his masters, surfacing in the narrative as self-doubt.

50. Joseph Conrad, *Heart of Darkness* (New York: Random House/Bantam Classics, 1969), 13.

51. Slavoj Žižek, *"Cogito,* Madness, and Religion: Derrida, Foucault and then Lacan," https://www.lacan.com/zizforest.html.

52. Ibid.

53. Olaudah Equiano, *The Interesting Narrative of the Life of Olaudah Equiano, or Gustavus Vassa, the African, Written by Himself*, ed. Vincent Carretta (New York: Penguin Books, 1995), 77.

54. Long, *Ellipsis*, 206.

55. Long, *Significations*, 65.

56. Toni Morrison, "Home," in Wahneema Lubiano, ed., *The House That Race Built: Black Americans, U.S. Terrain* (New York: Pantheon Books, 1997), 12.

57. Leah Kalmanson, *Cross-Cultural Existentialism: On the Meaning of Life in Asian and Western Thought* (New York: Bloomsbury Academic, 2021), 133–134.

58. Fredrich Nietzsche, *Beyond Good and Evil* VI. Aphorism #207, http://nietzsche.holtof.com/reader/friedrich-nietzsche/beyond-good-and-evil/aphorism-207-quote_b267781ea.html.

59. Mircea Eliade, *The Myth of the Eternal Return: Cosmos and History*, trans. Willard R. Trask (Princeton: Princeton University Press, 1973). See chapter 4, "The Terror of History."

60. Vincent Caretta, "Questioning the Identity of Olaudah Equiano, or Gustavus Vassa, The African," in *The Global Eighteenth Century*, ed. Felicity A. Nussbaum (Baltimore: The Johns Hopkins University Press, 2003), 226–238. His work set off a firestorm. For the discussions that followed, see James H. Sweet, "Mistaken Identities? Olaudah Equiano, Domingo Alvares, and the Methodological Challenges of Studying the African Diaspora," *The American Historical Review* 114.2 (April 2009): 279–306, fn. 4. Sweet goes on to argue that parts of the narrative indicate that Equiano did not invent his past (see 301-303).

61. Sweet 281.

62. Ibid., 281–283.

63. James Matlack, 20. "The Autobiographies of Frederick Douglass," *Phylon* 40.1 (1979): 20. 15–28.

64. Lawrence Aje, "Fugitive Slave Narratives and the (Re)presentation of the Self? The Cases of Frederick Douglass and William Brown," *L'Ordinaire des Amériques* [En ligne], 215 | 2013, mis en ligne le 27 novembre 2014, consulté le 16 octobre 2021. http://journals.openedition.org/orda/507; DOI: https://doi.org/10.4000/orda.507. https://journals.openedition.org/orda/507#quotation. James Olney, "'I Was Born': Slave Narratives, Their Status as Autobiography and as Literature," *Callaloo* 20 (Winter, 1984), 46.

65. John Sekora, "Black Message/White Envelope: Genre, Authenticity, and Authority in the Antebellum Slave Narrative," *Callaloo* 32 (Summer 1987), 503.

66. Teresa A. Goddu, "The African American Slave Narrative as Factual Compendium," in Teresa Goddu, *Selling Anti-Slavery: Abolition and Mass Media in Antebellum America* (Philadelphia: University of Pennsylvania Press, 2020), 56. Goddu is discussing *The Narrative of William James*, the first narrative published by the American Anti-Slavery Society, https://www.jstor.org/stable/pdf/j.ctv16t6gs4.6.pdf?ab_segments=0%2FSYC-6080%2Findeg-test&refreqid=fastly-default%3A5fd9231072bc25cd0e8b9953c850d6e1.

67. Jack Corp, "Misinformed: How a 1918 Narrative Shapes Our Discussion of Slavery and Race Today." The Humanities and Ethics Center at Drury University. https://humanities.drury.edu/misinformed-1918-narrative-shapes-discussion-slavery-race-today/.

68. "The Slave Narratives: A Genre and a Source," Gilder Lehrman Institute of American History, http://ap.gilderlehrman.org/history-by-era/literature-and-language-arts/essays/slave-narratives-genre-and-source. Ulrich Bonnell Phillips, *American Negro Slavery: A Survey of the Supply, Employment, and Control of Negro Labor, as Determined by the Plantation Regime* (Baton Rouge: LSU Press, 1966). Facsimile of the 1918 edition.

John David Smith, "The Construction of Ulrich Bonnell Phillips's Interpretation of Slavery," *American Studies Journal* 45 (Summer 2000): 4–9.

69. Robert Allison, "Reviewed Work: *Equiano, the African: Biography of a Self-Made Man* by Vincent Carretta," *Reviews in American History* 34.1 (March 2006), 14.

70. Ibid., 13.

71. Ibid., 12.

72. https://www.masterclass.com/articles/breaking-down-the-key-elements-of-a-memoir#what-is-a-memoir.

73. Monica Weis, "Olaudah Equiano at Sea: Adrift in White Culture," *CEA Critic*. 63. 1, *Literature of the Sea: A Special Issue of the "CEA Critic"* (Fall 2000), pp. 21–26, 25.

74. Allison, 13.

75. Ibid., 16.

76. Jesse M. Molesworth, "Equiano's 'Loud Voice': Witnessing the Performance of The Interesting Narrative," *Texas Studies in Literature and Language*, 48.2 (Summer 2006), 123–144.

77. Njoku, 194, 105.

78. Johnson, 1003–1004, 1019. Johnson examines the commentaries that Equiano . . . Vassa uses to establish this argument. Johnson is also very clear that Equiano . . . Vassa exercises a colonial consciousness that "demanded a knowledge about Africa and blackness that was demeaning, alienating, and haunting" (1012). He would have created a "racialized geography muted by colonial temporalities," whether he intended to do so or not (1014).

79. Ibid., 1019.

80. Ibid., 1021.

81. Equiano, *Interesting Narrative*, 251.

82. Qtd. in Paul, "'I Whitened My Face,'" 850.

83. Equiano, *Interesting Narrative*, 55.

84. Ibid., 10: he is torn from his home by the savage dealers and savage white men of England," for example.

85. Ibid., 56.

86. Rediker, *The Slave Ship*, 86.

87. Ibid., 89.

88. Ibid., 109, 111, 118. The term runs throughout the *Narrative*. Dr. Perkins is a "cruel" man and a drunk. The captain of one ship is cruel and bloody-minded (215). The whip is "cruel" (164) and punishments, in general, are cruel (171). To be cruel is to be without human feeling and the Christian capacity for the virtues of mercy and self-control. It is to act intentionally to harm and destroy, enjoying their pain.

89. Derek Hook, "Racism and Jouissance: Evaluation the 'Racism as (the Theft of) Enjoyment' Hypothesis," 6 in *Lacan and Race: Racism, Identity, and Psychoanalytic Theory*, ed. Derek Hook and Sheldon George (New York: Routledge, 2022), 35ff.

90. Virginie Bloch-Lainé, interview with Marcus Rediker, Verso Books (August 9, 2017), https://www.versobooks.com/blogs/3349-marcus-rediker-i-took-an-interest-in-pirates-and-sailors-because-they-were-poor.

91. Ibid.

92. Jeffrey J. Williams and Marcus Rediker, "History Below Deck: An Interview with Marcus Rediker," *symploke* 28.1–2 (2020): 551.

93. Ibid.

94. Williams and Rediker, 555.

95. Rediker, *The Slave Ship*, 84–85.

96. Virginie Bloch-Lainé.

97. Rediker, *The Slave Ship*, 79.

98. Njoku, 116.

99. Ibid., 85.

100. Ibid., 87. See the *Narrative*, 65ff.

101. Rediker, *The Slave Ship*, 85.

102. Allison, 15.

103. Matthew D. Brown, "Olaudah Equiano and the Sailor's Telegraph: The Interesting Narrative and the Source of Black Abolitinism," *Callaloo* 36.1 (Winter 2013), 191, 192.

104. Ibid., 193.

105. Ibid., 192.

106. See Ray Costello, *Black Salt: Seafarers of African Descent on British Ships* (Liverpool: Liverpool University Press, 2012), 182–183. Costello investigates the presence of black sailors from the "blue men" in the Viking age in the Irish Chronicles to the present.

107. A confounding variable is "an unmeasured third variable that influences the supposed cause and the supposed effect. To ensure the validity of your research, you must account for the confounding variable, or you may posit a cause-and-effect relationship that does not exist or over- or underestimate the impact of your variables. https://www.scribbr.com/methodology/confounding-variables/.

108. Rediker, 89–90. Rediker also points out that Equiano . . . Vassa does not tell us his parents,' his sister's or any other names, preferring not to exercise this power or to participate in the act of aggression that strips one of a name.

109. Johnson, 1023.

110. Njoku, 195.

111. Ibid.

112. Ibid., 194.

113. Rediker, 77.

114. On home, see, for example, Toni Morrison's now classic essay, "Home," in Wahneema Lubiano, ed., *The House That Race Built: Black Americans, U.S. Terrain* (New York: Pantheon Books, 1997), 3–12. Morrison argues that

> so much of what seems to lie about in discourses on race concerns legitimacy, authenticity, community, belonging. In no small way, these discourses are about home: an intellectual home; a spiritual home; family and community as home; forced and displaced labor in the destruction of home; dislocation of and alienation within the ancestral home; creative responses to exile, the devastations, pleasures, and imperatives of homelessness as it is manifested in discussions on feminism, globalism, the diaspora, migrations, hybridity, contingency, interventions, assimilations, exclusions. The estranged body, the legislated

body, the violated, rejected, deprived body—the body as consummate home. In virtually all of these formations, whatever the terrain, race magnifies the matter that matters. (5)

115. Ibid., 11.
116. Equiano, *Interesting Narrative*, 77.

BIBLIOGRAPHY

"The African Roots of Carnival," http://ayibamagazine.com/african-roots-carnival/.

Aje, Lawerence. "Fugitive Slave Narratives and the (Re)presentation of the Self? The Cases of Frederick Douglass and William Brown." *Open Edition Journals* (2013). https://doi.org/10.4000/orda.507. Open Edition Journals.

Allison, Robert. "Who Was Olaudah Equiano?" Review of *Equiano, the African: Biography of a Self-Made Man*, by Vincent Carretta, *Reviews in American History* 34, no. 1 (March 2006): 12–17.

Angelou, Maya. "The Mask" and Dunbar, Paul Laurence. "We Wear the Mask." https://www.poetryfoundation.org/poems/44203/we-wear-the-mask. Poetry Foundation.

Angelou, Maya. "We Wear the Mask." https://www.youtube.com/watch?v=_HLol9InMlc.

———. "The Mask." https://www.facinghistory.org/resource-library/mask-maya-angelou.

Back, Les. "Afterword: Giving Multiculture a Name." In *Studying Diversity, Migration, and Urban Multiculture: Convivial Tools for Research and Practice*, edited by Mette Louise Berg and Magdalena Nowicka. London: UCL Press, 2019, 192–196.

Borgatti, Jean. "Okpella Masking Traditions." *African Arts* 9, no. 4 (July 1976): 24–33+90–91. http://www.jstor.org/stable/3335050. JSTOR.

Brown, Matthew D. "Olaudah Equiano and the Sailor's Telegraph: The Interesting Narrative" and the Source of Black Abolitionism." *Callaloo* 36, no. 1 (2013): 191–201. http://www.jstor.org/stable/24264796. JSTOR.

Caretta, Vincent. "Questioning the Identity of Olaudah Equiano, or Gustavus Vassa, The African." In *The Global Eighteenth Century*, edited by Felicity A. Nussbaum, 226–238. Baltimore: The Johns Hopkins University Press, 2003.

Castle, Terry. *Masquerade and Civilization: The Carnivalesque in Eighteenth-Century English Culture and Fiction.* Stanford: Stanford University Press, 1986.

Conrad, Joseph. *Heart of Darkness.* New York: Random House/Bantam Classics, 1969.

Corp, Jack. "Misinformed: How a 1918 Narrative Shapes Our Discussion of Slavery and Race Today." The Humanities and Ethics Center at Drury University. February 24, 2019. https://humanities.drury.edu/misinformed-1918-narrative-shapes-discussion-slaveryracetoday/.

Costello, Ray. *Black Salt: Seafarers of African Descent on British Ships*. Liverpool: Liverpool University Press, 2012.

Curran, Douglas. "Masks and Ritual." *African Arts* 32.3 (Autumn 1999): 68–77.
    https://doi.org/10.2307/3337711. JSTOR.

Earley, Samantha Manchester. "Writing from the Center or the Margins? Olaudah
    Equiano's Writing Life Reassessed." *African Studies Review* 46, no. 3 (December
    2003): 1–16.

Edwards, Norval. "'Talking About a Little Culture': Sylvia Wynter's Early Essays,"
    Journal of West Indian Literature 10, nos. 1/2 (November 2001): 12–38.

Egwuda-Ugbeda, Felix U., and Ekwueme, Obiorah. "The Wheel of Life in African
    Worldview and Its Sustenance Through Performances." *Interdisciplinary Academic
    Essays* 8 (January 2016): Research Gate.

Eide, Elizabeth. "Strategic Essentialism." In *Wiley Blackwell Encyclopedia of Gender
    and Sexuality Studies.* Hoboken, NJ: John Wiley and Sons, Ltd, 2016. DOI:
    10.1002/9781118663219.

Ellison, Ralph. *Invisible Man.* New York: Vintage Books, 1995.

Equiano, Olaudah. *The Interesting Narrative of the Life of Olaudah Equiano, or
    Gustavus Vassa, the African, Written by Himself.* Edited by Vincent Carretta. New
    York: Penguin Books, 1995.

Falconbridge, Alexander. *Account of the Slave Trade on the Coast of Africa.* London:
    J. Phillips, 1788.

Gilder Lehrman Institute of American History. "The Slave Narratives: A Genre and
    a Source." http://ap.gilderlehrman.org/history-by-era/literature-and-language-arts/
    essays/slave-narratives-genre-and-source.

Goddu, Teresa A. *Selling Anti-Slavery: Abolition and Mass Media in Antebellum
    America.* Philadelphia: University of Pennsylvania Press, 2020.

Jaros, Peter. "Good Names: Olaudah Equiano or Gustavas Vassa." *The Eighteenth
    Century* 54, no. 1 (Spring 2013): 1–24. http://www.jstor.org/stable/23365023.
    JSTOR.

Johnson, Sylvester A. "Colonialism, Biblical World-Making, and Temporalities in
    Olaudah Equiano's Interesting Narrative." *Church History* 77, no. 4 (December
    2008): 1003–1024. https://www.jstor.org/stable/20618599. JSTOR.

Kalmanson, Leah. *Cross-Cultural Existentialism: On the Meaning of Life in Asian
    and Western Thought.* New York: Bloomsbury Academic, 2021.

LaRose, Michael. "History of the Caribbean Carnival." *Charleston Clarifest.*
    23 January 23, 2015. https://charlestoncarifest.com/information/history-of-the
    -caribbean-carnival/.

Lindahl, Carl. "Bakhtin's Carnival Laughter and the Cajun Mardi Gras" *Folklore* 107
    (1996): 57–70.

Long, Charles H. *Ellipsis: The Collected Writings of Charles H. Long: Ellipsis.* New
    York: Bloomsbury Academic, 2019.

———. *Significations: Signs, Symbols, and Images in the Interpretation of Religion.*
    Aurora, CO: The Davies Group, 1995.

"Marcus Rediker: 'I Took an Interest in Pirates and Sailors Because They Were
    Poor.'" Interview by Virginie Bloch- Lainé, Virginie-Bloch. Verso Books, August 9,
    2017. https://www.versobooks.com/blogs/3349-marcus-rediker-i-took-an-interest
    -in-pirates-and-sailors-because-they-were-poor.

Mardi Gras New Orleans. "Mardi Gras Masks." https://www.mardigrasneworleans.com/history/traditions/mardi-gras-masks.

Master Class Staff, "Breaking Down the Key Elements of a Memoir," last updated September 9, 2021. https://www.masterclass.com/articles/breaking-down-the-key-elements-of-a-memoir#what-is-a-memoir.

Matlack, James. "The Autobiographies of Frederick Douglass." *Phylon* 40, no. 1 (1979): 15–28.

Mbembe, Achille. *Critique of Black Reason*. Translated by Laurent DuBois. Durham: Duke University Press, 2017.

Medine, Carolyn M. Jones. "Ellipsis: The Deconstructive Practice in the Work of Charles H. Long." *American Religion* 2, no. 2 (Spring 2021): 5–24. muse.jhu.edu/article/811688. Project MUSE.

Molesworth, Jesse M. Equiano's "'Loud Voice': Witnessing the Performance of The Interesting Narrative." *Texas Studies in Literature and Language*, 48, no. 2 (Summer 2006): 123–144.

Morrison, Toni. "Home." In *The House That Race Built: Black Americans, U.S. Terrain*, edited by Wahneema Lubiano, 3–12. New York: Pantheon Books, 1997.

Nietzsche, Fredrich. *Beyond Good and* Evil, trans. Helen Zimmern. VI. 207, Project Gutenberg EBook (December 7, 2009). https://www.gutenberg.org/files/4363/4363-h/4363-h.htm#link2HCH0004. Project Gutenberg.

Njoku, Raphael Chijioke. *West African Masking Traditions and Diaspora Masquerade Carnivals: History, Memory, and Transnationalism. Rochester, NY: University of Rochester Press, 2020.*

Olney, James. "'I Was Born': Slave Narratives, Their Status as Autobiography and as Literature." *Callaloo* 20 (Winter, 1984): 46–73. https://doi.org/10.2307/2930678.

Ogunnaike, Ayodeji. "What's Really Behind the Mask: A Reexamination of Syncretism in Brazilian Candomblé." *Journal of Africana Studies* 8, no. 1 (November 2020), 146–171. https://doi.org/10.5325/jafrireli.8.1.0146.

Paul, Ronald. "'I Whitened My Face, That They Might Not Know Me,' Race and Identity in Olaudah Equiano's Slave Narrative." *Journal of Black Studies* 39, no. 6 (July 2009): 848–864.

Phillips, Ulrich Bonnell. *American Negro Slavery: A Survey of the Supply, Employment, and Control of Negro Labor, as Determined by the Plantation Regime.* Baton Rouge: LSU Press, 1966.

Rediker, Marcus. *The Slave Ship: A Human History.* New York: Penguin Books, 2008.

Sekora, Johbn. "Black Message/White Envelope: Genre, Authenticity, and Authority in the Antebellum Slave Narrative." *Callaloo* 32 (1987), 482–515. https://doi.org/10.2307/2930465.

Smith, John David. "The Construction of Ulrich Bonnell Phillips's Interpretation of Slavery." *American Studies Journal* 45 (2000): 4–9.

Spivak, Gayatri Chakravorty. "Subaltern Studies: Deconstructing Historiography, Crisis and Change." In Spivak, *In Other Worlds: Essays in Cultural Politics*, 197–221. New York: Methuen.

Sweet, James H. "Mistaken Identities? Olaudah Equiano, Domingo Alvares, and the Methodological Challenges of Studying the African Diaspora." *The American Historical Review* 114, no. 2 (April 2009): 279–306.

Thomas, Lauren, "Confounding Variables: Definition, Examples, and Controls." May 29, 2020. https://www.scribbr.com/methodology/confounding-variables/.

Warner, William B. *MLN: Comparative Literature* 103, no. 5 (December 1988); 1144–1147.

Weis, Monica. "Olaudah Equiano at Sea: Adrift in White Culture." *CEA Critic* 63, no. 1 (Fall 2000): 21–26.

Williams, Jeffrey J., and Marcus Rediker. "History Below Deck: An Interview with Marcus Rediker." *symploke* 28, no. 1 (2020): 547–566. muse.jhu.edu/article/773882. Project MUSE.

Žižek, Slavoj. "*Cogito*, Madness, and Religion: Derrida, Foucault and then Lacan," https://www.lacan.com/zizforest.html.

Chapter 3

Within the Veil and Between the Masks

Reflections on Unveilings and Unmaskings after the Apocalypse

Jacqueline M. Hidalgo

Imagining, perhaps somewhat futilely, that a future reader might wander upon these reflections, I must situate my remarks as a response to a digital exhibition that had once been planned to be in person, but the covid pandemic left us in a rather unpredictable world. Instead, the exhibition manifested virtually, but the digital version was perhaps more apropos to the logics of "Masquerade," to this play with and signification on the very notions of museum and exhibition, where we have all been challenged to ask of this "Masquerade," what is being exhibited, what is on display, for whom, and with what orientations?

As Vincent L. Wimbush pointed out in his opening remarks at the Masquerade Exhibition Symposium, we met virtually to reflect on masking in an era of mask mandates and struggles over them, where many of us must continue to literally mask, at least, in part, because of "counter-masquerades" (Wimbush 2023, 19) that demand all people should risk death so that some can maintain their freedom to infect, so they can maintain the lies of their domination. Directing our attention in stage 1 of this exhibition, Wimbush notes "that complex social life entails masking, the cult of masking, ritual masquerade for the sake of basic communication and structuring of and orientation to the world" (6). There is no social world unmasked; no one holds—or should hold—the power to fully expose. What I think this exhibition points us toward is not about becoming fully unveiled or unmasked so much as requiring that we all think more carefully and more pointedly about different masquerades and their consequences.

We live in a moment where we are more publicly and across platforms able to name lies that drive white supremacy, the particularly gruesome masquerade in which "the black-fleshed . . . serve as fraught synecdoche for the construction of modernities" (Wimbush 2023, 23). Among popular and current lies of a white-supremacist inflected masquerade is that "counter-masquerade," a refusal to mask for the sake of others, a refusal to wear a mask that might serve a complex social life. It manifests a fear of being marked, a yearning to keep one's mask seemingly unremarked, a fear and yearning that are so severe that vaccines must be avoided because of their potential to mark (Firebaugh 2021). In this peculiar era, many of us have read of or spoken with those specific anti-vaxxers who have chained themselves within a particular masquerade around the Book of Revelation, a masquerade in which they imagine themselves to be unmarked, to be especially capable of and especially anxious about evading the "the mark of the beast" described in Revelation 13.

Thus, this exhibition in November 2021 provided me an opportunity to return again to a text I keep attempting to flee but I seem never to evade. Its very title has too often served as a privileged metonym of scripturalization. I return to the Book of Revelation and to some of its legacies in the apocalyptic Americas it has helped shape because those legacies remind me that even as we may live under the legacies of the Apocalypse, this moment is not an apocalypse[1]—it is not *the* end of the world, nor is it necessarily a moment that unveils the ultimate.

As historical critics have often constructed Revelation, the text may be understood as a signifying play on Roman domination, on one historical empire's masquerade, and critics like Christopher A. Frilingos (2004) have drawn our attention to how the Roman empire used spectacle, how it attempted to put people and goods on display, perhaps not unlike our modern museums, as part of their own attempts to tell a smooth story of control. The Book of Revelation is itself not very smooth. Its narrative is almost impossible for moderns to follow, but perhaps that too is masquerade, an attempt to disrupt Roman management of meaning, to disrupt Roman spectacle through its own spectacular. In Revelation 13, the much-dreaded mark (χάραγμα in Greek) can mean many things, though I personally doubt a vaccine is among them. It may refer to the likeness of the Roman emperor on money or to the tattooed flesh of those enslaved. Few interpreters remark upon how all humans in Revelation are ultimately marked as enslaved, to Satan or to Christ, something that Shanell T. Smith examines more closely in her study of *The Woman Babylon* (2014). Even though I imagine there might be much to say about Revelation's metonymy in relationship to scripturalization as enslavement (see Wimbush 2012), I want to focus as Smith does on the veil, a central, if still fraught synecdoche of the Apocalypse.

Our very term for the book, apocalypse (ἀποκάλυψις), comes from the Greek verb to reveal/to unveil, but it can also mean to uncover the head, and it is close to the verb (ἀνακαλύπτω), for unveiling a bride (Huber 2013, 1). The name of the book in Greek encodes a notion of "revelation" that may have a certain gendered resonance of bridal unveiling. Even as we might understand the whole book as a long unveiling, it culminates in two particularly striking unveilings of two cities figured as women. Situated within a culture of spectacle, this insistence on removing a veil to expose another, truer story relies on the power of seeing and being seen and the capacity to see through. Demonic, Roman lies are unveiled in order to expose superior, divine truths.

At the same time, the exposed are figured as women. The Roman villain, presented to us in the guise of the woman Babylon is violently stripped and exposed as part of her destruction. Her counterpoint is the virginal bride-city, also to be unveiled, the new Jerusalem who descends from heaven near the end of the book.

As with all texts, especially ones as overly engaged as biblical texts, a lot depends on how you read Babylon and the new Jerusalem and who you are when you read about them and what you do with what you have read. When this privileged metaphor of veiling and unveiling entwines itself within modern structures of knowledge-making, something Eleanor Craig has traced in her examination of Giorgio Agamben's work on bare life (Craig 2019), a framework of revelation becomes a framework of power-knowledge, of meaning management, that is both gendered and raced, in terms of who has the power to unveil and to expose and who at the same time remains obscured, exposing truth but unexposed themselves. Here, I can only point to the colonial legacies, particularly for Muslim women and Muslims in general, of a modern European and Euro-North American Christian obsession with literal veiling and unveiling (Hoodfar 1992). This structuring of knowledge through metaphoric veiling relies on and perpetuates a binary framework, an epistemological hierarchy with those who are exposed subordinate to those who expose.

However, some modern minoritized critics model a different and less binary use of the veil. For Sara Ahmed, the critic is not the one who removes the veil, laying bare the other side: "The veil is not unveiled to reveal the truth; the veil is revealed, which is a revelation that must be partial and flawed" (Ahmed 2010, 166). Returning to Shanell T. Smith (2014) and her womanist hermeneutics of ambi*veil*ence, reading Babylon, presented both as imperial monster and enslaved woman reveals a veil in this world: "This veil reflects back to me the particularized veil in my own life" (loc 228 of 4125). In this way, Smith draws upon the Veil as found in W. E. B. Du Bois in order to reimagine the act of reading Revelation as an opportunity, perhaps akin to how Wimbush describes, "if not to throw off all the masks, at least to 'see through' their experiences and gestures, to gain heightened self-awareness of the masquerade that defines all human foibles and strivings in the world after Contact with difference" (15–16).

Smith's "ambi*veil*ence" and Wimbush's "seeing through" present a different metaphoric structure of knowledge, not the apocalyptic binary of exposer and exposed. In Du Bois's chapter (1994/1903) "Of the Passing of the First-Born," he describes his baby boy as born "Within the Veil," but he also says that he "heard in his baby voice the voice of the Prophet that was to rise within the Veil" (128). Du Bois here refers to the "Veil of Color," a way of understanding the "double consciousness" through which African Americans must encounter themselves and their world, seeing both through dominant white perceptions and their own. As Eboni Marshall Turman (2013) has argued, Du Bois does not necessarily only refer to a bridal veil in the Apocalypse, as he may also refer to the Jerusalem Temple veil that separates out the Holy of Holies. In this chapter, Du Bois articulates a sense of epistemic authority grounded in seemingly revelatory prophecy, but this prophet does not see beyond the Veil, rather the prophet speaks from within it. Du Bois offers a third space within the veil, a metaphor of knowledge-power that plays within and without the structuring binary of revelation.

Reviewing this online exhibition, itself structured around Olaudah Equiano/ Gustavus Vassa's capacity to speak to and within the Veil, to signify on the scriptural does not take us beyond the veil, but it instead offers a structuring metaphor for knowledge-making that is akin to but not the same as unveiling. This exhibition also offers the metaphor of masking: the exhibition as witness to and part of a masquerade that is scripturalization, the violence it has wrought on Black-fleshed peoples, and then in stage IV the presentation of Black Mimetics, here seeing "Equiano's/Vassa's . . . religious conversion [a]s metonymic of the larger ongoing attempt on the part of this particular black-fleshed person to be 'saved' within/into white men's world. . . . These attempts to 'convert' on the part of many if not most in the Black Atlantic worlds constituted a layered and complex history—of representations, resistance, flight, accommodation, survival. These attempts are all masquerade" (11–12). Even what we may think of as the most fundamental practices around our survival, those practices also fit into a social masquerade.

Here is an invitation, as Wimbush suggests, not out of masking but to greater and for many of us more distressing self-reflexivity about the multiple masks and masquerades in which we are entangled—distressing because they remind us, even and especially those of us who think we are above and beyond masks, that a play upon the logics of unveiling is itself a masquerade with veils. As Wimbush once said to me about a film we both watched (*Get*

Out 2017), no one can just get out. But I hope that for many of us, witnessing this virtual exhibition in a time of enforced masking is an invitation to the edges of apocalypse, a change in the forms of scripturalization that have relied on violent veilings and exposures.

As part of my own masquerade, I should admit that I always read from and think with Gloria Anzaldúa's (1984) mestiza consciousness, both within its limits (that is an appeal to the particularities of time and place with a fraught relationship to the construction of "mixed-race" consciousness), but also with its framework of the borderlands, of that space at the boundaries of seemingly distinct social worlds. Those of us who have lived between, among, and at the margins of many social worlds—and there are many of us along many different axes—know well how varied and ongoing masquerades are. As Fernando F. Segovia once described, for those of us who live in diaspora, "all worlds emerge as social constructions" (Segovia 1996, 212). Such recognition does not mean we can simply expose the constructions without participating in them, or that we are now freed from embeddedness within social constructions, but it can position us to recognize and navigate our masquerades differently.

As with all texts, this online exhibition will be experienced differently depending on who you are. For me, experiencing the exhibition offers not so much an apocalyptic unveiling but a less binary *apocalypso*. In *Decolonizing Diasporas* (2020), Yomaira C. Figueroa-Vásquez draws upon Michelle Cliff's (2008) notion of apocalypso, where "the Other appears to be the One." (159). Cliff, a paler-complected Jamaican-US author, reflected on an experience where her pale privilege brought her into spaces where her very presence triggered in (white) others a confusion around naturalized systems of categorization. Figueroa-Vásquez further describes "apocalypso" as "a cataclysmic failure" (160) of meaning regimes, a failure of dominants' smooth narration, a cracking in the epistemic armor. In short, apocalypso is not an unveiling but a space where the masks crack and the masquerade shifts.

Even as the metaphor of the veil has been scripturalized through certain readings of the Book of Revelation, perhaps this exhibition on masquerades viewed virtually during a moment of unending apocalypse, in forcing us to don literal masks, may offer something else. Perhaps many of us can follow an ex-centric apocalypso, a fracture of meaning regimes, a meta-exhibition played within the veil and between the masks.

NOTE

1. Here I follow the work of certain Indigenous environmental scholars in arguing that the "apocalypse" as we popularly think of it, in terms of a catastrophic end of the

world, already happened, especially for Indigenous peoples and the descendants of enslaved Africans in the Americas. In different ways, we in the Americas are post-apocalyptic peoples. See Powys Whyte 2017 and Simmons 2019.

BIBLIOGRAPHY

Ahmed, Sara. 2010. *The Promise of Happiness*. Durham, NC: Duke University Press.

Anzaldúa, Gloria. 1984. *Borderlands/La Frontera: The New Mestiza*. San Francisco, CA: Aunt Lute Books.

Cliff, Michelle. 2008. *If I Could Write This in Fire*. Minneapolis: University of Minnesota Press.

Craig, Eleanor. 2019. "Catastrophic Grammar, Bare Life, and the Fates of Other(ed) Bodies." Paper Presented at a "Colloquium on Coloniality, Race, Catastrophe." Cambridge, MA: Harvard Divinity School, November 1.

Du Bois, W. E. B. 1994 (1903). *The Souls of Black Folk*. New York: Dover Publications.

Figueroa-Vásquez, Yomaira C. 2020. *Decolonizing Diasporas: Radical Mappings of Afro-Atlantic Literature*. Evanston, IL: Northwestern University Press.

Firebaugh, Tiffany. 2021. "Covid-19 Vaccines: Why Some Christians Decry Them as the 'Mark of the Beast.'" *Religion & Politics*. October 11. https://religionandpolitics .org/2021/10/11/covid-19-vaccines-why-some-christians-decry-them-as-the-mark -of-the-beast/. (accessed June 16, 2022).

Frilingos, Christopher A. 2004. *Spectacles of Empire: Monsters, Martyrs, and the Book of Revelation*. Philadelphia: University of Pennsylvania Press.

Hoodfar, Homa. 1992. "The Veil in Their Minds and on Our Heads: The Persistence of Colonial Images of Muslim Women." *Resources for Feminist Research* 22, no. 3/4: 5–18.

Huber, Lynn R. 2013. *Thinking and Seeing with Women in Revelation*. New York: Bloomsbury.

Powys Whyte, Kyle. 2017. "Our Ancestors' Dystopia Now: Indigenous Conservation and the Anthropocene." *The Routledge Companion to the Environmental Humanities*, ed. Urusula Heise, Jon Christensen, and Michelle Niemann, 206–215. New York: Routledge.

Segovia, Fernando F. 1996. "In the World but Not of It: Exile as Locus for a Theology of the Diaspora." *Hispanic/Latino Theology: Challenge and Promise*. Ed. Ada María Isasi-Díaz and Fernando F. Segovia, 195–217. Minneapolis, MN: Fortress Press.

Simmons, Kali. 2019. "Reorientations; or, an Indigenous Feminist Reflection on the Anthropocene." *Journal of Cinema and Media Studies* 58, no. 2: 174–179.

Smith, Shanell T. 2014. *The Woman Babylon and the Marks of Empire: Reading Revelation with a Postcolonial Womanist Hermeneutics of Ambiveilence*. Minneapolis, MN: Fortress Press. Kindle Edition.

Turman, Eboni Marshall. 2013. *Towards a Womanist Ethic of Incarnation: Black Bodies, the Black Church, and the Council of Chalcedon*. New York: Palgrave Macmillan.

Wimbush, Vincent L. 2012. *White Men's Magic: Scripturalization as Slavery*. New York: Oxford University Press.

Wimbush, Vincent L. 2023. "Introduction: 'Everything about Me Was Magic': The Black-Fleshed and the Making and Management of Modernities." In *Masquerade: Scripturalizing Modernities through Black Flesh*. Edited by Vincent L. Wimbush. Lanham, MD: Lexington Books/Fortress Academic.

Chapter 4

Between the Veil and the Mirror

Josephine Baker and the Scripturalization of Black Modernity in France

Cécile Coquet-Mokoko

UN-SCRIPTING RACE, OR MUTING VOICES FROM WITHIN THE MASK

Race is a most unpalatable term in France these days. The first sentence of Article 1 of the Constitution of 1958 no longer reads, "France shall be an indivisible, secular, democratic and social Republic. It shall ensure the equality of all citizens before the law, without distinction of origin, race, or religion." In July 2018, by a unanimous vote of our equivalent of the U.S. House of Representatives, the word "race" was struck out of the French Republic's "living" Constitution—a text written in the wake of a coup prompted by the will to suppress Algerian natives' aspirations to independence by giving greater executive powers to a "strong man" in the person of General Charles de Gaulle.[1]

The lawmaking body, which was renewed in 2017 and was made up of 341 members of President Emmanuel Macron's newborn center-right party out of the 566 seats, boasted an unprecedented percentage of 38.8% women representatives, but few nonwhite faces or foreign-sounding last names. The previous Socialist President François Hollande (May 2012–May 2017) had called for the revision of constitutional language in a campaign pledge that he had made in 2012, but never delivered.[2] On the contrary, following terrorist attacks in Paris, Hollande's government considered stripping of their French citizenship any so-called "homegrown terrorists," in addition to the extant legal sanctions—a move that an overwhelming majority of legal scholars and his own minister of Justice Christiane Taubira, a Black female elected official from French Guiana and former presidential hopeful, deemed unnecessary and divisive.[3] Significantly, the last time French citizenship had been revoked by a French government, it was during Nazi occupation and Jews were the target; this is precisely the reason why the state has since then forbidden the collection of ethnic and racial statistics.

Today, the country's constitution thus only guarantees equality "without distinction of origin, sex or religion." Such language does not simply replace "race" by "sex," but deliberately assumes that "origin" and "religion" already encompass the social construction of race, even though neither is as immediately visible as skin color or the other phenotypes used in racializing a person or a group. This move effectively scripturalizes race while masking it. Indeed, on the one hand, it mirrors the conflation observed in the UK between race and ethnicity,[4] as if only cultural differences such as national origins and religion, not the racialization of individuals who otherwise conform to the cultural mainstream, were responsible for differential treatment. It also mirrors the conflation observed in twenty-first-century evolutions of uses of the French language among children and teenagers, who readily draw the strict binary distinction they perceive between being French (and therefore, by default, White with European origins only) and "having origins."[5] The latter phrase is a metonymy for visibly being the descendant of colonized subjects or other immigrant outsiders, whose right to belong in the nation may always be questioned by anyone curious of their presumably "real" identity, while their non-racialized peers are left unaccountable for their own origins if their names are not readable as foreign. In this case, they are free to choose whether or not to out themselves as descendants of Polish, Italian, Portuguese, or even Berber North African mothers or maternal grandparents. As in Equiano/ Vassa's case, claiming or not passing on a family name remains of utmost importance in being able or unable to pass for a full-fledged citizen and lift oneself above all suspicions of dual loyalty.

On the other hand, the reality of racialization within French society is further obliterated not only by having "origins" effectively mask the nation's history of enslavement and colonization of the native American, African, Asian, or Oceanian ancestors of contemporary citizens, but also by using the scripturalectics of assigning religious identities as a tool of racialization. This strategy was already implemented in colonial Virginia's 1662 statute, which defined any "negro man or woman" as presumably a non-Christian,[6] since conversion to Christianity was actively discouraged by planters concerned about their enslaved African workforce demanding equality with Europeans directly from the English monarch. Yet in the case of France—a nation that has insisted on wrenching its political independence away from the Catholic church since 1789, when it re-created itself as a secular Republic after centuries of divine-right monarchy—it is all the more paradoxical to see religion thus inscribed in the Constitution as possibly creating inequality among French citizens. Indeed, we are told from the cradle that religion belongs and should be restricted to the private sphere only, so that the State may treat all religious institutions in a neutral manner—although, in practical terms, this principle of invisibility of religion in public spaces is experienced as muting and concealing this dimension of our public personae. Following cases of suspensions of high school female students who insisted on wearing the hijab or Islamic headscarf, a ban on wearing "ostentatious signs of religious belonging" in public schools was even inscribed into law in 2004. More recent evolutions are now extending this principle of concealing religious affiliation to municipal swimming pools, where swimsuits for both men and women must be close-fitting for allegedly hygienic purposes, while French citizenship may be denied at the last minute to women who refuse to shake hands with men for religious reasons.[7]

The reason why religion was mentioned in the Constitution of 1958 was precisely the existence of a colonial status for Muslims in Algeria which made these natives second-class citizens, enfranchised only to elect their own representatives in a powerless lawmaking assembly. Conversely, their Jewish counterparts had been considered assimilable to the French Republic and thus enjoyed citizenship status, as well as representation in the Parliament in Paris along with the European colonists who had settled the country since 1830 and created a melting pot of European nationalities, many of which had no roots in metropolitan France or had fled the German colonization of the northeastern French provinces of Alsace and Lorraine.[8]

In twenty-first-century France, North African colonies are history. Still, whoever mentions "religion" is obliquely but transparently alluding to the unwelcome presence on metropolitan soil of Muslim French citizens, whose presumed or actual religious practice is made to be constitutive of their identities and loyalties. Like the "soft wax" analyzed by Wimbush, Islam is thus refashioned into a racializing category for anyone betrayed by a family name, a middle name or even an ambiguous Biblical first name (like Adam, Noah, or even Isaac). This, in turn, ironically scripturalizes anyone of European descent as presumably Christian, but from an ethnic perspective, regardless of actual adhesion to any brand of Christianity, in a country where fewer than 10% of the persons surveyed identify as practicing Christians—including an unknown but certainly sizable proportion of non-White French respondents.[9] With the rising popularity of avowed admirers of Donald Trump among presidential French hopefuls, the scripturalization of the Judeo-Christian roots of metropolitan France as evidence of the nation's Whiteness is no longer confined to the fringe discourse of the far right as it was ten years ago, but explicitly woven into conservative political rhetoric to resurrect the scrip-turalectics of the medieval and Renaissance geopolitics opposing Europe and Islam.[10] While claiming to embody the universal values of the Enlightenment, President Macron himself, along with his centrist ally Jean-Louis Bourlanges, president of the Parliament's Foreign Affairs Committee, unambiguously expressed preference for welcoming Ukrainian war refugees fleeing Putin's invasion of their land over Afghan or Syrian ones fleeing Islamic fundamentalism and a brutal authoritarian regime: the former were labeled "quality immigrants" only a few months after the latter were designated as a wave from which France and Europe should "protect ourselves."[11] In the May 2022 presidential elections, as many as 40% of French voters condoned this strategy of polarization of the nation over a racial binary masquerading as a clash of civilizations, and the Parliament is now home to 89 far-right lawmakers from Marine Le Pen's party—two record-breaking figures.

Ultimately, because racial and ethnic statistics are forbidden in France to make up for the anti-Semitic crimes of the Vichy regime under Nazi occupation, the erasure of the notion of race from the constitutional guarantee of equal treatment of course precludes any possibility of systemic racism on the part of the French state itself, or anyone acting in the name of the Republic. If only a person's detectable foreign origins, presumed biological sex, and religion inferred from a last name, physical appearance, or the nonconsumption of alcohol and pork can cause discrimination while the social construction and scripturalization of race are made literally un-thinkable, then the Republic can persuade itself that it has achieved colorblindness, and the citizenry must behave accordingly.

Ironically, the passing of the revision received next to no media coverage and was met with remarkable indifference in the midst of the fever around the Football World Cup, which was eventually won by a French national team of mostly African francophone descent. The players themselves objected to being seen as anything other than French, seeking to deflate controversy in social media (notably between the Daily Show host Trevor Noah and the French ambassador to the US[12]) over the unaddressed legacy of French imperialism and the silencing of daily discriminations suffered by Black French citizens—including high-profile athletes whenever they are defeated or found guilty of minor offenses.[13]

As the Canadian sociologist Danielle Juteau explains, the stubborn refusal by France's White elites to consider and even scientifically discuss the real implications of race and ethnicity as social constructs has strong political underpinnings. From the perspective of French sociologists, who are overwhelmingly of French or otherwise European descent,

[t]hat racial categories were originally constructed as part and parcel of a system of appropriation—that they served to justify slavery and other forms of domination, and to reproduce inequalities through monopolistic closure—justifies the rejection of racial and also ethnic categories, since the latter are equated with the former. Furthermore, recognising how racism naturalizes and excludes human beings and groups comforts the Republican ideal of equality for all through same treatment and the non-recognition of "difference." But as the confusion concerning racial and ethnic dynamics persists, the specific processes underlying ethnic trajectories, positions and identities keep on being misunderstood. . . . The idea of Republican integration . . . plays in French sociology a role similar to the dictatorship of the proletariat in orthodox Marxist sociology, transforming itself into a methodological nationalism which forbids the analysis of ethnic dynamics.

This flat refusal to discuss the very concepts of race and racialization, in the name of the universal values of the Enlightenment, finds its justification in the fear of the mutual distrust that, presumably, inevitably flows from acknowledging differences, as if this inevitably created separatist enclaves (referred to as "communities," necessarily incompatible with the unity of the nation), fostering "identity politics," political radicalization, and parochialism. The United States is regularly exposed as the counterexample and polar opposite of the racial harmony France has presumably achieved thanks to the subsuming of racial differences under a single national identity. The knee-jerk reaction triggered by the very use of the word "race" without inverted commas or a caveat like "so-called" preceding it, is strikingly similar to that caused among gun-rights defenders who accuse gun-control advocates of "politicizing" the grief of the bereaved after every mass shooting in the USA.[14]

Since the Black Lives Matter movement gained global exposure, and particularly after the murder of George Floyd in May 2020 triggered a wave of protests and toppling of statues symbolizing European nations' slaveholding heritage, French scholars and activists using and teaching the tools of Critical Race Theory and intersectionality have been increasingly anathematized by politicians across the political spectrum as introducing and seeking to normalize hate speech against straight White males. Most vocal among them have been conservatives like the former minister of education Jean-Michel Blanquer, himself the son of colonists expelled from Algeria in 1962, but also a number of high-ranking Army officers, persuaded of the existence of a plot by foreign agitators attempting to "Americanize" the minds of students, particularly from the African diaspora who, until then, had presumably been content with their lot.[15]

This polarization has led, in France as in the US, to calls to silence as dangerous radicals all those who challenge their invisibility as Black French persons or draw attention to the existence of a White norm underpinning the

French definition of citizenship. Mimicking the US culture wars, French public opinion is now invited to see defenders of racial, ethnic, and sexual minor-
ities as warriors engaged in a far-left fascist crusade against straight White
men, with some media commentators explicitly accusing those French intellectuals embracing CRT of being complicit with Islamic Fundamentalists.
Yet French-born theorists of race did articulate the scripturalization of Black
bodies as colonial bodies without necessarily having been influenced by prior
exposure to US theories of race.

As early as in 1957, the Tunisian-born thinker Albert Memmi shed light on
the systematically demeaning definitions of the colonized subject by the colonizer, prompting African American civil rights activists to marvel at the similarities with race relations between Blacks and Whites in Jim Crow America
(his book was not translated into English until 1965, while, conversely, Du
Bois's works were not available in French).[16] Memmi also demonstrated, as
Frantz Fanon had done in 1952, the inherent link between the colonial situation and the necessity for any European newcomer to embrace Whiteness
and all its racist underpinnings in order to enjoy citizenship rights not only
at the expense of the natives, but on the basis of their systemic exploitation and degradation.[17] He also emphasized the frustration of the members
of the French colonizer caste when considering the relative lack of racism
of metropolitan French visitors vis-à-vis the natives of North Africa: these
mediocre, ever-anxious colonizers' idealized version of France clashed with
the country's indifference to race matters as opposed to intraracial class and
regional issues.[18]

This indifference, of course, ceased when the colonizers were "repatriated"
and Arab and sub-Saharan African colonial subjects migrated to France. In
the sixty years that have elapsed since then, the country's political life has
evolved from negating the trauma of the loss of Algeria to an official effort,
led by President Macron, to acknowledge simultaneously the reality of war
crimes committed by the French (during the 8 years of Independence War
only, rather than from 1832 till 1962), the lack of socio-economic inclusion of the Muslim veterans who fought alongside French troops and were
grudgingly given refuge on metropolitan soil, and the present capitalization
by Algerian elites on the horrors of colonization to make excuses for their
own incompetence and corruption since 1962. In parallel with the young
President's efforts to come to terms with a past that he has no family ties with,
contrary to 39% of French citizens aged 18 to 25,[19] other politicians who do
have risen to prominence, further polarizing the political climate around the
inclusion or rejection of French Muslim citizens, with rhetoric around the
so-called Great Replacement on the one hand and on the Creolization of modern French culture on the other hand. Meanwhile and unsurprisingly, increas-
ing numbers of young French politicians are themselves representative of the

Black or Muslim segments of the nation, thirty years after a historic march where their forebears had demanded an end to their invisibility as French citizens. Precisely at the moment when these racialized French voices are beginning to make themselves heard on the political scene, another symbol of Black France, and more precisely Black Paris, is being extolled as a sign of national reconciliation, but also as a mask intended to mute any criticism of the very colonial heritage that shaped it.

JOSEPHINE BAKER, OR THE MIRROR EROTICIZING FRANCE'S COLONIAL PAST

Since the onset of the twentieth century and the successful photographic exhibition of Black American middle-class life by W. E. B. Du Bois at the Paris World Fair of 1900, African Americans have been the desirable Black Other, durably and visually distinguished from the colonized Black subjects from Africa and Oceania who were simultaneously penned half-naked in human zoos up to the 1930s, exposed as "savages" to the inquisitive gaze of French city-dwellers and made to perform daily activities while pretending to ignore their actor status (exactly like Buffalo Bill Cody's troupe of Native Americans, or Saartje Bartmann, the so-called Hottentot Venus).[20]

Du Bois's skillful carving of a distinctive place for Black Americans in French visual culture and imagination has been solidified since the 1920s, by virtue of the complex fostered by the two successive liberations of the country by US troops. Black Americans can be dealt with on an equal footing, particularly when they express appreciation for the treatment they receive in France: not only are they on the side of modernity and civilization, but their racial identity is always presented as the successful result of a harmonious mix, even as French White men and especially women were discouraged by institutions (the law or the Army) from building multiracial families with the country's colonial subjects on metropolitan soil.[21]

As the French Whites' Black men and women, American Blacks who choose to live in France are extolled as the wise and exemplary ones, because their presence helps public opinion avoid any discussion of the effects of France's slaveholding and colonial legacy on its social fabric, to focus instead on the purported success of the French assimilationist model of immigrants. Black yet comely, American Black bodies are nonthreatening, since their flesh has not been marked by the French slaveholding or colonial past. Their presence is useful to reiterate that here have been no lynchings of Blacks on metropolitan French soil; the killings by police of peaceful Algerian demonstrators who were beaten to death and/or thrown into the River Seine in 1961 remain scripturalized as signs of the importation of a colonial conflict into the hallowed metropolitan soil, not as symptoms of systemic racism. Besides, it is easy for the French public to keep believing in the country's untainted virtue and humanity, since only a handful of scholars know about the explicitly genocidal policy of colonization implemented by the French Republic from 1830 in Algeria and the efforts made by French monarchs in the previous century to have planters declare the slaves they took with them to metropolitan France and return them to "the colonies" of the Caribbean after a maximum period of two years, in order to nip in the bud any hope of liberation.[22]

For all his professions of love for French history, President Macron has proven a careful curator of its symbols, much like his predecessors. His claim to embody the nation's painful memory of World War I was embedded in his insistence on his own regional origins in the North of France, a formerly industrial hub which still bears the stigma of trench and landmine warfare. In a conjunction that could be compared with President Lincoln's consideration of the petitions tirelessly sent by Mrs. Sarah Josepha Hale to create a national feast of Thanksgiving, Macron's genuine appreciation for inspirational moments in French history found a convenient symbol of patriotism in the years-long request asking French Presidents since Nicolas Sarkozy (2007–2012) to formally induce the US-born performer Josephine Baker into the Pantheon—a former church turned into a secular temple celebrating the "ancestors" of the Republic, whose remains are always transferred into it in great pomp—along with other luminaries of French culture. Led by the left-wing intellectual Régis Debray since 2013 and supported by the members of Baker's "rainbow tribe" of twelve adopted children, the 2019 petition launched by the author Laurent Kupferman (which garnered 37,807 signatures) echoed the title and chorus of a famous song, "Osez Joséphine," implying that such homage would be a daring, possibly shocking move that would shake the status quo.[23] In fact, the proposal was met with remarkable consensus, proving the assumption wrong or the title misleadingly provocative. Indeed, no one could deny that Josephine Baker had enjoyed worldwide fame and had been a star and a sex symbol in France, particularly in the interwar period when US expatriates of the Lost Generation proclaimed that "Paris est une fête."[24]

Yet in November 2021, rather than a portrait of the boyish-looking flapper sporting either a top hat and a tuxedo or a topless costume, it was a much more conventional black-and-white portrait of an eternally grinning Josephine Baker in her uniform as a member of the French Resistance to Nazism that graced the entrance of the Pantheon. Although the coffin brought into the Pantheon was actually filled with earth from her native Saint Louis, Paris, Dordogne, and Monaco, where her body remains interred, she was hailed as the sixth woman to be admitted there, and the first woman of color, following only two French descendants of slaves. These were, following the chronology of their respective pantheonizations, first the colonial Governor Félix Éboué, who welcomed De Gaulle in Chad when French resistance to Nazism desperately needed the support of the country's colonies, and the writer Alexandre Dumas, who authored the famous *Three Musketeers* but whose African ancestry is hardly known to the French and the rest of the world. Significantly, the count of Black French luminaries leaves out the two iconic anticolonial figures Toussaint Louverture (the father of the Haitian revolution and a military genius equal to Napoleon) and Aimé Césaire (one of the fathers of the Négritude movement and an unforgiving critic of French Whiteness and colonialism in both the Caribbean and Africa) because they each have a plaque at the Pantheon and therefore did not benefit from the pomp of a national funeral.

Since August 2021, then, and without any discussion of her Black predecessors in the temple of the French Republic, Josephine Baker (1906–1975) has been iconized as the most modern symbol of France, with the scripturalectics of modernity building on her Blackness and queerness (persistently denied by her sons Jean-Claude and Brian) to spin the superficial narrative of "daring" while erasing the political implications of both her race and sexuality. Also forgotten in the process were the painful story of her eviction at age 62, with her twelve children, from the castle that was their home and her rescue by the US-born Princess Grace of Monaco. In the days prior to her induction into the Pantheon, the official message issued by the presidency read that Baker is "the embodiment of the French spirit" because "she fought all the good fights that gather citizens of good will, in France and throughout the world."[25]

"[E]very single choice that Josephine Baker made finds an echo in what we are living today. She is a mirror in which everyone may project themselves"— so President Macron said to justify the choice of the African American artist who made "the radical choice of eternal and universal France" to prove to the world "that emancipation and liberty could be won by willpower." The image of the mirror is a convenient avatar of the mask for a president who, like his predecessors, aims to indirectly celebrate his own idealized legacy by choosing a protective ancestor for the nation to worship, just six months before his own reelection bid—which he knew would eventually have him facing his far-right opponent Marine Le Pen.

Other prominent figures of Black men or women could have been chosen to embody French-speaking culture and democratic spirit, such as the Martiniquan Nardal sisters—one of whom, Paulette, criticized Baker for contributing to the dominant essentializing representations of Black women as sexually unrestrained. But to White French men and women, Josephine Baker was a particularly fascinating, festive celebration of Black flesh in her quasi-nudity, when she mingled the music-hall codes and the familiar erotic/pornographic visual codes of imperial France with imported minstrel show codes unknown to the Europeans, to become a sex symbol in the so-called *Revue Nègre* from 1925. Unexplained in this consensual celebration of Josephine as a pioneer of women's sexual emancipation was the role played by Chicagoan Caroline Dudley, a White patrician who had been sent to the segregated New York club The Plantation to recruit dancers for the Théâtre des Champs-Élysées, which was seeking a new exotic routine to offer its patrons after the end of the fad for Nijinsky's Russian Ballets. In unambiguously racial terms, Dudley had been told by the theater's new owner to bring back Black performers because the Parisian public craved all things primitive.[26] She spotted the teenage Baker in the routine of *Shuffle Along* that was run at The Plantation, offered her more than the $300 a week she made there, and later insisted that she dance topless. In her most memorable performance, wearing only a pair of yellow sandals and a banana skirt that revealed her curves, she climbed down a tree with simian gestures and offered herself in a syncopated dance to a White colonist lazily lounging under a tent, surrounded by scantily-dressed men who were all darker than Josephine.[27] Commentators today insist that the subtext was actually critical of colonization because the White man was shown doing nothing; yet the privilege of idleness was exactly what metropolitan spectators of the show envied in that character, as Memmi's portrait of the colonizer makes plain; much as the planter's idleness was coveted by the crowds going to minstrel shows to hear about "the good old days" of "the ole plantation." In his speech on the day of Baker's induction, President Macron contended that she had invented her routine in order to openly mock the racist clichés to which she was ordered to cater, as if she had not implemented the same survival strategies as other African American artists back home, such as Bert Williams who was forced to perform in blackface and speak Black vernacular English because he was too articulate for the White audiences' taste.[28] He admired her eccentric choice of a cheetah as a pet, apparently unaware that the oft-photographed pair represented a veiled echo of the racist figure of Little Black Sambo with the tiger, and in the same breath, he put this public presentation of her persona on a par with her spending one night in a man's arms and the next in a woman's—conveniently omitting to add that several years later, she disowned her adopted son Jari to punish him for being gay.[29]

Like so many before her who had to grin, roll and cross their eyes or carouse to hide more subtle signifyin' behind their performances of the grotesque, the interwar persona of Josephine Baker carved a place for herself in the hearts and fantasies of French *men* in particular, by comforting them in the belief that France was heaven to so-called "Negroes." Almost a century later, Macron chose to minimize the effects of European racism then and now by extolling Baker's humor and energy as the recipe to "turn the burlesque into sublime"—a convenient warning to those who would dare speak from within the mask instead of accepting success at the price of tokenism. Among the quotes by Josephine Baker, her pledge of patriotism when choosing the side of the Resistance to Nazi occupation is particularly effective in silencing any criticism today and scripturalizing French patriotism: "France has given me everything, use me as you will. I will save the country in my own way."

In a move that is typical of the refusal to acknowledge the existence of systemic racism by propelling to the forefront "the token Negro," the injunction to be grateful to France is constantly thrust by politicians and media influencers in the faces of any high-profile Black French person of African descent who dares suggest that the Republic's ideals of equality and fraternity have not yet materialized for non-American Blacks in France, or point out that not all Black French persons are of immigrant descent, or complain of the gratuitous, humiliating administrative hoops through which immigrants must jump when applying for French nationality.[30]

Josephine Baker's speaking before Martin Luther King at the March on Washington—and her being the only woman who was allowed to take the microphone on that occasion—are also largely extolled in France to showcase her antiracist credentials, especially as she appeared in her French military uniform and praised France as "a fairyland place" in front of a crowd who had few opportunities of traveling the world as she did. Few know that she took the trouble of sewing a miniature French flag as an insignia on her children's lapels in order to protect them when flying to the United States for Bob Kennedy's funeral, or that she was surveilled by the FBI for accepting Fidel Castro's invitation to visit Cuba with her family in 1966.[31] Just as Dr. King is now weaponized as an ancestor figure that may be used to silence anyone asking for affirmative action, in today's France, any attempt to criticize the commodification of Josephine Baker as a readily-accessible, ever-consenting colonized body—whose racial ambiguity led her to perform in films and songs alternatively as Indochinese or Arab, Caribbean or African[32] and, in 1933, accept to sing a jazz song that had her wish she saw "her breasts and hips turn white" instead of looking "like a small shriveled prune" on the snow[33]—is perceived as a breach of antiracist etiquette by the very same politicians who brand antiracists as "wokist" firebrands.

Among her twelve adopted children, only two regularly appear on screen to share childhood memories: Jean-Claude Bouillon-Baker, who publicly denied the racist connotations of the term "nègre" in 1925 (pace Césaire and the entire Négritude movement!) and appeared to lament the disqualification of the word attached to his mother's early success; and Brian, born Brahim in Algeria, whose presence in the "rainbow tribe" accounts for its presentation as a family uniting children of different origins and religions, although he was adopted at age two and does not seem to have had a particularly religious upbringing either before or after his adoption by Baker and her husband Jo

Bouillon.[34] When French television was invited into the castle of the Milandes in December 1960 to see how the children studied, each of them was asked to show in what country he or she was born—a constant, obsessive feature of French "colorblindness"—but Brahim pointed to Morocco instead of Algeria, on the off-the-record advice of his mother.[35] In spite of the age differences between the children, they were shown attending the same lesson with a private tutor. Baker's daughter Marianne explained in an interview that the children had private tutors only, after getting into fights with the other French children at the local school over the latter's calling their mother the N-word.[36]

Will the reader be surprised to hear that these jarring notes are muffled in the celebration of Josephine as Macron's France—unconventional, entertaining, and dazzling, but muted and willing to sacrifice herself? It is particularly significant that the body of a Black American woman is so astutely utilized, like "soft wax," Wimbush would argue, in the long-standing rivalry between two nations whose claims to embody universal aspirations to freedom and equality have been similarly grounded in the erasure of their own Black citizens—as Wimbush put it, "to make black-ness a supercharged/hypersignified 'reality' and in every respect the lack and the limit."

NOTES

1. See Lorraine Boissoneault, "Why Is France in Its Fifth Republic?" *Smithsonian Magazine*, April 20, 2017, https://www.smithsonianmag.com/history/why-france-its-fifth-republic-180962983/, Retrieved on June 20, 2022.

2. See Idris Fassassi, "Removing 'Race' and Adding 'Gender' to the French Constitution: On Constitutional Redundancy and Symbols," Voices From the Field, ConstitutionNet, August 24, 2018, https://constitutionnet.org/news/removing-race-and-adding-gender-french-constitution-constitutional-redundancy-and-symbols, Retrieved on June 19, 2022.

3. See Kim Willsher, "Hollande Drops Plan to Revoke French Citizenship of Dual-National Terrorists," *The Guardian*, March 30, 2016, https://www.theguardian.com/world/2016/mar/30/francois-hollande-drops-plan-to-revoke-citizenship-of-dual-national-terrorists. Retrieved on June 20, 2022.

4. See "A Guide to Race and Ethnicity Terminology and Language," The Law Society, February 10, 2022, https://www.lawsociety.org.uk/en/topics/ethnic-minority-lawyers/a-guide-to-race-and-ethnicity-terminology-and-language, Retrieved on June 20, 2022.

5. See Patrick Simon, "Nationality and Origins in French Statistics: Ambiguous Categories," *Population: An English Selection*, Vol. 11, 1999, 193–219, https://www.jstor.org/stable/2998696; and Roselyne de Villanova, "Espace de l'entre-deux ou comment la mobilité des immigrés recrée du territoire," *L'homme et la Société,* Vol. 3–4, No. 165–166, 2007, 65–83, https://doi.org/10.3917/lhs.165.0065, Retrieved on

June 20, 2022. For an example from Young Adult Literature, see Gérard Sogliano, "Grand-Mamie a des origines," Short Edition Jeunesse, https://jeunesse.short -edition.com/oeuvre/jeunesse-une-dizaine-de-minutes/grand-mamie-a-des-origines, Retrieved on June 20, 2022.

6. Higginbotham and Kopytoff, "Racial Purity and Interracial Sex in the Law of Colonial and Antebellum Virginia," in *Interracialism: Black-White Intermarriage in American History, Literature, and Law*, ed. Werner Sollors (New York: Oxford University Press, 2000), 102 and footnote 97.

7. See Cady Lang, "Who Gets to Wear a Headscarf? The Complicated History Behind France's Latest Hijab Controversy," *Time*, May 19, 2021, https://time.com /6049226/france-hijab-ban/, Retrieved on June 20, 2022; and Aurélien Breeden, "No Handshake, No Citizenship, French Court Tells Algerian Woman," *The New York Times*, April 21, 2018, https://www.nytimes.com/2018/04/21/world/europe/ handshake-citizenship-france.html, Retrieved on June 20, 2022. For an analysis of political uses of the veil in the context of the Algerian Independence War, see Neil MacMaster, *Burning the Veil. The Algerian War and the 'Emancipation' of Muslim Women, 1954–1962* (Manchester: Manchester University Press, 2020). Open access URL: https://doi.org/10.7765/9781526146182

8. See Amy L. Hubbell, *Remembering French Algeria. Pieds-Noirs, Identity, and Exile* (Lincoln and London: University of Nebraska Press, 2015).

9. Centre d'observation de la société, "Des croyances et pratiques religieuses en déclin en France," November 9, 2021, https://www.observationsociete.fr/modes-de -vie/des-croyances-et-pratiques-religieuses-en-declin-en-france/, Retrieved on June 20, 2022.

10. See the interview of Stanford professor Cécile Alduy "'Conquest, domination' at Heart of French Far-Right Presidential Candidate's Discourse," interview by Allison Heard, Radio France Internationale, March 17, 2022, https://www.rfi.fr/en /france/20220317-war-death-conquest-domination-at-heart-of-far-right-presidential -candidate-zemmour-discourse, Retrieved on June 20, 2022.

11. Gauthier Delomez, "Guerre en Ukraine: 'On aura une immigration de grande qualité dont on pourra tirer profit,'" podcast of Jean-Louis Bourlanges's interview on Dimitri Pavlenko's news show Europe Matin, Europe 1 radio station, February 25, 2022, https://www.europe1.fr/politique/guerre-en-ukraine-on-aura-une-immigration -de-grande-qualite-dont-on-pourra-tirer-profit-4095961; and Kim Willsher, "Macron Accused of Pandering to Far Right Over Afghan Crisis," *The Guardian*, August 17, 2021, https://www.theguardian.com/world/2021/aug/17/macron-accused-of -pandering-to-far-right-over-afghan-crisis, Retrieved on June 20, 2022.

12. See Benjamin Fearnow, "Trevor Noah, French Ambassador Spar Over 'White Supremacist,' African Identity World Cup Joke," *Newsweek*, July 19, 2018, https:// www.newsweek.com/trevor-noah-french-ambassador-racism-world-cup-african-joke -identity-politics-1032480, Retrieved on June 20, 2022. See also how star player Lilian Thuram had responded to Jean-Marie Le Pen's remarks on the proportion of non-Whites in the national team in 2006: Dominic Fifield, "We Are Frenchmen Says Thuram, as Le Pen Bemoans the Number of Black Players," *The Guardian*, June 30, 2006, https://www.theguardian.com/football/2006/jun/30/worldcup2006.sport3

and the echo offered in the wake of the 2018 World Cup by Yascha Mounk, "Trevor Noah Doesn't Get to Decide Who's French," *Slate*, July 24, 2018, https://slate.com/news-and-politics/2018/07/trevor-noah-and-the-french-ambassador-both-missed-the-mark-in-their-argument-over-the-world-cup-teams-africanness.html, Retrieved on June 20, 2022.

13. "Mbappé Accuses French Federation Boss of Ignoring Racist Abuse," *The Local*, June 20, 2022, https://www.thelocal.fr/20220620/mbappe-accuses-french-federation-boss-of-ignoring-racist-abuse/; Retrieved on June 20, 2022. On the French heptathlon champion Eunice Barber's claims of police brutality during a traffic stop in 2006, for which she was fined in 2008, see Fred Hirzel, "Le mystérieux tabassage d'Eunice Barber," *Le Temps*, March 25, 2006, https://www.letemps.ch/sport/mysterieux-tabassage-deunice-barber, Retrieved on June 20, 2022.

14. See Hayden Sparks, "'Sick Son of a Bitch,' Uvalde Mayor Blasts Beto O'Rourke for Crashing Abbott's Press Conference on Shooting," *The Texan*, May 25, 2022, https://thetexan.news/sick-son-of-a-bitch-uvalde-mayor-blasts-beto-orourke-for-crashing-abbotts-press-conference-on-shooting/, Retrieved on June 20, 2022.

15. See Norimitsu Onishi, "Will American Ideas Tear France Apart? Some of Its Leaders Think So," *The New York Times*, October 21, 2021, https://www.nytimes.com/2021/02/09/world/europe/france-threat-american-universities.html, Retrieved on June 20, 2022.

16. Albert Memmi, *The Colonizer and the Colonized*, trans. Howard Greenfield (London: Earthscan Publications, [1965] 2003).

17. Memmi, *The Colonizer and the Colonized*, 8, 51.

18. Memmi, *The Colonizer and the Colonized*, 89–120.

19. Paul Max Morin, *Les jeunes et la guerre d'Algérie* (Paris: Presses Universitaires de France, 2022), 133.

20. See Pascal Blanchard, Nicolas Bancel, Éric Deroo, Gilles Boëtsch and Sandrine Lemaire, eds., *Zoos humains et expositions coloniales* (Paris: La Découverte, 2011); and Nicolas Bancel, Thomas David and Dominic Thomas, eds., *L'invention de la race. Des représentations scientifiques aux exhibitions populaires* (Paris: La Découverte, 2014).

21. See Emmanuelle Saada, *Les enfants de la colonie: Les métis de l'Empire français entre sujétion et citoyenneté* (Paris: La Découverte, 2007) and Elisa Camiscioli, "Intermarriage, Independent Nationality, and the Individual Rights of French Women. The law of 10 August, 1927" in *French Politics, Culture and Society* Vol. 17, No. 3–4, Summer/Fall 1999, 62–65.

22. See Sue Peabody, *There Are No Slaves in France: The Political Culture of Race and Slavery in the Ancien Régime* (New York: Oxford University Press, 1996).

23. See Jean-Baptiste Urbain, "'Osez Joséphine': Une pétition pour panthéoniser Joséphine Baker," *Au fil de l'actu,* France Musique, May 7, 2021, https://www.radiofrance.fr/francemusique/podcasts/au-fil-de-l-actu/osez-josephine-une-petition-pour-pantheoniser-josephine-baker-5971054, Retrieved on June 20, 2022.

24. Pascal Blanchard, Nicolas Bancel, Gilles Boëtsch, Christelle Taraud and Dominic Thomas, eds., *Sexe, race et colonies* (Paris: La Découverte, 2018), 299–300.

25. https://www.elysee.fr/emmanuel-macron/2021/08/23/pantheonisation-de
-josephine-baker.

26. This information was provided by her son Jean-Claude Bouillon-Baker at a
public lecture given in honor of Josephine Baker, which I attended on June 14, 2022
at the town hall of Paris' 17th arrondissement. See also Olivier Roueff, "Politiques
d'une 'culture nègre.' La *Revue nègre* comme événement public," in *Anthropologie
et Sociétés*, "La mise en public de la culture," ed. Bob White, Vol. 30, no. 2 (2006):
65–85.

27. https://www.youtube.com/watch?v=wmw5eGh888Y, Accessed on June
20, 2022.

28. See Marlon Riggs, *Ethnic Notions.* Documentary film, 57 minutes, California
Newsreel, 1987.

29. See "Josephine Baker Exhibit: Jarry Baker Attending on Behalf of Jean-Claude
Baker," Artfix Daily ArtWire, July 21, 2019, https://www.artfixdaily.com/artwire
/release/5212-josephine-baker-exhibit-jarry-baker-attending-on-behalf-of-jean-c,
Retrieved on June 20, 2022.

30. See, for example, https://www.ozap.com/actu/alain-finkielkraut-maboula
-soumahoro-clash-lci/585727 or https://www.programme-tv.net/news/tv/102424
-onpc-echanges-houleux-entre-yann-moix-et-maitre-gims-sur-la-nationalite
-francaise/, Accessed on November 2, 2021.

31. This information was provided by her son Jean-Claude Bouillon-Baker at a
public lecture given in honor of Josephine Baker, which I attended on June 14, 2022
at the town hall of Paris's 17th arrondissement.

32. Alain Ruscio, "Chantons sous les tropiques . . . ou le colonialisme à travers la chanson française," in *Le livre noir du colonialisme. XVIᵉ–XXIᵉ siècle: de
l'extermination à la repentance*, Marc Ferro, ed. (Paris: Robert Laffont, 2003),
693, 698.

33. Josephine Baker, "Si j'étais blanche" (L. Falk/H. Varna/R. Lelièvre), https://
www.youtube.com/watch?v=GuEAUggKSY4, Accessed on June 20, 2022.

34. Although this lifestyle seems hardly practicable on a daily basis and questionable as regards the presumed heritage of the Ivorian-born child Koffi, the French
historian Yves Denéchère contends, "The children were all brought up in accordance
with their heritage and *the religions that Baker assigned to them.* Janot was Bud-
dhist, Jari Protestant, *Koffi animist*, Moïse Jewish, and so forth." (emphases mine;
in a filmed lecture given in 2012, he mistakenly designates Koffi's assigned religion as "fetishist"). Yves Denéchère, "Josephine Baker's 'Rainbow Tribe' and the
Pursuit of Universal Brotherhood," *The Conversation*, November 30, 2021, https:
//theconversation.com/josephine-bakers-rainbow-tribe-and-the-pursuit-of-universal
-brotherhood-172714, Retrieved on June 20, 2022. Josephine Baker's daughter Marianne explained in an interview that her mother had made sure each of the children had
a religious instructor from his or her faith. "Le Père Noël chez Joséphine Baker," *Cinq
colonnes à la une*, archives of the Institut national de l'audiovisuel, January 6, 1961,
https://www.ina.fr/ina-eclaire-actu/video/caf90021986/le-pere-nocl-chez-josephine
-baker, Accessed on June 20, 2022.

35. This information was provided by her son Jean-Claude Bouillon-Baker at a public lecture given in honor of Josephine Baker, which I attended on June 14, 2022 at the town hall of Paris's 17th arrondissement.
36. Marianne Baker, radio interview by Alba Ventura on the RTL Matin show, RTL, November 30, 2021, 5'37"–6'14", https://www.dailymotion.com/video/x85ynod, Accessed on June 20, 2022.

BIBLIOGRAPHY

Alduy, Cécile. "'Conquest, Domination' at Heart of French Far-Right Presidential Candidate's Discourse." Interview by Allison Heard. Radio France Internationale, March 17, 2022. https://www.rfi.fr/en/france/20220317-war-death-conquest -domination-at-heart-of-far-right-presidential-candidate-zemmour-discourse, Retrieved on June 20, 2022.
Baker, Josephine. "Si j'étais blanche" (L. Falk/H. Varna/R. Lelièvre), https://www .youtube.com/watch?v=GuEAUggKSY4, Accessed on June 20, 2022.
Baker, Marianne. Radio interview by Alba Ventura on the RTL Matin show, RTL, November 30, 2021, 5'37"–6'14," https://www.dailymotion.com/video/x85ynod; Accessed on June 20, 2022.
Bancel, Nicolas, Thomas David and Dominic Thomas, eds. L'invention de la race. Des représentations scientifiques aux exhibitions populaires. Paris: La Découverte, 2014.
Blanchard, Pascal, Nicolas Bancel, Éric Deroo, Gilles Boëtsch and Sandrine Lemaire, eds. *Zoos humains et expositions coloniales.* Paris: La Découverte, 2011.
Blanchard, Pascal, Nicolas Bancel, Gilles Boëtsch, Christelle Taraud and Dominic Thomas, eds. *Sexe, race et colonies.* Paris: La Découverte, 2018.
Boissoneault, Lorraine. "Why Is France in Its Fifth Republic?" *Smithsonian Magazine*, April 20, 2017. https://www.smithsonianmag.com/history/why-france -its-fifth-republic-180962983/, Retrieved on June 20, 2022.
Breeden, Aurélien. "No Handshake, No Citizenship, French Court Tells Algerian Woman." *The New York Times*, April 21, 2018. https://www.nytimes.com/2018/04 /21/world/europe/handshake-citizenship-france.html, Retrieved on June 20, 2022.
Camiscioli, Elisa. "Intermarriage, Independent Nationality, and the Individual Rights of French Women. The law of 10 August, 1927." *French Politics, Culture and Society* Vol. 17, no. 3–4 (Summer/Fall 1999): 62–65.
Centre d'observation de la société. "Des croyances et pratiques religieuses en déclin en France," November 9, 2021. https://www.observationsociete.fr/modes-de-vie/ des-croyances-et-pratiques-religieuses-en-declin-en-france/, Retrieved on June 20, 2022.
de Villanova, Roselyne. "Espace de l'entre-deux ou comment la mobilité des immi-grés recrée du territoire." *L'homme et la Société*, Vol. 3–4, no. 165–166, (2007): 65–83. https://doi.org/10.3917/lhs.165.0065, Retrieved on June 20, 2022.
Delomez, Gauthier. "Guerre en Ukraine: 'On aura une immigration de grande qualité dont on pourra tirer profit.'" Podcast of Jean-Louis Bourlanges' interview on Dimitri

Pavlenko's news show Europe Matin, Europe 1 radio station, February 25, 2022. https://www.europe1.fr/politique/guerre-en-ukraine-on-aura-une-immigration-de-grande-qualite-dont-on-pourra-tirer-profit-4095961.

Denéchère, Yves. "Josephine Baker's 'Rainbow Tribe' and the Pursuit of Universal Brotherhood." *The Conversation*, November 30, 2021. https://theconversation.com/josephine-bakers-rainbow-tribe-and-the-pursuit-of-universal-brotherhood-172714, Retrieved on June 20, 2022.

Fassassi, Idris. "Removing 'Race' and Adding 'Gender' to the French Constitution: On Constitutional Redundancy and Symbols." Voices From the Field, ConstitutionNet, August 24, 2018. https://constitutionnet.org/news/removing-race-and-adding-gender-french-constitution-constitutional-redundancy-and-symbols, Retrieved on June 19, 2022.

Fearnow, Benjamin. "Trevor Noah, French Ambassador Spar Over 'White Supremacist,' African Identity World Cup Joke." *Newsweek*, July 19, 2018. https://www.newsweek.com/trevor-noah-french-ambassador-racism-world-cup-african-joke-identity-politics-1032480, Retrieved on June 20, 2022.

Fifield, Dominic. "We Are Frenchmen Says Thuram, as Le Pen Bemoans the Number of Black Players." *The Guardian*, June 30, 2006. https://www.theguardian.com/football/2006/jun/30/worldcup2006.sport3

Higginbotham, A. Leon, Jr. and Barbara K. Kopytoff. "Racial Purity and Interracial Sex in the Law of Colonial and Antebellum Virginia." In *Interracialism: Black-White Intermarriage in American History, Literature, and Law*, edited by Werner Sollors, 81–139. New York: Oxford University Press, 2000.

Hirzel, Fred. "Le mystérieux tabassage d'Eunice Barber." *Le Temps*, March 25, 2006. https://www.letemps.ch/sport/mysterieux-tabassage-deunice-barber, Retrieved on June 20, 2022.

Hubbell, Amy L. *Remembering French Algeria. Pieds-Noirs, Identity, and Exile.* Lincoln and London: University of Nebraska Press, 2015.

"Josephine Baker Exhibit: Jarry Baker Attending on Behalf of Jean-Claude Baker." Artfix Daily ArtWire, July 21, 2019. https://www.artfixdaily.com/artwire/release/5212-josephine-baker-exhibit-jarry-baker-attending-on-behalf-of-jean-c, Retrieved on June 20, 2022.

Lang, Cady. "Who Gets to Wear a Headscarf? The Complicated History Behind France's Latest Hijab Controversy." *Time*, May 19, 2021. https://time.com/6049226/france-hijab-ban/, Retrieved on June 20, 2022.

"Le Père Noël chez Joséphine Baker." *Cinq colonnes à la une*, archives of the Institut national de l'audiovisuel, January 6, 1961. https://www.ina.fr/ina-eclaire-actu/video/caf90021986/le-pere-noel-chez-josephine-baker, Accessed on June 20, 2022.

MacMaster, Neil. *Burning the Veil. The Algerian War and the 'Emancipation' of Muslim Women, 1954–1962.* Manchester: Manchester University Press, 2020. Open access URL: https://doi.org/10.7765/9781526146182

"Mbappé Accuses French Federation Boss of Ignoring Racist Abuse." *The Local*, June 20, 2022. https://www.thelocal.fr/20220620/mbappe-accuses-french-federation-boss-of-ignoring-racist-abuse/, Retrieved on June 20, 2022.

Memmi, Albert. *The Colonizer and the Colonized.* Translated by Howard Greenfield. London: Earthscan Publications [1965] 2003.

Morin, Paul Max. *Les jeunes et la guerre d'Algérie.* Paris: Presses Universitaires de France, 2022.

Mounk, Yascha. "Trevor Noah Doesn't Get to Decide Who's French." *Slate*, July 24, 2018. https://slate.com/news-and-politics/2018/07/trevor-noah-and-the-french -ambassador-both-missed-the-mark-in-their-argument-over-the-world-cup-teams -africanness.html, Retrieved on June 20, 2022.

Onishi, Norimitsu. "Will American Ideas Tear France Apart? Some of Its Leaders Think So." *The New York Times*, October 21, 2021. https://www.nytimes.com/2021 /02/09/world/europe/france-threat-american-universities.html, Retrieved on June 20, 2022.

Peabody, Sue. *There Are No Slaves in France: The Political Culture of Race and Slavery in the Ancien Régime.* New York: Oxford University Press, 1996.

Riggs, Marlon. *Ethnic Notions.* Documentary film, 57 minutes, California Newsreel, 1987.

Roueff, Olivier. "Politiques d'une 'culture nègre.' La *Revue nègre* comme événement public." In *Anthropologie et Sociétés*, "La mise en public de la culture," edited by Bob White, 65–85. Vol. 30, no. 2, 2006.

Ruscio, Alain. "Chantons sous les tropiques . . . ou le colonialisme à travers la chanson française." In *Le livre noir du colonialisme. XVIe–XXIe siècle: de l'extermination à la repentance*, edited by Marc Ferro, 927–37. Paris: Robert Laffont, 2003.

Saada, Emmanuelle. *Les enfants de la colonie: Les métis de l'Empire français entre sujétion et citoyenneté.* Paris: La Découverte, 2007.

Simon, Patrick. "Nationality and Origins in French Statistics: Ambiguous Categories." *Population: An English Selection*, Vol. 11 (1999): 193–219. https://www.jstor.org/ stable/2998696, Retrieved on June 20, 2022.

Sogliano, Gérard. "Grand-Mamie a des origines." Short Edition Jeunesse, https:// jeunesse.short-edition.com/oeuvre/jeunesse-une-dizaine-de-minutes/grand-mamie -a-des-origines, Retrieved on June 20, 2022.

Sparks, Hayden. "'Sick Son of a Bitch,' Uvalde Mayor Blasts Beto O'Rourke for Crashing Abbott's Press Conference on Shooting." *The Texan*, May 25, 2022. https://thetexan.news/sick-son-of-a-bitch-uvalde-mayor-blasts-beto-orourke-for -crashing-abbotts-press-conference-on-shooting/, Retrieved on June 20, 2022.

The Law Society, "A Guide to Race and Ethnicity Terminology and Language," February 10, 2022. https://www.lawsociety.org.uk/en/topics/ethnic-minority -lawyers/a-guide-to-race-and-ethnicity-terminology-and-language, Retrieved on June 20, 2022.

Urbain, Jean-Baptiste. "'Osez Joséphine': Une pétition pour panthéoniser Joséphine Baker." Au fil de l'actu, France Musique, May 7, 2021. https://www.radiofrance .fr/francemusique/podcasts/au-fil-de-l-actu/osez-josephine-une-petition-pour -pantheoniser-josephine-baker-5971054, Retrieved on June 20, 2022.

Willsher, Kim. "Hollande Drops Plan to Revoke French Citizenship of Dual-National Terrorists." *The Guardian*, March 30, 2016. https://www.theguardian.com/world

/2016/mar/30/francois-hollande-drops-plan-to-revoke-citizenship-of-dual-national
-terrorists, Retrieved on June 20, 2022.

Willsher, Kim. "Macron Accused of Pandering to Far Right Over Afghan Crisis."
The Guardian, August 17, 2021. https://www.theguardian.com/world/2021/aug/17
/macron-accused-of-pandering-to-far-right-over-afghan-crisis, Retrieved on June
20, 2022.

Chapter 5

·Whose Flesh?

Flesh Tone as Scripturalization in the Art and Practice of Ballet

P. Kimberleigh Jordan

Dancing is an essential human practice occurring everywhere on our planet. Human beings dance for every reason and for no reason at all, among cultures and societies in the past, present, and will presumably, in the future. Dance occurs as intentional movement through space in grand collective presentations, or in minimized individual gestures embedded in everyday human experience. Exploring the potential of human bodies to carve through space with or without music, with or without rhythm, with or without emotion, ecstasy, or purpose is recognized as dancing. Dance is a ubiquitous practice in human life.

Conversely, ballet is a rarefied and specialized form of dance that is not a ubiquitous human dance form. Rather, ballet is a highly refined complex of movements, positions, gestures, and "techniques of the body"[1] that have been and continue to be practiced among particular human bodies. The shapes, postures, and high commitment to specialized training are not necessarily accessible to *every* human *body*. The historical development and practice of ballet dancing adds complexity to the core premise herein that dancing is an essential element of human life. Ballet dancing was cultivated in opulent, aristocratic European contexts among royal bodies—bodies in which sovereign, monarchic power was vested. The rise and codification of ballet dancing is historically synchronous with the rise of modernity and its enlightenment-suffused ways of thinking, knowing, and producing knowledge.

The digital exhibition, *Masquerade: Scripturalizing Modernities through Black Flesh* around which our discourse moves, seeks to explore scholar and curator Vincent Wimbush's generative provocation of "scripturalizing" as a kind of play instantiating "the production of the racialized world" in historical and theoretical tandem with the formation of modernity.

I bring a multiply informed perspective to Wimbush's discursive "dance party." While I have academic training in the post-discipline of Performance Studies, I also spent the first half of my life in the ballet world. My first ballet classes were at the same time that I entered kindergarten. Approximately twenty-five years later I concluded my dancing vocation in New York City as a professional dancer. I was a member of an endangered species: Black ballet dancers.

Within the ballet world, race matters. Ballet is what Dr. Wimbush names a "racialized world," as the art and practice of ballet simultaneously (hyper) visibilize and invisibilize race through dancing flesh. Ballet dancing is a practice shaped and formed in Europe and circulated in the western world as modernity was forming. Ballet has been the domain of white-skinned bodies in contexts of hereditary affluence and sovereignty since its earliest formations in sixteenth century Renaissance Europe. Ballet has been established on the premise that it exists as the aesthetic pinnacle in the performing arts, offering ultimate notions of sublime beauty and human grace. Therefore, through much of its half-millennia history the art and practice of ballet has been performed by white bodies, to the decided exclusion of other bodies.

While the following quotation may cause a reader to cringe in 2022, it is not unique; instead, the statement is a relatively ubiquitous expression of the ways in which notions of race and color have been normalized in the ballet world.

> By and large, he [Black persons have] been wise enough not to be drawn into it [ballet], for its wholly European outlook, history and technical theory are alien to him culturally, temperamentally and anatomically.[2]

John Martin, then chief dance critic of the *New York Times* wrote in 1963, a not insignificant year in US civil and human rights history. Rather than obscure expression of a closeted racist, Martin, from his international journalistic platform of "the paper of record," expressed common societal presumptions about ballet and "its wholly European outlook." While dance is essential human activity, ballet is specialized movement in which Europeanness and whiteness have been made canon. Note the ease of the language in the Martin quotation. It makes tangible the scripturalization of whiteness, and white flesh in ballet.

Nonetheless, as a child I loved the look and feeling of ballet dancing, whether live in-person or on television. By my fifth birthday, my mother and grandmother enrolled me in one of only two dance schools known in the

Black community of my southern US hometown to welcome Black families, even though all the teachers were white. True to its grapevine reputation, the Leocarta School of Dance welcomed me and others like me from my side of town.[3] Through my seven years of study there, Mr. Jimmy Leocarta maintained a racially diverse student body. However, in the continuing years of my ballet training after Leocarta School, I never again experienced diverse ballet studios. As I advanced as a ballet student, I was either one of a pair, or the only Black girl in the studio or ballet company. As is customary in daily ballet training, I wore the required uniform for female ballet students: black, short-sleeved leotard on my upper body; pink tights as legwear, and pink soft leather ballet shoes or later, pink satin pointe shoes.

Ballet tights and shoes were all manufactured in the same light buff shade of pink called "flesh tone." I wore the required "flesh tone" uniform without question from my first ballet class until, as an advanced dancer in ballet training in New York City, the seamless representation of "flesh tone" was finally disrupted. In hindsight, I wish that I could say that my racial pride and maturing intellect caused me to assert the disruption. The truth is that my geographical, cultural, and artistic context caused the disruption in the five-hundred-year accepted ballet tradition of "flesh tone."

By this time, I was invited to enroll on scholarship in the Professional Training Program at the Dance Theatre of Harlem. There I polished and refined my ballet technique with other dancers from around the African diaspora. Brown and Black ballet dancers studied and rehearsed together for six to eight hours each day. We performed in theatres, workshops, and monthly Open Houses for our Harlem neighbors, under the leadership of artistic director Arthur Mitchell. We learned the works of classical ballet choreographers, emergent ballet dance makers, as well as several resident ballet choreographers.

We did all this wearing flesh tone tights and shoes. However, as an aesthetic and political intervention at Dance Theatre of Harlem, the uniform included tights and shoes that were the color of the flesh of the human dancer wearing those tights and shoes. More precisely, as a medium brown complexioned dancer, I was responsible for wearing uniform tights that matched my very own medium brown complexion. This intervention meant that no longer was a white skin/pink buff color the default uniform of ballet and signifier for all ballet dancing flesh.

Ballet technique and performance in the Dance Theatre of Harlem school and company represented the best of the art and praxis as it had originated in Europe, first in Florence and Paris, and subsequently circulated through outposts in the United Kingdom, the Netherlands, and most especially Russia. Late nineteenth and early twentieth century Russia was where the art of ballet dancing reached the apex of its development of the form birthed in the French courts centuries earlier. The political disruptions and eventual dissolution of Imperial Russia created a dispersion of Russian dancers, choreographers, and musicians first to Paris, and subsequently to the twentieth century United States. Among the dispersed Russian artists were Igor Stravinsky and George Balanchine. Balanchine later co-founded the New York City Ballet, and by the 1950s laid aside US racialized laws and customs of segregation such that he hired a Harlem teenager named Arthur Mitchell as a permanent member of his ballet company.[4]

In the vast worlds under consideration in this digital exhibition, *Masquerade: Scripturalizing Modernities through Black Flesh* and related discourses, perhaps a reader might inquire why such a seemingly nanoscopic point of attention should hold space among these deliberations. I respond to this query with this confident assertion: ballet is the progeny of modernity. The origins and practices of ballet are an ideal lens through which to view modernity and Wimbush's theory of scripturalization of flesh. Plainly, white complexioned skin has been canonized—scripturalized—into ballet praxis since its earliest origins. The effect therefore of scripturalization of flesh in this aesthetic context is that traditional ballet flesh tone causes white skin to be hypervisible. White-complexioned skin became the signifier of the art and practice of ballet, as white skin became signifier of modernity/ies. The hypervisibility of white skin as signifier of flesh tone has normativized the condition in which brown and black skin, though present, is hyperinvisibilized.

The term flesh tone exists in ballet, at its most benign, as a presumption of whose flesh is valorized. However, at the essence of this usage is a kind of malignancy in which flesh tone expresses a socio-political and economic ordering of human flesh in which whiteness is the apogee of humanity. White flesh has been valorized in the ballet world as flesh tone has been equated to white colored skin.

Flesh tone in ballet made whiteness hypervisible, such that "others" were masked, concealed, and hyperinvisibilized. "Others," in this context, means Black and brown bodies. In the tradition of western modernity, the invisibility of Black and brown bodies was not an actuality, but philosopher Charles Long proffers that the invisibility "represents a suppression" concealing the human lives that made the wealth, intellectualism, and vast conquest inherent in modernity possible.[5] Imagine a ship sailing on the Atlantic Ocean in bygone centuries. The ship would be visible from a distance due to the several masted sails extending upward. Below those sails would be various members of the crew performing maritime labors. However, as this imagined ship sails for the purpose of transporting humans from the African continent to one of many 'new world' ports of disembarkation, the most significant part of the ship's purpose would be invisible: the hundreds of Black and brown bodies below deck. This ship is a metaphor for the scripturalizing of the flesh that is the focus of this chapter

As with modernity/ies, the artform and practice of ballet has made white bodies suitable and hypervisible, while simultaneously constructing an under-hold, in which Black bodies are invisible, yet hyperproductive of the resources to support the formation of the Enlightenment. The simultaneously invisible and hyperproductive Black bodies made possible the material resources that funded the monarchies and the empires which European aristocrats and regents sought to build throughout the non-European world to establish hegemonic domination and plunder natural and human resources.

In this chapter, I contend that ballet is the offspring of modernity. I will endeavor to frame a perspective on scripturalization that casts moving and dancing bodies centerstage as a means of fathoming the weight of modernity on whole persons—at once, flesh and intellect. This contributes to the discussions launched in response to the *Masquerade: Scripturalizing Modernities Through Black Flesh* exhibition, while showing how dance and embodiment studies expand the discourse and theoretical analysis surrounding the exhibition.

In the five hundred years of synchronous formation and histories of ballet and modernity, whose flesh has been seen and valorized? Likewise, whose laboring and suffering flesh has been unseen? Whose dancing bodies have been perceptible and appropriate, and under what conditions? Whose flesh is "discoursed away?" Engaging the *Masquerade* exhibition and resources from ballet histories and dance studies, I will explore the effect of the formation of the modern on Black flesh at three sites of performance.

Ballet provides an ideal exemplar for this important exhibition at Emory University's Pitts Library curated by Vincent L. Wimbush. Wimbush has curated an exhibition-as-window "onto the construction, naturalization, maintenance, defense, disruption, and destabilization of modernities" explicating "modernities" as those "social-cultural and political-economic arrangements, performances and practices, politics . . . that we are made to differently experience, . . . [and] negotiate in different types of bodies." The generatively curated exhibition invites analyses behind the mask to see what can be revealed, even in hiding, as well as what is revealed by modernity. Wimbush argues:

> The silence . . . here signifies a blocking—keeping black-fleshed persons from seeing/being seen, from hearing/being heard on their own terms, through their own agency, being represented as human and experiencing full humanity. Various expressive practices and ideologies in the maintenance of such silence

is masquerade and so become the chaotic impetus behind the production of modernities as we know them.[6]

Had I been a prescient five-year-old when I was first assigned to put on "flesh tone" to learn the fundamentals of pliés and relevés, I would have asked: whose flesh, not my flesh? But I did not ask "whose flesh?" in my earliest days of dance training, nor did I ask, "whose flesh?" when I was a minoritized Black girl at barre in a sea of white dancers through most of my intermediate and advanced training. Even when I initially arrived at Dance Theatre of Harlem and auditioned in pink tights and shoes—the only thing I knew then as "flesh tone"—I still did not ask "whose flesh?" Eventually however, my experiences in the Dance Theatre of Harlem context made me ask the question to my very own, brown-skinned dancing self.[7]

PERFORMANCE SITE: OLAUDAH EQUIANO/ GUSTAVUS VASSA IN WEST AFRICA

The exhibition and its surrounding discourse engage Olaudah Equiano/ Gustavus Vassa's *Interesting Narrative and Other Writings*.[8] *The Interesting Narrative* provides a launchpad for these discussions as it offers as the author's letter to a world in the process of becoming the modern west, while, in this scene, presenting dance as essential human behavior among community members. He writes with the force of his own and his people's full humanity, even through many developmental stages and conditions of freedom and/or oppression of brown and black-skinned descendants of Africa.

The Interesting Narrative is Equiano/Vassa's epistle to western world's setting in motion elements that came to comprise modernity/ies. He narrates from the theoretical and geographical location which modernity masked and invisibilized: continental Africa. From Equiano/Vassa's uncommon autobiography and unique life experiences, we learn that he was born a free person in West Africa. He was brought up in a family within a community to such an age that his life experiences became transferable memories, even after he was kidnapped from home and made to be chattel, purchased and sold in the circum-Atlantic commerce in enslaved humans. His memories of life in West Africa were immaterial, yet imperishable freight that he carried through his multiple sea journeys and life experiences—whether freed or enslaved.

Equiano/Vassa's *Interesting Narrative* offers multiple examples; however, my focus herein is on the significance of enfleshed bodies moving in public spaces. Particularly resonant for this project is the description that Equiano/ Vassa's offers of moving bodies in his homeland:

We are almost a nation of dancers, musicians, and poets. Thus every great event, such as a triumphant return from battle, or other cause of public rejoicing, is celebrated in public dances, which are accompanied with songs and music suited to the occasion. The assembly is separated into four divisions, which dance either apart or in succession, and each with a character peculiar to itself.[9]

In this description, the reader imagines multiple senses engaged by onlookers at such "great event(s)": e.g., sounds of singing and polyrhythmic music; touch and scent of crowds of gathering familiar family and friends; sights of bodies moving in sync with some, and contrapuntal to others; and finally, an affective sense of communal belonging. These moving bodies are visible and offer images of historic West African life in motion and in full human expansiveness. The formation of European modernity precludes the imagination of such a dynamic communal performance, and yet there it is richly described in his text.

Whether as modern subjects or subjugated to modernity, all humans have been struck by the formation of modernit/ies. In this scene from the *Interesting Narrative*, before "first contact" with Europe, visible bodies move and dance. They gathered prosocially to sing, parade, and celebrate. Nevertheless, the formation of European modernity concealed these dancing Black and brown bodies. While scripturalization embedded in the formation of modernity/ies served to reveal and make visible European-ness, it simultaneously concealed the agential sociality evident in Equiano/Vassa's poignant description. In the suppressed or masked place resides the violence of caste, colonialism, racism, and hierarchical difference in the psycho-politics of modernity.[10] The term flesh tone affirmed the manufacture of a superior place of white-fleshed persons on the hierarchy and normalized the term "flesh tone" as signifier of whiteness intricately bound up with white-fleshed superiority.

PERFORMANCE SITE: *BALLET COMIQUE DE LA REINE*

Consider another such "great event" occurring a century and a half earlier and approximately 2,500 miles to the north of Equiano/Vassa's description. The *Ballet Comique de la Reine* provides a myth of origin for ballet praxis. The performance occurred at the beginning of western European production of modernity and holds the historical distinction for inaugurating what is now known as classical ballet. In 1581, the *Ballet Comique de la Reine* was a spectacle of multimedia performance, this nearly six-hour performance was comprised of music, poetry/spoken word, elaborate mobile sets, extravagant costuming, and, of course, ballet dancing—at its earliest form of development. Staged in rarefied environs of the Salle de Bourbon in what is now the

Louvre, in Paris, the evening performance was sponsored and produced by French monarchs and their aristocratic geopolitical relatives during Catherine de' Medici's reign.[11]

Created to celebrate a monarchical wedding, *Ballet Comique* borrows from Greek mythology's narrative on Circe, a minor Greek goddess. In the ballet, dancing was one of many performance media; yet the event was propelled forward by staged bodies in motion.[12] Balthasar de Beaujoyeulx, choreographer, and librettist of the *Ballet Comique de la Reine* described his intention in this way:

> I enlivened the ballet and made it speak, and made the Comedy sing and play; and, adding some unusual and elaborate décor and embellishments, I may say that I satisfied the eye, the ear, and the intellect with one well-proportioned creation.[13]

It seems that the only missing element of the performance was humility. The event lasted nearly six hours. There was no stage, all action occurred on the floor of the hall. The nine hundred audience members sat in galleries, above the main floor on which a platform was built for immediate monarchic family members at one end of the hall.[14]

The *Ballet Comique* performers danced and made intricate figures on the floor, accompanied by newly commissioned music played on a wide array of instruments from cornets to violins. The performers recited long monologues approximately related to the theme. Large mobile set pieces were moved on and off the floor on cue. Picture the spectacle through this excerpt of Beaujoyeulx's text:

> the fountain, which contained three basins adorned with sculptures of dolphins, mermaids, and tritons made of burnished gold and silver. Scented water flowed from the topmost basin into the third and largest basin, which had twelve golden pulpits on its rim. In these sat the queen and eleven other royal ladies representing naiads, dressed in silver cloth, and wearing many precious stones. The mermaids joined this company. Then, to music and singing, the fountain moved toward the king, made a turn in front of him, and slowly withdrew.[15]

The above recounting offers a workout for the imagination; yet the reader is invited to extend perception further and multiply the sets, the music, the storyline, the moving bodies by six hours.

Furthermore, I invite an extension of the readerly imagination beyond the Salle de Bourbon, and even beyond Paris. Through this imaginative extension, our perceptual portals open past those 1581 aristocrats and their grandiose and aggrandizing spectacle of a forgettable Greek myth. In this invitation to look beyond, we begin to apply more acute perspective on focal point of this exhibition: the masquerade embedded in enfleshed performance as ballet and its world of modernity were being born. The project herein offers "counterpoint," shadowing Wimbush, to the canonical view of this (kind of) performance as evidence of a (re)birth of classical modes of intellect and interpretation, and the once-and-for-all establishment of the top of the human hierarchy of aesthetics, beauty, and perfection in the "family of man."

While the history of this performance has given rise to a kind of "scripture" of the modern, it also masks, or veils "conflicting sources, objects, alter-representations, of instability if not impossibility of storytelling . . ."[16] The canon of the formation of the modern valorizes their (re)interpretation of Hellenic knowledge and epistemes from a perceived past, while seeking to discover other lands, other tastes, other humans ("first contact"). European wealth expanded through conquest, commerce, and trade. The Holy Roman Empire was in the societal rear-view mirror, though the powerful Roman Catholic church held immense power over European people and ideas; nonetheless Roman Catholic totalizing societal power declined to the extent that the secular was becoming an identifiable category of European life in modernity/ies.

Various family groupings established themselves as, not just rich, and contextually famous; but came to understand themselves to have bloodlines that made them particularly superior to all other human beings, thus asserting themselves in the category of monarchs. Resourcing interpretations of "classical" Hellenic thinking, "first contact" with distant lands and peoples leading to conquer, plunder, and commodification, notable increase in the transnational flow of persons and capital, and the establishment of the absolute monarchy are all concretized as hallmarks of modernity. All are evident in the performance of the *Ballet Comique de la Reine.*

While the nyads, mermaids, goddesses and dancing queen reveal the mind of the choreographer/producer, and the power and wealth of Queen Mother Catherine de' Medici, the moving bodies in the *Ballet Comique* also conceal aspects of the modern that continue to burden society in later centuries. As an origin story for the art and practice of ballet, *Ballet Comique* was built on the backs and necks of those who existed at the bottom of stringent hierarchy that ran the gamut from the superhuman on the one end, to the beneath human on the other. This modern sense of humanity was surfacing at the time, and especially through this performance. Is it an oversimplification to say—from the mind of modernity—that those who established themselves as monarchs thereby proclaimed themselves to be the zenith of humanity? No others in their world, or any other, had their notable value and domination. The scripturalization of this hierarchy materialized through the ballet performance and canonized in social, political, economic, and cultural spheres also constructed a veil that occluded other, different human experiences.

Illustration of *The Ballet Comique de la Reine in 1581* performance in Paris, the Salle de Bourbon of the Louvre before and including the French Monarchy. The image is a re-engraving from an original on copper by Balthazar de Beaujoyeulx (Paris: Ballard, 1582). This work is in the public domain.

Ballet Comique is a notable signifier of the formation of modernit/ies. While it must be supposed that the evening of October 15, 1581, was astonishing and delightful for the audience of invited dignitaries, Beaujoyeulx endeavored to extend the evening's history-making sparkle beyond the live audience out to far flung European locales by way of the publication of detailed libretto. I imagine that the publication and distribution of the text was something of a public relations power move on behalf of its monarchic sponsors and their regime. However, the textualization of the *Ballet Comique* also performed a scripturalization of facets of modernity that still, five centuries on, require excavation.

It was a performance site which affirmed the superior place on the hierarchy of white-fleshed persons, thus naturalizing the term "flesh tone" as signifier of whiteness intricately bound up with white-fleshed superiority and presumed supremacy. *Ballet Comique* scripturalized white-fleshed persons' claims, which have been elemental to modernity, to be seen, heard, esteemed, and exalted through the actual performance, as well as through the later international distribution of the libretto.

PERFORMANCE SITE(S): AGON PAS DE DEUX[17]

Another ballet, almost four hundred years later: *Agon*, choreographed by George Balanchine is the final site of enfleshed performance.[18] The spotlight herein is on the pas de deux (*dance for two*) within the slightly longer ballet danced by Arthur Mitchell and Diana Adams. The duet for one male dancer and one female offers a punctuation mark to the 1581 *Ballet Comique*, while making hypervisible elements of modernity that were invisible in earlier histories of ballet.

Agon premiered on an unseasonably on December 1, 1957, at City Center for Music and Drama—the foremost theatre presenting classical ballet to New York audiences at the time. The New York City Ballet (NYCB) is the only company on program. Founded by George Balanchine and Lincoln Kirstein in 1948, nine years prior to this premiere, this company was and perhaps is the most prominent ballet organization in the US. The entire evening consists of collaborative works by Russian compadres in the United States, Balanchine and composer Igor Stravinsky. In the *Agon* premiere, its centerpiece, *Agon* pas de deux is danced by Diane Adams and Arthur Mitchell. Adams was a white, female ballerina and soloist in NYCB. She known to have the image of a "porcelain princess."[19] Arthur Mitchell was a Black man trained in ballet, who was the first Black dancer to receive a contract and be

employed full-time at NYCB, or any major ballet company in the world. To
be clear, Arthur Mitchell was the "Jackie Robinson of ballet."

As the house lights went down, the curtain rose on *Agon*. The dance, in
three parts, lasts a mere twenty-five minutes and included a total of twelve
dancers who gathered in a duet, quartets, and an octet. The stage is sparse,
with no sets and only a plain backdrop upstage. There is no unifying story or
plot that makes a structure for the dance. Against this bare backdrop, dancers wore standard studio practice clothes: the four men in white ballet shoes
and white socks, black tights on their legs and bright white cotton T-shirts.
The female dancers wore black leotards on their upper bodies and flesh
tone-colored tights and flesh tone-colored pointe shoes.

Contrasting the *Ballet Comique*, the stage for the premiere of *Agon* is unen-
cumbered by decoration and costuming. Instead, the audience sees a blank
stage with dancers in simple practice uniforms. In the *Agon* pas de deux,
the two dancers enter upstage left. Adams puts forth the metaphorical image
of unadorned porcelain, while Mitchell puts forth the image of Benin, West
African sculpture. Her skin is white and opaque, sharply contrasting to the
jet-black leotard she wears, and more so contrasting her dance partner. Arthur
Mitchell is the complexion of polished mahogany. His bone structure and
musculature are an anatomical lesson in precision. His complexion directly
contrasts with the bright white T-shirt, shoes, and socks that he wears. His
upper body is dressed in bright white, while her torso is sheathed in black.
In the dance, their colors—their costume flesh tones and their contrasting
complexions—intertwine as they braid and bind, temporarily loosen and then
weave again. Their stark flesh colors and clothing colors integrate and mix
with each other. Choreography is axiomatically defined as "problem-solving
in space and time." In this pas de deux, the "problem" of the flesh is the
"problem" seeking resolve.

Costume contrasts aside, mental sparks perhaps exploded in the brains of
some in this 1957 premiere audience as Mitchell's his black flesh wove in
and out of her "white" flesh. Their flesh colors index the problems of vis-
ibility and hypervisibility in the construction in the formation of modernity/
ies. While the colors of their outfits gesture toward academic dance wear, the
colors of their flesh signify modernity's sweep of history. In some paradisical
world, the flesh colors would be as inconsequential as the color of their dance
attire. The world that modernity has made, though, is by no means paradise.

On the same night that Adams and Mitchell made their upstage left
entrance to begin the pas de deux, US President Dwight Eisenhower continued the federalization of National Guard troops in Little Rock, Arkansas.
The National Guard was in Arkansas to protect the lives of nine Black high
school students attempting to matriculate and study in previously all-white
Central High School.[20] The Black and brown students attempting to enter and

Arthur Mitchell and Diana Adams dancing the pas de deux of *Agon*, choreographed by George Balanchine (1957). Photograph by Martha Swope.

Image used by permission of the Jerome Robbins Dance Division, The New York Public Library for the Performing Arts

learn in Central High School were performing a kind of refusal to the vortex of modernity/ies' hierarchy. Like Arthur Mitchell, their Black enfleshed performance disrupted their invisibility and smashed the foregoing disguise of modernity.[21]

In the opening phrase of the *Agon* pas de deux, the two dancers play a choreographic cat-and-mouse game: Adams takes two steps and a small leap, and Mitchell responds with a step and leap that echoes her move. When Mitchell catches up to Adams, the pair is at center stage. She then makes a preparation for a turn from fourth position, while he places his hands just above each of her hipbones. Adams then does a fast double pirouette on half pointe with Mitchell's support. Mitchell holds her, causing her to finish the turn facing the audience and standing on one leg. As she leans forward on her standing leg, she stretches the other leg behind her and upward, such that Adams' flesh tone-covered leg wraps around Mitchell's white bedecked upper body, contrasting with the mahogany brownness of his face and head.

Beyond the stage at City Center, there was national upheaval on the topic of flesh colors mixing in the same spaces. The nine Black high schoolers in Little Rock had no such aspirations as these two NYCB Dancers. The students, in their quest to attend the seemingly better resourced Central High School, only sought the nonphysical intimacy of "reading, writing, and arithmetic" in the presence of white-fleshed persons. Yet, their lives were at highest risk every day of the school year.

The *Agon* pas de deux offers a punctuation mark to the 1581 *Ballet Comique*. The 1581 performance spurred the production and dissemination of modernity and made white-fleshed aesthetics, epistemes, and wealth hypervisible. At the same time, it violently rendered black-fleshed persons invisible, though powerful by way of commodification and wealth production. The *Agon* pas de deux made elements of modernity visible that had previously been invisibilized.

I noted above that my ballet experience spanned twenty-five years of my life. I began dancing in flesh tone. On my final day in the studio at Dance Theatre of Harlem, I concluded my ballet experience wearing flesh tone. Whose flesh? My own flesh. Medium brown tights and pointe shoes remarkably like my own brown skin. No longer rendered invisible through concealment under another's flesh tone. This is not a claim to liberation or redemption through balletic performance. Modernit/ies and its offspring of colonialism, racism, and human hierarchies continue to effect humans on the planet. Yet, the Masquerade that has been theorized and articulate in this exhibit has offered a clear site from which to continue interrogating and undoing the scripturalization in modernity.

NOTES

1. Marcel Mauss, "Techniques of the Body," *Economy and Society* 2 (1973): 70–88.
2. John Martin, *John Martin's Book of Dance* (New York: Tudor, 1963), quoted in Joselli Audain Deans, "*Arabesque en noire*: The persistent presence of Black Dancers

in the American ballet world" in Adesola Akinleye, editor/curator, *(Re:)Claiming Ballet* (Bristol, UK/Chicago, IL: Intellect, 2021), 48.

3. A question that might rise in reader's mind is this: "Why did my mother and grandmother enroll me in ballet, if the practice of ballet was so inherently European and white?" Over the years, they offered these reasons: (1) I lacked physical grace and had flat feet, which they hoped to remedy with ballet classes; and (2) I consistently danced "with" ballerinas at our local theatre and on television, so my mother and grandmother were responding to my nonverbally expressed desire.

In retrospect, I am personally struck by the ways that participation in ballet by Black children in the twentieth century has been bound up with the all-encompassing project of racial uplift in the "on-going project of Emancipation," particularly in the US. Though not always stated, racial uplift was never far from the minds and plans of my parents and grandparents. For an interesting exploration of this matter in Black middle-class Philadelphia, see chapter 2, "Spectacularly Black on Black—1940s–50s" in Brenda Dixon Gottschild, *Joan Myers Brown and the Audacious Hope of the Black Ballerina: A Biohistory of American Performance* (New York: Palgrave Macmillan, 2021), 33–83.

4. On the relationship of the ballet to the political changes in Tsarist Russia, and its eventual European and US dispersion, see Jennifer Homans, *Apollo's Angels: A History of Ballet* (New York: Random House, 2010) Location 5775–5914, Kindle Edition.

5. Charles H. Long, *Significations: Signs, Symbols, and Images in the Interpretation of Religion*. Philosophical and Cultural Studies in Religion Series (Aurora, CO: The Davies Group, 1995), 156–158 and 165–168.

6. Vincent L. Wimbush, "Introduction: 'Everything about Me Was Magic': The Black-Fleshed and the Making and Management of Modernities," In *Masquerade: Scripturalizing Modernities through Black Flesh*. Edited by Vincent L. Wimbush (Lanham, MD: Lexington Books/Fortress Academic, 2023), p. 11.

7. The one exception in the professional ballet industry in the twentieth century is the Dance Theatre of Harlem, founded by Arthur Mitchell in 1968. When Mitchell launched the Dance Theatre of Harlem School and company, the original dancers wore classical flesh tone, i.e., pinkish-white tights and shoes. This created the conundrum in which brown, beige, and black ballet dancers, dancers of African descent from the far reaches of the worldwide African diaspora, studied and performed ballet wearing tights and shoes in a shade that was in decided contrast to their skin. By 1977, Mr. Mitchell made the significant choice to require that DTH dancers wear flesh tone that matched the actual color of their skin. TK Notable for at least two reasons: (1) Mitchell's requirement affirmed that white flesh was not the only proper status or the only color of ballet dancers; and (2) black people, or people of African descent have varied complexion colors which can be reflected in their tights and shoes. More later on Arthur Mitchell. The author thanks Dr. Joselli AuDain Deans of the University of Utah College of Fine Arts, and former Dance Theatre of Harlem company member, for this information. Personal interview, May 22, 2022.

8. Olaudah Equiano. *The Interesting Narrative and Other Writings* New York: Penguin Books/Penguin Random House, 2003 (1789). Kindle Edition.

9. Equiano, Olaudah. *The Interesting Narrative and Other Writings*, 34. Kindle Edition.

10. Vincent L. Wimbush, "Introduction: 'Everything about Me Was Magic': The Black-Fleshed and the Making and Management of Modernities." See also, Charles Long, *Significations: Signs, Symbols, and Images in the Interpretation of Religion*, 155–158.

11. The transnational cultural and political power of Catherine de' Medici deserves greater attention in the future. To apprehend a sense of her power from a twenty-first-century perspective, imagine a leader with the political power of Hillary Rodham Clinton, the diplomatic finesse of Madeleine Albright, and the artistic, cultural, and economic investments of Oprah Winfrey—this juncture of personalities may offer a sense of who Catherine was and the power she wielded in Florence, France, and geopolitically across Europe. See Broomhall, Susan, "The Game of Politics: Catherine de' Medici and Chess," *Early Modern Women* 12, no. 1 (2017): 104–18, https://www.jstor.org/stable/26431524; see also John Brackett, "Race and Rulership: Alessandro de' Medici, first Medici duke of Florence, 1529–1537," in T. F. Earle and K. J. P. Lowe, eds, *Black Africans in Renaissance Europe* (Cambridge: Cambridge University Press, 2005), 303–325.

12. See Selma Jeanne Cohen, ed., *Dance as a Theatre Art: Source Readings in Dance History from 1581 to the Present*, Second Edition (Hightstown, NJ: Dance Horizons/Princeton Book Company, 1992); Jack Anderson, *Ballet & Modern Dance: A Concise History*, Second Edition (Hightstown, NJ: Dance Horizons/Princeton Book Company, 1992); J. Homans, *Apollo's Angels: History of Ballet* (New York: Random House, 2010), Kindle Edition.

13. Balthasar de Beaujoyeulx, "Ballet Comique de la Reine," Mary-Jean Cowell, trans. (Paris, 1582) in Selma Jeanne Cohen, ed., *Dance as a Theatre Art: Source Readings in Dance History from 1581 to the Present*, Second Edition (Hightstown, NJ: Dance Horizons/Princeton Book Company, 1992). The author, who was also the choreographer and producer, was, like Catherine de' Medici, originally from Florence. He migrated to Paris around 1555 as a member of a musical ensemble. Once in Paris, he changed his name from Baltazarini di Belgiojoso and was eventually hired as court valet to Catherine de' Medici. Belgiojoso/Beaujoyeulx's position included planning and executing royal performances for the Franco-European monarchs, their families, and attendants.

14. Anderson, 31–33.

15. Balthasar de Beaujoyeulx in Selma Jeanne Cohen, 25–27.

16. Vincent L. Wimbush, "Introduction: 'Everything about Me Was Magic': The Black-Fleshed and the Making and Management of Modernities," p. 2.

17. *Agon*, choreographed by George Balanchine, music composed by Igor Stravinsky, premiered December 1, 1957, by New York City Ballet, at City Center of Music and Drama. Original Cast: Todd Bolender, Barbara Milberg, Barbara Walczak, Roy Tobias, Jonathan Watts, Melissa Hayden, Diana Adams, Arthur Mitchell. The repertoire notes offer the following: "*Agon* ('The Contest') is not a mythical subject piece . . . it has no musical or choreographic subject beyond the new interpretation of the venerable dances that are its pretext. It was even conceived without provision

for scenery and was independent, at least in Stravinsky's mind, of décor, period, and style." New York City Ballet—The Repertory, accessed 2 August 2022, https://www.nycballet.com/discover/ballet-repertory/agon/.

18. *Agon* (pas de deux), George Balanchine, choreographer, filmed in 1960, dancers: Diana Adams and Arthur Mitchell, https://youtu.be/w7sKrI5daZM, Accessed 18 March 2022.

19. "Arthur Mitchell coaching the pas de deux from Agon [videorecording]," 2006, New York Library of the Performing Arts in the Performing Arts Research Collections—Dance *MGZIDVD 5-3246.

20. The effort to make matriculation possible for Black high school students to in the previously all-white Central High School in Little Rock, AK was covered widely in news across the country and internationally. Little Rock was just one front in the US Civil Rights movement and ongoing project of emancipation. Examples of headlines from the time reveal much about the situation for the Black students, who came to be known as the Little Rock Nine: "U.S. Troops Invade Little Rock: Take Over Central High School"; & "President [Eisenhower] Orders Negro Children In" on the front page of the African American newspaper *Arkansas State Press*, September 27, 1957, https://infoweb-newsbank-com.us1.proxy.openathens.net/apps/readex/.

21. Lilian G. Mengesha and Lakshmi Padmanabhan, "Introduction: Performing Refusal/Refusing to Perform," *Women & Performance* 29.1, February 2019: np, https://www.womenandperformance.org/bonus-articles-1/29-1/intro.

BIBLIOGRAPHY

Akinleye, Adesola, ed. *(Re:)Claiming Ballet*. Bristol, UK/Chicago, IL: Intellect, 2021.

Anderson, Jack. *Ballet & Modern Dance: A Concise History.* 2nd ed. Hightstown, NJ: Dance Horizons/Princeton Book Company, 1992.

Cohen, Selma Jeanne, ed. *Dance as a Theatre Art: Source Readings in Dance History from 1581 to the Present*. 2nd ed. Hightstown, NJ: Dance Horizons/Princeton Book Company, 1992.

Equiano, Olaudah. *The Interesting Narrative and Other Writings*. New York: Penguin Books/Penguin Random House, 2003 [1789]. Kindle.

Long, Charles H. *Significations: Signs, Symbols, and Images in the Interpretation of Religion*. Philosophical and Cultural Studies in Religion Series. Aurora, CO: The Davies Group, 1995.

Mauss, Marcel. "Techniques of the Body." *Economy and Society* 2 (1973): 70–88.

Chapter 6

"Relentlessly Pursu[ing] All Who Live in Darkness"

The African Read as Bondage through Devotional Missionary Life Writing[1]

Rachel E. C. Beckley

INTRODUCTION—HOW THE MASK WAS MADE OR HOW THE BUZZARD FLEW

As a graduate student, I was fascinated by Dr. Wimbush's introduction in *Theorizing Scriptures*. There, he recounts Robert Penn Warren's 1940s poem "Pondy Wood." Wimbush notes that, in the poem, Big Jim Todd is fleeing a southern town,

> "As Warren's Jim Todd runs, he is hovered over and tortured by a clacking, talking buzzard. Jim Todd was, shall we say, very well-defined by the talking buzzard as the Western cultural standard bearer—" . . . nigger your breed ain't metaphysical . . ." Jim Todd was silent and on the run—the way most of U.S. society . . . assumed or wanted him to be. How is it that the buzzard could speak—using that violent epithet that hunts us even today—as though he knew Jim Todd? Knew who he was, what he was about? How could the silent Jim Todd . . . be said or be assumed to be known? How was it possible for him to know himself?" How can it be that certain things and peoples are assumed to be so clearly defined and located in the cultural imaginary and discourse, so much talked about, so much gazed upon, engaged, scripted, exegeted, yet remain unknown?[2]

The purpose of this provocative exhibition at Pitts Theological Library is surely to displace the scriptural work of the dominant culture, that is, to displace the buzzard and turn to Jim Todd. It is to examine the deep processes of what Wimbush calls the "counterpoint(s) to the canonical show-and-tell."[3] It is to hear from those behind the mask, as/if we are able.

As a scholar who examines white evangelicalism in the United States, I find myself drawn to the active creation of masks in the masquerade, or the creation of the buzzard. How was it made to fly, anyways? Where did it come from? And why is it that a buzzard clacking was somehow more believable to Warren's audience than Big Jim Todd speaking with his own voice? My hope is that this chapter can provide a type of "un-veiling"[4]—my own counterpoint of the traditional narrative—of exactly *where* scripturalectics takes place and how it takes place. In this way, this essay will attempt to respond to Wimbush's call to "take off as many layers of the masks as possible; . . . going forward with a new orientation,"[5] to "open wider many more windows beyond Equiano/Vassa."[6]

By understanding the where and how of power, we remove layers of the mask. We can track, as Wimbush puts it so eloquently, how the "black-fleshed phantasm" was "made (-up) to be and to produce and reflect a certain construal of hierarchicalization of 'reality.'"[7] This essay examines the "poisonous and burdensome scheme"[8] of scripturaletic-led masquerade in which black-fleshed people are made to signify through white man's magic, like the soft wax.

Before beginning, I would like to situate my own understanding of Wimbush's definitions. *Script* I take to mean the texts we use to make sense of the world around us. These texts do not need to be physical. *Scripturalization* is the act of making everything into a text that can be read and understood as if a complete whole. As Wimbush states in his introduction, "the scriptural claims . . . universal reach,"[9] understood the same way in all times and all spaces by all people. Of course, we know that people have vastly varied interpretations of what they "read," but the assumption is that the interpretation does *not* change across time, space, and person. This is one reason "scripture" is such a good term for this act. Western perceptions of scripture portray it as unchanging and unchangeable, sacred in its transcendence and absolute in its meaning.

Scripturalization takes place through the process *scripturalectics*. Scripturalectics refers to the ways the dominant culture makes texts be read and legible in the world—binding, labeling, categorizing them, and most deadly of all, enforcing them. When scripturalectics occurs, it produces *modernities*, the myriad of ways we exist, perform, and masquerade as we are categorized, bound, labeled, and enforced. Specifically, Wimbush, and others answering his call, examine racial modernities, understanding that black-fleshed peoples have been made to be read without reference to their own voices and humanity.

Importantly, scriptures do not need to have their origins in a faith practice or a religiously-based text (however we define that), but my work does happen to look toward religiously-inflected texts. However, I prefer to push the boundaries of what is considered "scripture." Protestant practitioners do not only read "The Bible" but also read other forms of literature that create meaning in a similar way to the biblical text. By pushing the boundaries of scripture, scholars can better track how white Protestant Christians in the United States have formed their ideas, (re)inscribing the mask. In this chapter, I will examine how scripturaletics is made to work on black-flesh peoples through a set of autobiographical missionary texts of the 1990s published by the Christian and Missionary Alliance called *The Jaffray Collection of Missionary Portraits*.

SECTION I: THE C&MA AND *THE JAFFRAY COLLECTION*

Dr. A. B. Simpson felt called by god to leave his Presbyterian pastorate for a New York City mission. This audacious move developed out of the growing Holiness movement of the mid-1800s. A. B. Simpson founded the Four-Fold Gospel, a theological doctrine claiming Christ is savior, healer, sanctifier, and coming king. Originally, congregations formed Alliance "branches," a missionary society made up of members of diverse congregations. These branches often met outside of Sunday worship times so that members could continue to attend their home parish.

Quickly, Alliance branches formed independent churches with a full governmental body, a general council, a president, and district superintendents. However, the Christian and Missionary Alliance (hereafter C&MA) only became an official denomination in 1974. Because of doctrinal similarity, many Pentecostal ministers received training at Simpson's Missionary Training Institute (later to become Nyack College).[10] The C&MA was heavily influenced by famous evangelists such as A. W. Tozer, but its focus always remained with overseas missions rather than forming a new denomination.

The C&MA purports to build churches in order to encourage autonomy, forming what they call "sister," rather than "daughter," churches. These churches, while begun by C&MA missionaries and receiving some aid from the denomination, are encouraged to build their own buildings, create their own statement of faith and governmental structure, ordain their own pastors and then send out their own missionaries. Global councils are loosely affiliated under the Alliance World Fellowship (AWF).[11] Importantly, missionaries from the C&MA also build schools and medical infrastructure, not just church buildings.[12]

The C&MA-owned Christian Publications (CPI) published a series starting in 1990 entitled *The Jaffray Collection of Missionary Portraits* (hereafter *Collection*). Named for the C&MA missionary R. A. Jaffray,[13] the *Collection* is a series of books written either by the missionary or a close acquaintance, who recount the missionary journey for readers. The missionaries are heroized in these books, allowing the reader to go with them on their missionary adventures. For example, the second book in the *Collection* series entitled *"Weak Thing" in Moni Land* is described in the magazine *Alliance Life* as an exciting and exotic adventure:

> "Bill Cutts, with a congenitally deformed body, went to a rugged, desolate corner of the world and with his wife . . . ministered . . . [h]is accounts of his labors and physical hardships, the backwardness of the people and spiritual battles with the forces of Satan provide for compelling, inspirational reading."[14]

Marilynne Foster, marketing coordinator for CPI,[15] volunteered to edit the book series, collecting manuscripts from a variety of missionaries. Each book has a similar style: chapters are generally chronological and are between 3 and 6 pages long, recounting a particular experience in the missionary's life. Every chapter ends with a particular biblical verse or general moral epitomized by that chapter's story. Importantly, god (and Satan) is an active, albeit invisible, agent throughout the text. Finally, these books are meant to exotify the life of a missionary *while at the same time* demonstrate that miracles and godly intervention can happen all the time, anywhere.

Paradoxically, the adventurous missionary journey in a "desolate" land with "backward" people, is banal. The books beg the question that god teaches all people similarly; god provides similarly; god performs miracles similarly, whether in a desolate place or in the readers' own backyard. In this way, the authorial and editorial intent of these books is to invite readers to look inward reflectively and expect to encounter the inbreaking of the transcendent in their own lives. In telling exotic, miraculous, adventure stories, these books *de*mystify the Christian life. In this way, the *Collection* represents a melding of autobiography and devotional Christian literature, with a unique ability to perform scripturalectics and (re)create the Other (as we shall see, specifically the African Other.) In other words, this type of literature performs masking and masquerade.

To demonstrate this, I will draw from *On Call*, the third book in the Jaffray Collection of Missionary Portraits series by missionary doctor David C. Thompson, a white male. Thompson was the son of C&MA missionaries to Cambodia. Both his parents were killed by the Viet Cong when he was a young adult. He went to medical school at the University of Pittsburgh and went on to serve with his wife and family at the Bongolo Mission Hospital in south-central Gabon, near Lebamba, about 400 kilometers south of the city of Libreville. I will draw from chapter 27, the story of a Gabonese man (ironically) named Christian.

In the next section, I will discuss Protestant autobiography and devotional literature generally in an attempt to situate *On Call* and show how this form of literature uniquely produces scripturalized meaning. In section III, I will briefly recount the entire story of chapter 27 and Thompson's interaction with Christian. Then, in section IV, I will apply the stages found in Dr. Wimbush's exhibition to demonstrate how this devotional chapter not only exemplifies each stage of the masquerade, but actively helps to (re)create it. *On Call* uses its authorial authority produced through autobiography and devotional literature in order to make black-fleshed people in Gabon signify as continuously, persistently in bondage.

SECTION II: NARRATED LIVES AND DEVOTIONAL LITERATURE

Protestant missionary narratives are common in American literature, both fiction and nonfiction.[16] In the case of *On Call*, Thompson writes an autobiography, which I will call "life writing" for the purposes of this chapter.[17] Authors of life writing are not innocent tellers of truth, creating a singular, coherent, and true Self. Life writing is entirely about performing identity and constructing meaning.

Life writing is performative of identity in two ways. First, the author produces a particular version of themselves that will impart ultimate meaning by quilting experiences together to create a coherent pattern. Martha Watson describes it as a form of "personal mythology," but a mythology that must also justify itself as worth the trouble of telling.[18] It is not self-evidently important—after all, what makes anyone's life worthy of note? The author must persuade readers that their life narrative has a meaning worth imparting. As she states, "[t]he 'I' of the autobiography is a rhetorical construct, the images of what the author wants to convey about the world."[19] In life writing, the author constructs a self and then "encodes or reinforces particular values . . ."[20]

The second form of identity creation in life writing refers to the audience. Not knowing what sort of reader will actually pick up their text, the autobiographer also writes to a "given audience."[21] That is, they create their own audience who understands and accepts their rhetoric. The "actual" audience—the nonimaginary one—who reads the book may or may not agree with the author. But, in their own writings, the author constructs a reader who will interpret and apply the autobiographer's ultimate meaning. In the *Collection*, this imaginary audience is present as each chapter ends with a biblical verse or presumed-universal Christian truth. Thompson speaks directly to an imagined audience who understands the bible and Christian worldview as a complete and singular whole, with an absolute and transcendent meaning.

The autobiographer, in writing to an imagined audience, disciplines the actual interlocutors. The autobiographer believes that their lives can be a model for others (that is, their readers) to follow.[22] Thus, the author interprets their own experiences, hoping that their reader will internalize that meaning and live it out (or, perhaps, avoid mistakes the author made). This involves the reader accepting the author's construction of the world.

Watson hypothesizes that this creates a unique intimacy between the author and the reader.[23] The reader must trust the author's authority: trust that the autobiographer is not lying about their experiences (not a hoax); trust that the meaning the autobiographer constructs is worthwhile and helpful; trust that the author's worldview is correct. It is this language of intimacy that caused me to reach for another type of literature: Christian devotional literature.

Christian devotional literature is mainly examined by scholars of the Medieval and Early Modern period. In this field, devotional literature is well theorized. Specifically, it is meant to produce receptivity in the reader—that receptivity may ready them for an experience with the transcendent, or simply prepare them to be taught.[24]

The missionary life writing of the *Jaffray Collection* represents, I argue, a unique form of devotional literature that masquerades as autobiography. Missional autobiographies are particularly able to construct reality because these missionaries base their authority not just on the implicit connection between the autobiographer and the reader, but they also cement the narrative in the confines of the biblical text—a text that the author presumes already has a transcendent meaning for their imagined reader. The bible is "[the missionary's] paradigmatic narrative, through which [missionaries] recognize new situations and even their own actions."[25] In other words, the new narrative told by the missionary author inherently has meaning and power because it is based on the old narrative, that is, the biblical narrative. The bible provides legitimacy for the missionary autobiographer as they recount experiences from their lives that they believe mirror the biblical text.

I posit that because autobiography is performative of identity and meaning creation, it is didactic. This teaching quality connects the autobiography to devotional literature. Devotional literature hopes to construct, teach, and discipline its reader to interpret the world by a certain framework and expect the inbreaking of the transcendent. As Terrance Craig argues in *The Missionary Lives*, "missionary life-writing constructs sub-mythologies in support of a central mythology." Missionary lives "more obviously than others—are broad statements of ideology," they stand as "public monuments."[26] Using the autobiographical genre, the author is able to write to an imagined audience who will interpret that public monument within a certain framework. The autobiographical author has a unique ability to discipline their audience to see and interpret the world in a certain way, giving that interpretation an immediacy and necessity unparalleled, because they can appeal to the biblical.

Because the author constructs the ideal audience, the author does not explain terms, and this is particularly true in *On Call*, as we shall see. The author views every situation through a particular lens of interpretation that the author believes is stable. The devotional author assumes that biblical truth is the same in all places, at all times, for all people (especially for the evangelical protestant this must be true, because if truth can change then perhaps god would change). The missionary autobiographer hopes the reader can identify the same interpretive meaning in their own lives, leading to interior self-reflection, self-discipline, and mimicry of the missionary life. Interestingly, this creates a cycle of proof in this type of devotional literature: the fact that people can have different experiences, but there is still (presumably) only one interpretation, demonstrates over and over again the implacability and universality of the author's and imagined reader's Christian faith.

Whether or not the reader *actually* interprets any of this when they do read the missionary autobiography is not the main point and would require a different type of methodology to find out. My interest is in what the missionary life writing *purports* to do. Autobiographical devotional literature, like the *Jaffray Collection*, sees the world as a constant reenactment of biblical stories and scriptural interpretation.[27] This reenactment is, paradoxically, new and old. Because the new experiences of the missionary rest in old biblical narratives, they have an added a level of authority. The missionary autobiographer writes to an imagined audience who has an already-constructed perception of the divine and the bible. I argue that it is in delving into these already-constructed perceptions and seeing how they are wielded and utilized in the narrative that the scholar can see scripturalectics at work.

On Call as a form of autobiographical devotional literature gives an excellent examination of mask-making—scripturalectics—because the Evangelical reader and writer co-construct meaning from the text, expecting both old meanings and new, and then that devotional mentality is used to interpret the world in which the reader lives.

SECTION III: THE BUZZARD TELLS A STORY

In one of the longest chapters in the book, chapter 27 recounts the story of a man named Christian. Christian stays at the Bongolo hospital for days complaining of pain. When discharged, he panics, telling Thompson that he was a student at the University of Libreville.[28] He became haunted by spirits who encouraged him to do violence and had to drop out of school.

> For years, he said, spirits had talked to him at night, telling him to do certain things . . . When someone told him that our hospital was a place where God was, he decided to come. The moment he stepped onto the hospital grounds the spirits became subdued.[29]

Thompson posits that Christian might be a "budding schizophrenic"[30] but was overjoyed when Christian converted. Christian is discipled (that is, mentored) by another missionary. Thompson tells his reader that Christian's family life is a mystery: Christian spoke of his uncle with fear, believing his uncle had cursed him with the spirits who haunted him.

Three months later, Christian is baptized. Importantly, throughout the chapter, Thompson recalls that he had doubts about Christian—that he was so silent about his family, that he wouldn't tell his family about his intention to be baptized, and about the fact that he had fetishes. Multiple times, Thompson or another missionary, "on a hunch"[31] asks questions that reveal more concerns. It provides a sense of ominousness throughout the chapter.

One year later, Christian expresses a desire to become a pastor and attends the local Bible School. However, Christian is also told by his mentors that he must visit his family and tell them of his intentions to be a Christian and a pastor (even though Christian has repeatedly refused to do so). Christian claims he went to talk with his family but remains evasive about the visit. Christian then stops eating meat or anything made from palm nuts (a main ingredient in oil used to cook most foods). He loses weight, purposefully fasts for multiple days, sings songs into the night, and then stays out all night. Thompson clarifies the oddness of being out all night for his reader,

> [t]he Gabonese are afraid to be out alone at night because thy believe the night belongs to the spirits . . . The windows must be closed. If asked, they will tell you that they do it to keep out thieves, but even if the window has security bars, they will be uneasy until it is shuttered . . . [to stay out all night] could only mean . . . that he was either mad or consorting with the spirits.[32]

Christian admits to his pastor that an angel of light and beauty has told him to stop eating certain foods, taught him songs to sing, and to stay out at night. Once again, Christian is asked if he got rid of all his fetishes and Christian again states that he has done so. The pastor of the Bible School asks Thompson to meet with Christian.

Thompson meets with Christian on his porch in the evening. After a silence, Christian speaks, "I have learned many wonderful things since I left [the Bongolo Hospital compound]." Thompson assumes that at the Bible School he has been learning from the Bible exclusively. Christian answers, "Well, in the Bible, but from other places as well."[33] Christian tells Thompson that the angel of light has taught him other things and has encouraged him that he is "on the right path" following God. The angel claims to be the spokesperson and messenger of Jesus. Thompson then asks:

> "Is it true that you have not destroyed all your old fetishes?" . . . His friendly mood changed immediately.
>
> "Who told you I have kept fetishes?" There was anger in his voice now and I began to sense the presence of great evil.
>
> "Do you still have your old fetishes? . . . if you have kept even one, it gives Satan the right to oppress you."
>
> "The angel told me to keep them, so I did."
>
> " . . . the Bible says that Christians must have nothing to do with things that belong to Satan. Why would an angel of God contradict God?"
>
> "It is an angel of God, I tell you!" he almost shouted . . . "Do you want to see him for yourself?"[34]

At this point, Thompson describes a strong sense that they are not alone on the porch, goosebumps appearing all over his arms. But Thompson rebukes Christian's offer,

> An angel of God would never permit you to keep a fetish! He is taking you off to hell! Christian, if you want to follow Jesus, you must renounce this evil angel. Otherwise he will have you in his power forever! . . . you are being deceived by an angel of light. That is Satan's oldest tactic. It's what he did in the garden of Eden when the world began. . . . when he has finished with you he will destroy you. I beg you . . . let me help you get free of this thing.[35]

Christian storms off into the jungle and "[h]is bare feet on the lawn made his departure noiselsss [*sic*] and the black night seemed to swallow him whole."[36]

The next day, Christian leaves the Bible school with his machete and shoulder bag. "We never saw Christian or heard from him again . . . [his uncle] told us that he had not seen Christian since he had gone to the university in Libreville two years before. The family had thought that Christian was dead" (confirming Thompson's hunch that Christian lied when he said that he had visited his family after his baptism). "Christian's whereabouts remain a mystery. Perhaps he wandered into the nearby Republic of Congo. Perhaps he is among Libreville's masses. Perhaps he is dead."

Finally, Thompson interprets this story for his reader,

> The reasons behind his strange behavior . . . are not a mystery. In consulting with a sorcerer and buying his sacred object and charms, Christian acquiesced to evil spiritual beings. When he came into the light of Jesus Christ he was temporarily free of their harassments—until he decided to keep several of the fetishes as a safety net . . . he turned back into the night of Satan's power and bondage . . . seduced by an evil angel of beauty and light who appeared to him and promised him success and power . . . [o]nly prayer and the overcoming power of God can deliver him from Satan's grasp now.

Strikingly, as recounted to us in the story, Christian never says the angel told him he would be successful. Thompson only tells the reader that the angel of light and beauty has said, " . . . the Bible is true and that [Christian] [is] on the right path. God sent him to lead [Christian] on that path."

What is the critical scholar of scripturalization to make of this story?

SECTION IV: THE MASQUERADE

Stage I: "He was a muscular, healthy-looking 20-year-old, but he moaned and groaned so effectively . . . I finally admitted him to the hospital."[37] Or, Knowing the World through/as Masquerade

Earlier in the book, in chapter 17, Thompson states, "Staging and symbolism play an important part in much of Africa. . . ."[38] Thompson shows this "staging" in Christian's story in two main ways. One clear and straight-forward, the other more roundabout.

First, Christian playacts in order to be admitted to the hospital, and Thompson's is clear that he doubted Christian's "effective" shows of pain. The playacting went on for two weeks so that Thompson and the nurses "began to suspect he was a shirker."[39] This will not be the only time Christian is accused by the narrator of lying, or playacting.

Before Christian is baptized he "assured the pastor that he had destroyed all his fetishes."[40] Thompson says that Christian, always the persuader, convinced them that he could be baptized without declaring it to his family. A year later, he "argued convincingly" about becoming a pastor and separating from his family.

Thompson has shed doubt on this man, portraying him as a potential danger and con-man. He is convincing, healthy and muscular, but a shirker, possibly conniving. In fact, Thompson cast such a doubt that he feels the need to assure his audience of the truth of Christian's conversion.

Later, after supposedly returning from visiting his family, Thompson begins to doubt Christian's performance: "I felt for some reason Christian was hiding something from us . . . [s]omething did not ring true."[41] But, what has caused Christian's cultural play, his masquerade, to deteriorate? Thompson has one answer, and it is this answer that leads us to our second point concerning cultural play: fetishes.

Wimbush's Stage I in the Exhibition focuses on masks. "The fetish" in Thompson's book plays a similar role. To Wimbush, the African mask is a basic representation of the masquerade. Similarly, the fetish is a site of sociality, revealing the complex cultural life of Gabonese people. Yet, Thompson, in regular fashion of white-fleshed people looking *at* and *upon* Black-fleshed peoples' cultural play, deems the fetish as "frenzied . . . magic."[42]

To Thompson, the fetish is a space both of inconsequential and primitive ritual practice *and yet* a site of unparalleled and real evil power. There are two ways I'd like to unpack the way that Thompson talks about the fetish that removes the cultural complexity housed within these figures of masquerade and remakes them into a signifier of black-fleshed enslavement.

First, the fetish is portrayed as a primitive magical thing, one-dimensional and simplistic. Thompson never explains what a "fetish" is in the Gabonese context. The reader does not have a sense for what a fetish looks like, smells like, feels like, how or where they are obtained. Instead, the author is willing to accept whatever his reader *thinks* is a fetish. This takes us back to the unique ability of autobiographical devotional literature. Thompson speaks to an imagined audience who already knows what a fetish is and categorizes it as primitive and diabolical. The western interlocutor is taught/disciplined to minimize and deconstruct the complex Gabonese fetish without any input from the Gabonese themselves. The cultural complexity of the fetish object is rendered silent in Thompson's refusal to describe what it is or looks like.

After stripping the Gabonese fetish of any cultural or personal context, reorganizing it as a western imaginary of primitive magic, Thompson will scripturalize the fetish according to his own western gaze. The Gabonese fetish houses great power, but not *African magic*. Thompson dismisses (and thus leads his reader to dismiss) African magic as superstition. He talks about Gabonese fears of the night (quoted above in section III) and notes that many people in Gabon buy fetishes in order to increase their intelligence:

> While a student, [Christian] consulted several sorcerers to enhance his ability to learn. This is not unusual in Gabon. The sorcerer also sold him a sacred object called a fetish to give him special intelligence, a sort of good luck charm.[43]

And Thompson finally demonstrates that the Gabonese people are the source of their own problems, putting their faith in a meaningless superstition:

> Soon [after buying the intelligence fetish], [Christian] began hearing voices at night, but he never associated the voices with the fetish. In fact, he went back to the sorcerer to try to obtain protection and relief from the voices, which he concluded were spirits. Additional fetishes did not help . . . [u]ntil coming to our hospital he had been unable to find relief.[44]

Thus, Thompson disassociates the Gabonese fetish from *African* power or *African* magic. African magic is superstition. However, Thompson does believe that the fetish has power. Instead, the power that *actually* exists in the fetish is satanic power, importantly the understanding of Satan from a western framework developed since the medieval period in Europe. The Gabonese fetish becomes a mask! It masks the hidden, real, satanic, western power behind all things African. There is nothing real about the African fetish itself. The only thing that is real is how it is used and fetishized by Satan and the powers of western perceptions of evil.

The fetish performs work of enslavement that then signifies on African people as constantly enslaved. This is even more apparent in a previous chapter (also about fetish-use ominously entitled "Casualties of the Warfare" meaning the spiritual warfare between good and evil). In this chapter, Thompson says:

> What the Africans do not recognize, however, is the principle which is clearly taught in the Scriptures: that those who enlist the help of spirits will be enslaved by them. The only deliverance from this slavery is through the Name and power of the Lord Jesus Christ.[45]

This perspective that the Gabonese cause their own enslavement is found constantly in Christian's chapter as well. As Thompson says several times, keeping a fetish gives Satan the right to oppress—not just an opportunity to oppress, but a clear allowance to do it, as if Christian is owned because he owns the fetish. "Christian acquiesced to evil" in keeping this fetish, and thus Christian "turned back into the night of Satan's power and bondage."[46] This will mimic the last line of *On Call* in which Thompson says that God has power "over the dark and malevolent spirits that so relentlessly pursue all who live in darkness."

Living in darkness is an enslavement to that darkness, even as Thompson talked about Gabonese fears of the dark, claiming that Gabonese people are not at ease until the window is shuttered. Thompson is saying that they are enslaved to their fears and to the spirits. As a result, (ironically, given Thompson's reference to a general Gabonese fear of the dark), Gabonese people live in perpetual spiritual darkness. Thompson makes it an essential-ized feature of Gabonese people who do not go out at night and buy intel-ligence fetishes at the university.

In these several quotes, we can see that Thompson believes a fetish—no matter what it looks like or how it is used—is a tool of enslavement. The Gabonese (a synecdoche for all Africans, a slippage Thompson makes occa-sionally in his book) enslave themselves because of their masquerade with fetishes and spirits. Their cultural play is not a matter of perceiving the world differently; it is bondage.

In Thompson's worldview, resting on biblical narratives (like the Garden of Eden which Thompson references during his talk with Christian), scriptural-izes African people as enslaved no matter what they have done or what they do. Their very worldview creates enslavement. And the only saving grace (literally) for African people, is a white, western doctor bringing the salvation of a western deity, scattering the evil power of a western Satan who "puts on" the Gabonese fetish as his own mask.

In Christian's chapter, Thompson uses scripturalectics that have already taken place. African people are manipulatable and manipulating; superstitious and magical. Their own cultural play not recognized as such by Europeans, colonizers mask black-fleshed people so their lifeways could be read or made legible, and at the same time, render the people behind the masks unreadable, invisible, and silent. Their complex masquerade with fetishes is signified as primitive, containing no power in-and-of-itself, but used as a mask by a west-ern concept of anthropomorphized evil.

Stage II: "He showed remarkable ability to understand the Word of God . . ."[47]
Or, *Translatio studii et imperii* (Transfer of Learning and Power) as Scripturalization

Christian expressed "white man's magic" quite clearly at the beginning of the narrative. In Thompson's narration, Christian explained that he was so plagued by the voices of spirits that he had to drop out of school. Christian is palpably afraid as the spirits began to threaten him and instruct him to do things (Thompson is not clear what the spirits were telling Christian to do, leaving the reader to construct this silence for themselves. Were the spirits encouraging him to be violent? To harm others? The reader's imagination is

given space to run wild) even as he tried to resist the things they were telling him to do. Thompson described how a haunted Christian found his way
to the Bongolo hospital, "When someone told him that our hospital was a
place where God was, he decided to come. The moment he stepped onto the
hospital grounds, the spirits became subdued."[48] Thompson hires Christian to
do odd jobs and eventually to be a groundskeeper so he never needs to leave
the compound. Note that Christian understands god as being present on the
hospital grounds. He interprets god in a similar way as he interprets the spirits—present, active, powerful.

As soon as Christian "pray[s] to receive Christ as his Savior," he is
immediately put on a delineated trajectory to understand western, dominant
regimes of representation.[49] Christian is discipled (or mentored) by a visiting missionary, Rev. Cook.[50] Unable, or deemed unqualified, to study his
own religious development, he must receive guidance from a white, western,
missionary. The schedule is hefty: Christian went to Rev. Cook's office after
work every day. There, they would do an hour of Bible study reading, they
would discuss, and they would pray. Thompson is impressed with Christian's
ability "to understand the Word of God."[51] Christian is then baptized. He
would sing hymns as he worked and he would talk about Christ all the time
to anyone who would listen. Christian then wants to be a pastor, and goes to
the local Bible School to study, read, and be trained for that profession. This
is a long process that takes upwards of four years.

We can see that Thompson, Rev. Cook, and the Bible School all mobilize
western ways of knowing and believing. Christian is not allowed to hear god
in any other way—he must read the book; he must be discipled; he must go to
a "legitimate" Bible school. These western norms devalue the orally received
knowledge that first brought Christian to the hospital—that god was present
at the hospital. This was not deemed a proper understanding of Christianity.
He must convert in a clearly perceived and legible way.

But what is understood as legible? Thompson (ironically?) fetishizes the
Bible. Thompson understands the text to be perfectly meaningful, across
space, place, time, and people. It must mean the same thing and no other truth
or worldview can exist alongside it. As I stated above in my introduction, the
scriptural claims the universal.

Hence, Thompson betrays his own view of conversion. A convert is meant
to leave all previous relationships, all previous worldviews, and turn to a
western interpretation of the sacred text. Christian is made to get rid of all
his fetishes (although, as we will learn, he apparently did not do this). He is
to cast off the things of his old life and be made new. This includes view-
ing his family structure with a western hierarchy. His mentors insist that he
must speak to his family—as if to come clean to them. Becoming a Christian
but not telling one's family, is a betrayal of the patriarchal, western, familial

system. It is not only confusing, but *sinful*, for Christian to retain his own perception of his family, which is clearly encased in fear for reasons Thompson does not reveal or does not know.

By privileging western ways of being and knowing as a mimetic of the only way to exist and be as a Christian, demanding black-fleshed people like Christian follow it precisely, this chapter demonstrates minstrelsy. Christian is made to perform and dance, minstrel-like, for the audience around him. "Christian was one of the most exhuberant (*sic*) Christians I've ever known" Thompson raves. Christian is meant to perform Christianity and western-ness without referencing his own worldview and past at all. He must be made anew in his baptism—leaving behind all other things, fetish and family, but also his *understanding of how the fetish and family work.*

Stage III: "I have learned many wonderful things . . . in the Bible, but from other places as well."[52] or, Scripturalization as White Violence on Black Flesh; and Stage IV: "When asked why he was so happy, he would smile and say, 'Because Jesus set me free!'"[53] or Black Mimetic Translation of Scripturalization

I decided to take these two stages together. Christian attempts, again and again, to mimic western forms of Christian behavior. He is read as Christian by Thompson and others. He appears legible in their framework even as their scripturalization process performs a violent minstrelsy upon Christian. Christian sings. Christian proclaims that he has been "set free." Christian invites Jesus into his heart. But, in doing all of this, Thompson and the others assume that Christian means what they mean.

My Stage III quote strikes me as remarkably similar to Ottobah Cugoano's *Thoughts and Sentiment* quote that Wimbush chose for Stage III. The Inca wanted to know where Valverde had learned so many things.

> In this book, replied the fanatic Monk . . . The Inca opened it eagerly, and . . . lifted it to his ear: This, says he, is silent; it tells me nothing . . . The enraged father of ruffians . . . cried out "To arms, Christians, to arms; the word of God is insulted; avenge this profanation on these impious dogs.

Wimbush encourages his viewer/reader to think how frustrating African and Native peoples would be when missionaries described learning from a book, but the book did not talk. However, he also asks us to go further in our analysis.

Wimbush notes that, at a certain point, many Black Atlantic people (and Indigenous people as well) did indeed learn how to read. Meaning that the book was no longer silent for them. However, their interpretations of the book—that is, their construal of what the book speaks to them—is constantly veiled, silenced, and masked when it appears differently from white European interpretation.

By rejecting Black and Indigenous perspectives on the "talking book" Black and Indigenous people are rendered less human, unable to be heard. Wimbush posits that "[v]arious expressive practices and ideologies in the maintenance of such silence are masquerade and so become the chaotic impetus behind the production of modernities. . . ."[54] Like so many other black-fleshed people before him, Christian can read the book, and he unites it with his own understanding of the world. When he does this, he tries to speak it to others. But, Christian cannot leave behind his own profound cultural play, that is, his fetishes. Indeed, he believes that they *add* to the talking book, they do not take away from it.

Thompson reads this as a demonstrable, physical sign of Satan's bondage of all of Africa. Notice, again, in Thompson's view, Africa is already and remains enslaved. It is enough to make the reader believe that perhaps the physical bondage of the sixteenth to nineteenth centuries was somehow an improvement to their spiritual bondage! And, in that moment, the black-fleshed African person signifies only bondage. Whether spiritual or physical, they wear the mask of the slave, in perpetual darkness. In this chapter, Christian is a synechdoche of all African people—unable to truly understand the western text, even though he is discipled and taught at a legitimate bible school. Christian can only signify bondage. And, more than this, Thompson is clear, it is a bondage of his own making! By keeping fetishes, Christian gives Satan "the right" to oppress. Christian is asking for it, not through speech, but through action. *Qui tacet consentire videtur* (silence gives consent). The silence of the African gives consent to bondage.

But, of course, the African is always rendered silent by the masking of the white missionary. The missionary attempts to place a white mask on Christian, and then condemns him when he tries to speak through it, telling Christian that his silence is what gives consent to his own enslavement. The irony and disturbing nature of the scripturalization of Christian is appallingly clear in this chapter.

Stage V: "Without saying a word to anyone he walked into the forest."[55] or, Signifying on Mimetic Scripturalization of Black Flesh

But, Christian, in an interesting flip of the script, refuses the mask. Christian votes with his feet, as it were, and leaves. Thompson, of course, interprets this as Christian turning his back on god. Christian, thinks Thompson, chooses the fetish and embraces Satan rather than trusting god. Thompson once again renders Christian's actions silent. Christian recognizes that he cannot exist and be fully human—fully himself—in this space created by Christians. Trying desperately to find a place where the book can speak alongside, with, and to, his fetish, Christian heads out into the forest. In this sense, Christian could not "make do" with the white man's fetish.

CONCLUSION

I have argued that *On Call* represents a form of missionary life writing that also expects to serve the purpose of devotional literature. I argue that this form of literature has a unique ability to scripturalize because of identity construction and intimacy.

The autobiographer constructs themselves and an imagined audience. The writer can then attempt to discipline their actual interlocutors to interpret the world within particular frameworks. And because the autobiography style produces intimacy with its reader the disciplining of the reader is given an added sense of immediacy and necessity. Further, the missionary autobiography has added authority because it is a mirror of the biblical narrative. The new and the old interact together to produce a seemingly unchanging Truth in the world.

For this chapter, I have focused in on racialized modernities and the way that Thompson (re)produces them upon Christian, a Gabonese man. Thompson presumes masquerade and magic on the part of Christian, then judges Christian by western standards of "proper" education and "the book," and rejects (and eventually condemns) any form of Black mimetic scripturalization by Christian. Thompson's autobiography replays the exact types of scripturalectics that Equiano/Vassa notes in his own life.

Thompson believes his autobiography stands as a monument to the work of god in the world. Thompson's life does mirror, but it does not mirror a transcendent biblical text. Instead, it mirrors complex historical processes of scripturalectics that render Black-fleshed people silent and continuously in bondage, unable to break free without western, divine intervention. Thompson attempts to pass this framework on to his reader through autobiography and devotional literature, hoping that the reader will emulate and refract this framework in their own lives.

NOTES

1. I was deeply honored when Dr. Wimbush asked me to moderate one of the panels for this exhibition. Not being as established, nor as well-spoken, as the members of the two panels, I was relieved when my role would be no more than commenting. To my surprise, joy, and abject horror, Dr. Wimbush invited me to contribute a chapter. My thanks to him, and to the leniency of my reader.

2. Vincent Wimbush, "Introduction: TEXTureS, Gestures, Power: Orientation to Radical Excavation." Pages 1–20 in *Theorizing Scriptures: New Critical Orientations to a Cultural Phenomenon.* Edited by Vincent Wimbush. *New Brunswick, NJ*: Rutgers University Press, 2008, 2. See also original discussion in "Reading Darkness, Reading Scriptures," in *African Americans and the Bible*, ed. V. L. Wimbush (New York: Continuum, 2000) 3–8, 18, passim.

3. Wimbush, see Introduction above, 2.

4. Ibid., 3.

5. Ibid., 28.

6. Ibid., 30.

7. Ibid., 5.

8. Ibid., 29.

9. Ibid., 24–25.

10. "Our History," Christian and Missionary Alliance, accessed July 14, 2022, https://cmalliance.org/who-we-are/our-story/; "CMA History," Fellowship Bible Church, accessed July 14, 2022, http://cmafellowshipbible.org/index_files/cmahist.htm

11. "Our History," Alliance World Fellowship, accessed June 29, 2020, http://awf.world/history/.

12. In full disclosure, my father was a C&MA pastor, as was my maternal grandfather, and my maternal great-great grandfather. My great-great-great grandfather was a farmer who helped start the Locus Street Church, later called Chapel Hill Akron branch of the C&MA in 1916. He was one of the founding families who followed the lead of Mrs. Grace Butts who attended services with A. B. Simpson in New York City. See "History," Chapel Hill Church, accessed July 14, 2022, http://www.chapelhillchurch.org/our-history. I am no longer affiliated with the C&MA or a member of an Alliance church, but I am an example of how devotional history still resonates, even among those of us who are no longer practitioners. The book *On Call* that I reference throughout this essay, along with almost 20 other books in the Jaffray Collection, were all in a box that has been in my basement for 6 years now, moved along with a portion of my father's library when he came to live with us after his ALS diagnosis. I remember vividly when I was a child that these books sat in a bookshelf at the end of the hallway, sandwiched between my parent's room and my brother's room. I would sit in that hallway and pour over the covers, the miracles within them, and feel deeply deficient in my own spiritual journey.

13. R. A. Jaffray was born to a wealthy Canadian senator who owned and operated the Toronto Globe newspaper, heard A. B. Simpson speak and after enrolled in what would become Nyack College. In 1897, he left for missions work in the Guangxi

province of China and later in Indonesia, specifically the islands of Kalimantan and Sulawesi. He died in a Japanese internment camp in Kampili, Indonesia on July 29, 1945. For a biography see, "Jaffray Legacy," *Alliance Life*, accessed May 24, 2022, https://legacy.cmalliance.org/about/history/jaffray. A more complete biography can be found at F. Randall Whetzel, "A Man to Follow: Memories of China's Pioneer Missionary," *Alliance Life*, August 2008, https://legacy.cmalliance.org/alife/issue /2008-08/.

14. Darolyn Irvin, "Book Review: Pioneer Missions," *Alliance Life*, August 1990, 13.

15. For an interview with Marilynne Foster, see Pamela Taylor, "Missions Her Lifelong Passion: The Jaffray Series of Missionary Portraits Is a Love Gift to the Lord," *Alliance Life*, November 1998, 18–19.

16. For the role of fictional missionary accounts see: Albert Triconi, *Missionary Positions* (University Press of Florida, 2011); Jan Blodgett, *Protestant Evangelical Literary Culture and Contemporary Society* (Connecticut: No. 51 Greenwood Publishing Group, 1997); A. Gandolfo, *Faith and Fiction: Christian Literature in America Today* (Connecticut: Praeger Publishers, 2007).

17. For an examination of the term "autobiography" and "life writing" as an alternative, see Smith and Watson (eds), *Reading Autobiography: A Guide for Interpreting Life Narratives* (University of Minnesota Press, 2010), 3–4.

18. Martha Watson, *Lives of Their Own: Rhetorical Dimensions in Autobiographies of Women Activists* (University of South Carolina, 1999), 3–4.

19. Ibid., 30.

20. Smith and Watson, *Reading Autobiography*, 16–17.

21. Watson, *Lives of Their Own*, 5.

22. Ibid., 13. See also J. P. Tompkins. *Sensational Designs: The Cultural Work of American Fiction, 1790–1860* (Oxford: Oxford University Press), 1986, ix. "These novelists have designs upon their audience, in the sense of wanting to make people think and act in a particular way."

23. Watson, *Lives of Their Own*, 19.

24. Anne Clark Bartlett and Thomas H. Bestul (eds), "Introduction" in *Cultures of Piety: Medieval English Devotional Literature in Translation*, eds. Anne Clark Bartlett and Thomas H. Bestul (New York: Cornell University Press, 1999), 2–3.

25. J. D. Y. Peel, "For Who Hath Despised the Day of Small Things? Missionary Narratives and Historical Anthropology," *Comparative Studies in Society and History* 37, no. 3 (July 1995): 595.

26. Terrence L. Craig, *The Missionary Lives: A Study in Canadian Missionary Biography and Autobiography* (New York: Brill, 1997), 89.

27. Susan Friend Harding, *The Book of Jerry Falwell* (Princeton, NJ: Princeton University Press, 2018), 54–56.

28. Thompson notes offhandedly that Christian consulted with sorcerers, receiving a fetish to increase his intelligence. "This is not unusual in Gabon." Thompson notes in David C. Thompson, *On Call*, The Jaffray Collection of Missionary Portraits #3 (Pennsylvania: First Christian Publishers, Inc., 1991), 194.

29. Ibid., 194.

30. Ibid., 194.
31. Ibid., 199.
32. Ibid., 198.
33. Ibid., 200.
34. Ibid., 200–201.
35. Ibid., 202
36. Ibid., 202.
37. Ibid., 194.
38. Ibid., 129.
39. Ibid., 193.
40. Ibid., 195.
41. Ibid., 197.
42. Ibid., 10.
43. Ibid., 194.
44. Ibid., 194.
45. Ibid., 130.
46. Ibid., 203.
47. Ibid., 195.
48. Ibid., 194.
49. Wimbush, Introduction above, *10–11*.
50. Importantly, Rev. Raymond Cook was a missionary 20–30 years prior to the Bapounou Tribe, to whom Christian also belonged. He was at Bongolo for a year special assignment.
51. David Thompson, *On Call*, 195.
52. Ibid., 200.
53. Ibid., 196.
54. Wimbush, Introduction above, *11*.
55. David Thompson, *On Call,* 202.

BIBLIOGRAPHY

Alliance World Fellowship. "Our History." Accessed June 29, 2020. http://awf.world /history/.

Bartlett, Anne Clark, and Thomas H. Bestul. "Introduction." In *Cultures of Piety: Medieval English Devotional Literature in Translation*, edited by Anne Clark Bartlett and Thomas H. Bestul, 1–17. New York: Cornell University Press, 1999.

Blodgett, Jan. *Protestant Evangelical Literary Culture and Contemporary Society*. Connecticut: No. 51 Greenwood Publishing Group, 1997.

Chapel Hill Church. "History." Accessed July 14, 2022. http://www.chapelhillchurch .org/our-history.

Christian and Missionary Alliance. "Our History." Accessed July 14, 2022. https:// cmalliance.org/who-we-are/our-story/.

Craig, Terrence L. *The Missionary Lives: A Study in Canadian Missionary Biography and Autobiography*. New York: Brill, 1997.

Darolyn, Irvin. "Book Review: Pioneer Missions." *Alliance Life*, August 1990.

Fellowship Bible Church. "CMA History." Accessed July 14, 2002. http://cmafellowshipbible.org/index_files/cmahist.htm.

Gandolfo, A. *Faith and Fiction: Christian Literature in America Today.* Connecticut: Praeger Publishers, 2007.

Harding, Susan Friend. *The Book of Jerry Falwell. Princeton, NJ*: Princeton University Press, 2018.

Peel, J. D. Y. "For Who Hath Despised the Day of Small Things? Missionary Narratives and Historical Anthropology." *Comparative Studies in Society and History* 37, no. 3 (July 1995): 581–607.

Taylor, Pamela. "Missions Her Lifelong Passion: The Jaffray Series of Missionary Portraits Is a Love Gift to the Lord." *Alliance Life*, November 1998.

Thompson, David C. *On Call.* The Jaffray Collection of Missionary Portraits #3. Pennsylvania: First Christian Publishers, Inc, 1991.

Tompkins, J. P. *Sensational Designs: The Cultural Work of American Fiction, 1790–1860.* Oxford: Oxford University Press, 1986.

Triconi, Albert. *Missionary Positions.* University Press of Florida, 2011.

Whetzel, F. Randall. "A Man to Follow: Memories of China's Pioneer Missionary." *Alliance Life*, August 2008. https://legacy.cmalliance.org/alife/issue/2008-08/.

Wimbush, Vincent L. "Introduction: 'Everything about Me Was Magic': The Black-Fleshed and the Making and Management of Modernities." In *Masquerade: Scripturalizing Modernities through Black Flesh.* Edited by Vincent L. Wimbush. Lanham, MD: Lexington Books/Fortress Academic, 2023.

Wimbush, Vincent. "Introduction: TEXTureS, Gestures, Power: Orientation to Radical Excavation." Pp. 1–20 in *Theorizing Scriptures: New Critical Orientations to a Cultural Phenomenon.* Edited by Vincent Wimbush. *New Brunswick, NJ:* Rutgers University Press, 2008.

Smith, Sidonie, and Julia Watson, eds. *Reading Autobiography: A Guide for Interpreting Life Narratives.* Minneapolis: University of Minnesota Press, 2010.

Watson, Martha. *Lives of Their Own: Rhetorical Dimensions in Autobiographies of Women Activists.* University of South Carolina, 1999.

Chapter 7

Seeking Solace

Finding Hush Harbors for Healing Scripturalization Horrors

Velma E. Love

What exactly is *scripturalization horror* and where might hush harbors for healing be found? Here I offer a collage of reflections, a curated public narrative of my seeking and finding . . . glimpses of the past, ponderings and musings in the present, and imagined possibilities for the future. Scripturalization horror could be defined as what Wade Nobles refers to as an infected meme, a deeply embedded and engrained mode of thought that fuels a furtive attack at the level of psyche and soul wounding. The scripts are based on a particular value system and worldview that expresses itself in behaviors that devalue human life.

Vincent Wimbush uncovers the documentation of such in the Equino narrative, which he posits as a scriptural story, an epic story in which he can see his own life. In my reflective analysis of his intensely thought-provoking essay, I am inspired to examine some of the ways in which black people have constructed healing responses to scripturalization horrors. Starting with my own social location as a black woman in America, descendent of enslaved Africans from the original homelands now known as Mozambique, Guinea Bissau, and Sierra Leone (according to African Ancestry DNA testing), l have come to know that I live and work in haunted spaces.

I haven't always known this, but I have often felt some nagging feeling of discontent, some "troubling" in my soul, some undefined presence that compelled me to ask curious questions and search for answers in strange places. Perhaps this lingering presence is a "phantom narrative," a culture complex, a constellated force from the past showing up in the present, visible in plain sight and yet not perceived because it shapeshifts and masquerades, appearing as one thing and then another. I borrow the phrase "phantom narrative" from Samuel Kimbles, a Jungian psychologist who argues that "We are all acculturated through attitudes that are absorbed into our notions of self and other long before we are conscious of these attitudes as factors that have shaped the way we hold ourselves in the world . . . noting that some responses are just as powerful as gods in shaping a complex response that will last for generations."[1]

I became conscious of this haunting presence at a young age, growing up during the era of segregation in the rural south of the US, keenly aware of racial injustices, social suffering, and the ongoing struggles, strife, and strivings of my people. Like most young children growing up in the South in the 1950s and 1960s, my siblings and I played church and store and school. We learned to love the land, the Red Bank, the Sandy Field, the Mitch Hill, the springs, the creeks, the bottoms, the caves and canyons and woods of my grandfather's multi-acre farm. The places that I roamed all seemed so real, so alive to me, with unique personalities and distinctive characteristics. The cotton fields, potato patches, vegetable gardens, fruit trees and flower gardens that defined the land were my friends, as were the fireflies that fascinated me with their twinkling lights on warm summer nights.

So when did the phantom appear? I think it was always there, lurking in the background, moving in the shadows, creating culture complexes that crept into our spaces of play . . . the church, the school, the store. The phantom wore a mask. How was I to know? I was just a child. It was much later that I began to suspect its true identity, but early on I began to ask questions and now I know that even then I was seeking a fugitive space, a place of sanctuary, a place where I did not have to be on guard, where the color of my skin was not what dictated the opening and closing of doors in my comings and goings. Perhaps I was always seeking a "Hush Harbor for Healing."

Where do we, as people of African descent, find the origin story of "scripturalization horror"? Wimbush suggests, and I agree, that we start the gaze with the "first contact, between the West and the rest," the missionaries who played an integral role in the transatlantic slave trade and the far-reaching colonial project, those who taught our ancestors that their cultural practices were demonic and the only way to be "saved" was to disavow all that was African. There is little need to repeat this well- known story here. It is, in the words of Samuel Kimbles, a phantom narrative, an unseen contribution of culture to psyche, that shows up when and where it pleases, leaving fragmentation in its wake.

Its memetic infection has for generations impacted the lives of black people, like a curse that refused to go away, functioning as "psychological incarceration and epistemological entrapment," as black psychologist, Dr.

Wade Nobles argues. Wimbush refers to it as "white men's magic." He identifies five stages or themes around which Equino's Narrative is structured and builds his essay from those foundational blocks, including the following: Stage I: We are a nation of dancers, musicians, poets; Stage II: The white man had some spell or magic; Stage III: The book remained silent; Stage IV: The Ethiopian was Willing to be Saved by Jesus Christ; and Stage V: The Scriptures became an unsealed book of things that can never be told" (14–21).

Equino's Narrative and Wimbush's analysis of it makes clear the horrific script that drives slavery, oppression, colonialism, racism, and capitalism and the devastating outcomes for black racialized people. In my quest for healing responses, I turn to the work of Wade Nobles and other black liberation psychologists who are advocates for "the self-conscious centering of psychological analyses and applications in African realities, cultures, and epistemologies," focusing on the illumination of the human spirit.[2] With this framework in mind, I point to illuminating activity in three areas, including (1) New Mythmaking, (2) Immersive Ritual, and (3) Sankofa Practices, identifying some contemporary cultural responses by runagate interpreters who seek solace and I would argue "redemption" in a culture that is highly charged and racialized in multiple ways.

NEW MYTHMAKING

"Scripturalization horror" has for multiple generations kept black people "singing our dirges and our ditties" as "poor pilgrims of sorrow tossed in this wide world alone, with no hope for tomorrow, trying to make Heaven our home." This weighted narrative left its characters void of power, but there have always been the runagate interpreters who dared to find the cracks in the ground where counter narratives might find a space to emerge. It is to the runagate interpreters that I devote the bulk of this discussion. Runagate interpreters fashion themselves from different mythic matters as they seek solace from scripturalization horrors.

Constantly seeking spaces from which to maneuver, they are adept in operating within the energy matrix of "Esu, the Yoruba divinity that represents intersecting ideas and unlimited possibilities." Esu, the god who knows no boundaries, crossed the Atlantic, with full knowledge of the traumatic experience of enslavement and displacement from the African homeland. The violence, dehumanization, soul level fragmentation, intergenerational transmission of trauma, are all understood by Esu and he comes with healing powers. As noted by Toyin Falola, the redemptive powers of Esu are no less potent in the Diaspora than in the land of origin. Those who practice the cultural traditions of Ifa, affirm that "Invoking the powers of Esu offers an assurance that all has not been lost or forgotten, that by connecting with the powers of Esu within, one can remember, recreate, and birth oneself anew."[3] The Esu mythic magic is, then, an important aspect of seeking solace and finding healing from scripturalization horrors.

In fact, Esu could be described as the muse that re-scripts and shape shifts the victim narrative, suggesting that flipping the script is a tool for personal and cultural empowerment. For example, what if the story posits that "Esu allowed the transatlantic slave trade to happen in order to change the face of humanity and spread the genius of the black body throughout the world?" What a different lens this story might provide for the descendants of the enslaved Africans.

Here I offer Anita Kopacz's debut novel, *Shallow Waters*, as an example of counter narrative mythmaking in the order of Esu principles. In the author's note, Kopacz shares her inspiration for penning this novel. She describes this mythmaking endeavor as a fantasy tale of the African goddess Yemaya with healing powers, acknowledging that her own ancestral story and healing are wrapped in the mythmaking work. Yemaya's myth history fashions her as the nurturing mother, the one who accompanied the enslaved Africans during their long treacherous journey to the strange land, providing comfort and care during the passage and upon arrival. She is driven by a combination of love and wisdom, embodying the Ifa concept of *egbe*, a term with multiple meanings, but one of which is the "heart" of the group, the heart as the center of ancestral wisdoms and passions that sustained the uprooted and displaced Africans.[4]

I consider it an honor to have been invited to write the Foreword to *Shallow Waters*. As I summonsed the muse to come sit with me for the writing, my thoughts centered on the importance of mythmaking as healing strategy for the intergenerational transmission of psyche wounds, which I believe to be closely related to Wimbush's concept of scripturalization horrors. Also of relevance here, is the way in which Burton Mack's work on mythmaking and social formation highlights the Christian myth as problematic to the ideals of freedom and equality. Certainly, Mack and Wimbush are conversational partners and I have learned from the provocative and often perceived as "controversial" work of each. Burton suggests that "humans have always painted themselves into big picture of the world," pictures that we call myths.[5] Those "big pictures," those "myths" then are part of how humans imagine and construct societies and make meaning of life . . . even when the meaning making leads to the destruction of psyche, soul, and body.

But there is also the big picture painting, meaning making that seeks to heal, restore, and repair. Case in point is *Shallow Waters*, a fantasy novel, mythmaking project by Anita Kopacz, that is infused with all of the magic one could imagine as important for today's healing and recasting of mythic structures that have eroded beneath the feet of those who are descendants of displaced Africans. *Shallow Waters* speaks to those who seek a spiritual journey that does not center on "scripturalization horrors," but instead on enduring love and possibility.

It is the answer to *Black Imagination*, a curated collection of personal narratives and sayings expressed by marginalized persons who were asked to reflect on three questions: (1) What is your origin story? (2) How do you heal yourself? (3) How would you describe a place where you are loved completely? Natasha Marin organized a field research project that served as the basis of this collection of personal expressions after a devastating experience of the viral reaction to her "Reparations Project."[6]

The web-based project asked the descendants of enslaved Africans to discuss their feelings of harm and asked Euro Americans to offer a "reparations" response. The project demonstrated how difficult it is to successfully engage in the practice of "leveraging privilege" and likewise, I believe, the practice of healing *scripturalization* horrors. However, it also shows creative acts of self-healing. Consider, for example, Reagan Jackson's response to the question, "How do you heal yourself?"[7]

> First, I listen. This is hard when my feelings are screaming, when my body, my heart, the pieces of me are aching. . . . There is a guiding light that talks to me. (Jackson, 97)

Isn't this what we are all seeking, some relief from the screaming feelings, the anguish of the heart, some form of self-soothing, some light that will show the way beyond the horrors we witness through psyche and spirit?

> I don't know her name or even her language. Mostly she is a dream walker of pictures, sounds, and feelings and I awake knowing what is mine to do. (Jackson, 97)

Lucid dreaming, evening and morning deep meditation is, for some, a healing strategy. Ancestral communications, tapping the field of all knowing to draw forth from deep wells of wisdom is implied.

> Is she ancestor or unborn child, guardian angel, spirit guide, or interdimensional healing practitioner—I don't know. I just know that when I listen and I follow directions, healing happens. (Jackson, 97)

The focus on healing is the critical point and the point of unmasking the horrors of scripturalization, the power dynamics that continue to impose harm on those who have for generations been blind-sided by the phantom narratives that show up in the psycho-social political realms of existence:

At these times I feel most acutely the loss of my cultural traditions. We the children of the unchosen diaspora—the progeny of the stolen, the kidnapped, the shackled, the tortured, the enslaved, are in many ways still lost. Lost to our heart language, lost to our indigenous practices. We pray to white Jesus, god of colonizers, and wonder why our prayers aren't answered. (Jackson, 98)

This passage and the one that follows reflects a problematizing of the Christian myth and a hope for a repair of the breach, the estrangement from the African gods and their ways of being. The quest is to find the way forward. The fantasy novel, *Shallow Waters*, offers new mythmaking as an answer, the creation of a counter narrative to the scripturalization that has created fear and limitation.

. . . so long estranged, I can only listen and guess, make do with plastic cowrie shells and white fabric, pray in English and hope that there is something beyond my colonized words, that some part of me is still me enough to be heard and healed anyway. (Jackson, 98)

Web-based projects, such as Natasha Marin's *Reparations* and its sequel, *Black Imagination*, an audio installation, as well as Vincent Wimbush's *Masquerade Exhibit* are conceptual projects that break free of the "psyche incarceration and epistemological entrapment," as Dr. Wade Nobles would term it, that are embedded in the Christian myth/scriptures and profoundly impactful in social and cultural life.

These case studies of new mythmaking (Mack) fall within the thematic focus of Wimbush's Stage I, representative of the artists, the cultural creatives whose play was loaded with lived experience stories, active imagination, and epistemological agency for knowing and acknowledging what counts as knowledge.

Both Antia Kopach's fantasy novel, *Shallow Waters*, and Natasha Marin's curated collection of marginalized voices, *Black Imagination*, are representative of what is presented in Stage I, a nation of dancers, musicians, poets, those who represent sociocultural dynamics in creative form. These authors take epistemic control as they channel creative energies into new life forms.

Immersive Ritual

The second area that I want to direct attention to in the quest for solace is "immersive ritual." The Hush Harbor Lab, a dramaturg workshop and community space for creatives, provides a case study in play building as immersive ritual design. "Hush Harbor Lab is a brave space for the development and production of new and innovative digital, live, and multimedia performance work by Black Atlanta based artists. Hush Harbor strives to be a space that promotes wellness, self-care and the sacred within the Black arts community with the recognition that caring for the full person (body, mind, spirit) encourages better art" (www.hushharborlab.com).

Cassie's Ballad, an immersive ritual/play written by Addaé Moon and produced by the Hush Harbor Lab, is based on the documented stories of Atlanta's "missing and murdered children," the traumatic occurrences during the mid-1980s in Atlanta, Georgia of the Southeastern United States. *Cassie's Ballad* as immersive ritual is "play," participatory, interactive, multisensory and often designed for cultural healing and social awareness.

The play/ritual invites its collaborative audience to enter an outdoor space and join the search for missing body parts (symbolically represented by scraps of paper) as Cassie, a young girl, silenced by her traumatic experiences also seeks to find her voice. A plague has ravished the land and, in its wake, has left a landscape littered with infected body parts. The charge is to "reassemble the pieces" to make the damaged body whole. The possible metaphorical and symbolic interpretations are extensive. What if one were to interpret the "plague" as capitalism, oppression, or racism and the missing body parts as the people of African descent, dispersed throughout the Diaspora? What if the plague were interpreted as "scripturalization," to use Vincent Wimbush's term, or "epistemological entrapment" to use Wade Nobles' term? Either way, the quest at hand is that of cultural repair.

An audience participating in immersive ritual/ play is engaging a different sort of textual field, another space of consciousness, one in which time is not linear and symbolic meanings morph into emotional realities, evoking promises and possibilities for the emergence of new speech, and unmuffled voices. The characters speak in plain language. . . .

> We don't know anything for sure,
> > But it's effecting our children in ways we never anticipated
> > > Our neighbor's little girl, Cassie, . . .
> > > Hasn't spoken a word in months . . .
> > And I think its shock . . . These kids grow up in the middle of a plague
> > > And they are vulnerable to contamination,
> > > Based on the color of their skin
> > > And where they live . . . (Moon)

As the ritual play progresses, the scene changes to that of a graveyard. The characters are directed to form a circle and share what they have found. The names of the dead are spoken, their ages, how they died, when they died.

They were all young, between the ages of 7 and 31. This roll call of Atlanta's missing, and murdered children is interspersed with epithets from well-known literary artists.

These words are powerful and evocative, noting that . . .

"People are trapped in history and history is trapped in them."—
James Baldwin

After having collected shards of memory and verse, one of the main characters announces:

I think we have enough . . .
It might not cure the plague,
But they will make the body whole
so that the healing can begin.
Maybe it's what Cassie needs?
Truth.
A balm to heal the voiceless. (Moon)[8]

With this the ritual moves into its final scene with talk of spirits, bottle trees, ancestors, safe harbors and healing balms, with a very potent line, "the land is the plague and the killings will not stop until the terrain changes." *Cassie's Ballad* is an example of designing immersive ritual, based on archival research, in service to an evolution in collective consciousness. Indeed, "we are a nation of poets, dancers, singers and artists" whose creative genius unleashes itself in service to the people and the conscious efforts to alter the terrain that produces the plague that hurts, harms, fragments, and destroys the people. Confronting cultural harms through "truth telling" in the form of immersive ritual is one means of seeking solace from scripturalization horrors experienced by the black-bodied person. Immersive ritual is cultural play that creates an experiential context through intentional design, which in many ways can derail the power of phantom narratives and scripturalization harms.

As described above, Addae Moon's ritual play, *Cassie's Ballad*, meets the criteria of radical ritual, as defined by Malidoma Somé, who reminds us that there are two parts to ritual, one part is planned, and the other part is what happens when the people who are included in the ritual space collectively engage their spirit energies. Something of an effervescence bubbles up with the power to heal and repair a fractured or broken spirit. Somé calls radical ritual a dramatic interaction with Spirit, one of the most ancient and most effective ways of building human community. In his words:

The ritual will push out the energy that is keeping the person trapped and will open a new space to fill with appropriate energy. This ritual must be done in community. (Somé, 154)

This is what happens in *Cassie's Ballad*. The people are summoned to action that involves gathering "shards of memory and verse," for an act of healing and recovery.

Ultimately, the young child, Cassie, recovers her voice. The ritual journey has been successful. Why ritual? Malidoma Somé argues that ritual is an activity for change, that some problems cannot be solved without the intervention of Spirit and the release of tensions "from which words alone can not release us" (Somé 154).

Immersive ritual is an important radical ritual strategy for survival, repair and healing. Somé also refers to other types of ritual, known as maintenance rituals, designed to restore the psyche in the face of everyday wear and tear of human interaction, especially for those in the healing arts and helping professions. Ritual encapsulates the blues song of black-bodied people and the need for maintenance ritual. Seems that we are always "running" to get away from, distance ourselves from scripturalization horrors.

Several years ago, I participated in a radical ritual as part of a training program with Malidoma Somé. Our cohort included a diverse group of seven or eight trainees in the year-long Dagara Medicine Wheel Diviner's Practitioner Training, held at a retreat house in the mountains near Asheville, NC. During our final weekend session, we were informed that the agenda included an Earth ritual that required a burial. Together the group dug four shallow graves, just deep enough and long enough for a tall person to lie down in and be covered with dirt from the neck down to the feet. Just the thought was unsettling for me.

I imagined that the grave could include bugs, ants, and all sorts of critters crawling over me. I told myself that if I had known this I never would have signed up for the training, but since I was here, I might as well settle my mind and make the best of it. So, I dressed in a jogging suit, lined my grave with towels and climbed in. My team members carefully covered me with dirt and told me that the attendant would be close by and I could call for help when I was ready to come out. By this time, it was night, and the only light was that of the fire burning brightly a little ways off. I had decided that I would stay in the grave a respectable amount of time, which I imagined would be about five minutes, or maybe seven at most. I closed my eyes and began a meditation breathing exercise.

To my surprise my body began to relax, and I drifted into another level of consciousness. I felt held by the earth in a way that I never could have imagined. I lost track of time and was summoned back to my physical space when my body signaled me with a kind of numbing sensation. I called for the attendant to come and "unearth" me. They helped me climb out and supported me as I walked to the fire and quietly took my seat among the others who were part of this ritual group. I could not then and cannot now describe how I felt. It was some deep soulful level of comfort, ease, release, and restoration.

That night I slept well and entered a space of lucid dreaming. I received information about the pending demise of a business venture in which I was involved. I shared the dream in our mourning debriefing. My teacher/mentor, Malidoma Somé said that the ancestors were giving me a warning in my dream of what would happen if things continued as they were. He said the burial ritual had opened up my receptive channels and allowed me to receive this information. The demise of the business was unfolding, even as I was dreaming. The dream was accurate. The whole experience was incredibly amazing, teaching me in an experiential way the power of immersive ritual.

Malidoma is now among the land of the ancestors, but he devoted his life to teaching the strangers of the West, the indigenous wisdoms of the African people. He embodied the essence of the Sankofa practice of bringing forward the goodness of the past so that it might inform new cycles of life and living. Every time I sit down with my divining cloth, I think of him and express gratitude that his teachings are still alive. I now turn to a fuller discussion of Sankofa practices.

Sankofa Practices

The term "Sankofa" became popular in the mid-1990s following the release of the independent film, *Sankofa*, by Haile Gerima, author and director. Iconic images of the Sankofa bird with its feet facing forward and its head tilted in a backward glance became a popular cultural symbol for gathering the goodness of the past to propel a flight into the future. The emphasis on turning to ancestral wisdoms to source healing medicines is an important Sankofa practice. *Cassie's Ballad* as a community healing ritual gave a prominent role to the ancestors. The following story, from the sacred texts of Ifa, the Holy Odu, also highlights the role of ancestral wisdoms in African indigenous cultural traditions. This is an oral tale that was passed on to me by an initiated priest of Ifa:[9]

> *Aworonke was the beloved wife of Orunmila. They had been happily married for years, but had no children, which made them sad. This is what prompted Orunmila to go and consult a diviner to see what could be done.*

The diviner told Orunmila to do something that had never been done before on Earth. . . . That was to fashion an ancestral costume and icon and to hold an annual festival in honor of the ancestors.

Since nothing like this had been done on Earth, Orunmila had to visit the ancestral society in the heavens to get instructions.

He did that. And came back with a set of instructions which he followed. He made the costume and consecrated it, performed all of the prescribed rituals and arranged for the Masquerade to dance around the town. The dancer prayed for Aworonke and a year later she gave birth to a beautiful daughter who was named Awodola. Awodola was the joy of her family. She grew up to be both beautiful and wise. She remembered the masquerade and honored her ancestors at the Annual Festival.

Awodola got married and gave birth to a daughter, Egunbola, who was as beautiful as her mother. She was brilliant and good nature, but she did not believe in the old ways. She refused to embrace the lineage of the ancestral Masquerade. She found other people's ancestral traditions more attractive.

Before long, all of the good in her life collapsed. Her health deteriorated. Her money disappeared. Things got so bad that Egunbola decided to go see a diviner to consult Ifa.

Ifa said her troubles came from abandoning her ancestral traditions . . . that the only solution to her problems was to return to the ways of her ancestors . . . to ensure that the masquerade costume was repaired and maintained and the Annual Festival was held.

Egunbola listened to this advice. She performed all of the prescribed rituals, repaired the Egun Masquerade and organized the Annual Festival. Her health began to improve and her fortune was restored. She became a great guide for others. She was known near and far as an advocate for ancestral memory. Teaching the people to never, ever abandon their ancestral traditions.

I share this story because it is the story of many black-fleshed bodies who now seek out the road of return to ancestral ways. As descendants of enslaved Africans, we carry in our DNA ancestral wisdoms that were demonized by the oppressive forces and *scripturalization* horrors that incarcerated the minds of our people. So long disconnected from their ancestral knowledge systems and the rituals of access, many seek answers outside of themselves.

The journey to freedom and the decolonization of the mind has been long and arduous, but one need only to visit the exhibits of the National Museum of African American History and Culture in Washington, DC, or search the annuals of history to realize that there have been torchbearers along the way who have carried the light in the darkest hours. Some of those were high-lighted in the Masquerade exhibition. Their words are sacred utterances that ignite black passion, love, and imagination. Like the legendary Egungun masquerade dancers they are the conduits of psycho-social healing.

This story of the Egun dancers is a reminder that black genius is often obscured by the suffering and sorrows, the social pestilence and plagues that continue to cover the land, but the healing antidote can be found beneath the mask. I use the term "masquerade" here in contrast to Wimbush's con-cept of masquerade and the power dynamics of scripturalization. The Egun represents an excavation of the healing wisdom power embedded in one's ancestral lineage.

A historical cultural tradition, the Egun Masquerade Festivals continue to be a part of ancestral reverence practices in Nigeria as well as other locations throughout the African Diaspora. The masked dancers emerging from the sacred igbodou (forest), completely covered from head to toe by their swirl-ing multicolored costumes generate an air of mysticism and awe. I recall my experience at an Egun Festival at Oyotunji African Village in SC. It was a celebratory, high energy ritual event that seemed to be part theatrical and part spiritual, but totally engaging as a small crowd of 50 or so participants cheered and followed the dancers about the village. The masquerade danc-ers may represent lineage ancestors or cultural ancestors, depending on who organizes and sponsors the festival. Regardless, the intent is to bring healing energy that redefines the spiritual, moral and cultural priorities of the com-munity. Ancestral spirits are consulted for guidance, protection and wisdom for everyday life concerns.

As explained by Griffith and Griffith, this dramatic communal ritual func-tions as a cultural philosophy that is beneficial to the well-being of the com-munity, serving as a reminder that appeals can be made to one's ancestors for help in everyday life.[10] Traditionally, the masked dancer emerges from the forest, blesses the towns folk, and recedes into the forest without leaving a trace of his human existence. Creating a sense of awe and mystery, it could be said that the Egungun Masquerade Festival functions in a way that is consis-tent with the "broaden and build" theory of positive psychology. This theory posits that the experience of positive emotions such as interest, joy, awe, love, and belonging broadens one's awareness and provides an emotional baseline that is conducive to hope, creativity and possibility thinking that leads to a more expansive thought-action repertoire leading to a range of health enhanc-ing behaviors.[11]

The broaden and build theory has interesting implications for countering the impact of scripturalization horrors. Consider for example, the traditional black church experience of "getting happy," tapping into a reservoir of ecstatic spiritual power and vibrational energy that elicits a therapeutic emotive response. "Getting happy" is not unlike the somatic exercises suggested by Resmaa Menakem in his book, *My Grandmother's Hands: Racialized Trauma and the Pathways to Healing Our Hearts and Bodies*, Menakem argues for bodied-centered practices like singing, humming, chanting, movement, to metabolize the trauma that the black body has stored for generations. He calls his approach "somatic abolitionism," and defines it as a resourcing of energies that live in the body, arguing that our (black) existence is permeated by white bodied supremacy and that we must be intentional abut practices that decolonize the mind by releasing the aftermath of trauma stored in the body. In the opening pages of his book, Resmaa acknowledges the ancestors with these words, "Our bodies exist in the present. To your thinking brain, there is past, present, and future, but to your traumatized body there is only *now*. That *now* is the home of intense survival energy."[12] His far-reaching global educational program trains people to temper body, mind and soul by re-membering, re-storing, and re-covering the wisdom of the body.

This conversation on the Sankofa practice of remembering and recovering would not be complete without bringing Ayi Kwei Armah into the conversation. Armah, a Ghanaian novelist and essayist based in Popenguine, Senegal, is a prolific writer who devotes his tine, energy, and attention to advocating for the embrace of Africa's philosophical and cultural values as the "surest path to a regenerative future." In his collection of essays, *Remembering the Dismembered Continent*, Armah issues a stern rebuke and a strong challenge to African intellectuals:

> So disoriented African intellectuals adopt alien gods, myths, thought systems and ideals thinking they can make them their own, believing they will work for them. What such disoriented African intellectuals do not know is that Africa possesses its own ideal projections and they cover the entire range of human possibility. . . . Intellectually disoriented Africans, in their inertia, remain ignorant of the fact that the ideational resources required in war and peace, reaction and revolution, stagnation and dynamic growth, are in fact present in the original lodes of African culture and history, awaiting only rediscovery and reuse by thinking Africans.[13]

Sankofa practices, then, must surely be a part of the treatment plan for healing scripturalization horrors. Armah reminds us that the human consciousness creates its myths, its gods, and spirits or projects itself as such for a purpose, that purpose being the development of itself. When reference points are stripped away, as in colonization and enslavement, the colonized mind becomes hostile to its own reference points, its own balm for soul level healing. In this essay, I have argued that a narrative counter to the masquerade of western scripturalization horror can be constructed though three practices, including (1) new mythmaking, (2) immersive ritual, and (3) Sankofa practices. In these ways, I suggest, folk of African descent are known for seeking solace and finding hush harbors for healing.

Ashé!

NOTES

1. Samuel Kimbles, *Phantom Narratives: The Unseen Contributions of Culture to the Psyche* (New York: Rowman & Littlefield, 2014).

2. Wade W. Nobles, *The Island of Memes: Haiti's Unfinished Revolution* (Baltimore: Black Classic Press, 2015), 33.

3. Toyin Falola, "Esu: The God without Boundaries," in *ESU: Yoruba God, Power, and the Imaginative Frontiers*, ed. Toyin Falola (Durham: Carolina Academic Press, 2013), 3–36.

4. Anita Kopacz, *Shallow Waters: A Novel* (New York: Simon & Schuster, 2021).

5. Burton L. Mack, *The Rise and Fall of The Christian Myth: Restoring Our Democratic Ideals* (New Haven: Yale University Press, 2017).

6. Natasha Marin, curator, *Black Imagination* (San Francisco: McSweeney's, 2020), 9–12.

7. Reagan Jackson in *Black Imagination*, ed. Natasha Marin (San Francisco: McSweeney's, 2020) 97.

8. Addae Moon, author of *Cassie's Ballad*, is co-founder of the Hush Harbor Lab, a play development company and workshop space that supports innovative, multimedia performance work by Atlanta based Black artists. In May 2022, I was invited to serve on a virtual panel to discuss *Cassie's Ballad* and the significance of immersive ritual as a community healing art. The excerpts above are from the unpublished script used as the basis for the panel discussion.

9. This tale was shared with me verbally by a Babalawo in Atlanta, GA, in 2022. I have never seen it in print but have referred to it myself in other written material.

10. Griffiths, David, and D. Griffiths. *Touch and the Masquerades of Nigeria: The Masquerades of Nigeria and Touch*, Taylor & Francis Group, 1998, *ProQuest Ebook Central*, http://ebookcentral.proquest.com/lib/atlunivctr/detail.action?docID=238704. Created from atlunivctr on 2022-06-28 15:06:55.

11. Fredrickson, Barbara L. "What Good Are Positive Emotions?" *Review of General Psychology* 2, no. 3 (198): 300–319.

12. Resmaa Menakem, *My Grandmother's Hands: Racialized Trauma and the Pathway to Mending Our Hearts and Bodies* (Las Vegas: Central Recovery Press, 2017), xv.

13. Ayi Kwei Armah, *Remembering the Dismembered Continent: Seedtime Essays* (Popenguine, Senegal: Per Ankh, 2010), 71.

BIBLIOGRAPHY

Armah, Ayi Kwei. 2010. *Remembering the Dismembered Continent: Seedtime Essays.* Senegal: Per Ankh.

Falola, Toyin. 2013. *Esu: Yoruba God, Power and the Imaginative Frontiers.* North Carolina: Carolina Academic Press.

Frederickson, Barbara L. 1998. "What Good Are Positive Emotions?" *Review of General Psychology* 2 (no. 3), 300–319.

Kimbles, Samuel. 2014. *Phantom Narratives: The Unseen Contributions of Culture to Psyche.* New York: Rowman & Littlefield.

Kopacz, Anita. 2021. *Shallow Waters: A Novel.* New York: Simon & Shuster.

Mack, Burton L. 2017. *The Rise and Fall of the Christian Myth: Restoring Our Democratic Ideals.* New Haven: Yale University Press.

Marin, Natasha, curator. 2020. *Black Imagination.* San Francisco: McSweeney's.

Menakem, Resmaa. 2017. *My Grandmother's Hands: Racialized Trauma and the Pathways to Mending Our Hearts and Bodies.* Las Vegas: Central Recovery Press.

Moon, Addae. 2022. *Cassie's Ballad.* Unpublished Script Panel Discussion. Hush Harbor Lab. Atlanta, Georgia.

Nobles, Wade W. 2015. *The Island of Memes: Haiti's Unfinished Revolution.* Baltimore: Black Classic Press.

Somé, Malidoma. 1998. *The Healing Wisdom of Africa: Finding Life Purpose, through Nature, Ritual, and Community.* New York: Penguin Putnam.

Wimbush, Vincent L. 2021. "'Everything about Me Was Magic': The Black-Fleshed and the Making and Management of Modernities." Masquerade Virtual/Digital Exhibition Lecture. Pitts Library Candler School of Theology, Emory University and The Institute for Signifying Scriptures.

Chapter 8

Toni Morrison and the Masquerade of Black Oral Imprint with a Meditation on the Preparation of Soft-Boiled Eggs

Miles P. Grier

MASQUERADE, ALIENATION, MALDISTRIBUTION

In his opening address, revised as the Introduction for this book, Vincent Wimbush convened a Symposium to discuss culture-as-play, a *masquerade* that entails "the necessarily layered and indirect ways that humans and other living creatures communicate with one another and negotiate their shared space, including the psychosocial and political environments" (Introduction, 5).[1] In suggesting that masquerade is essential to sociality, Wimbush exhorted the speakers and audience to take critical stock of the sideshow of modernity and to foster "underground" counter-formations to the repeated enactment of vulnerability for some and enjoyment for others (16).[2] To his invocation of Blue Magic's opus "Sideshow," the DJ in me wants to respond with that haunting bossa nova, "This Masquerade" (George Benson's recording): "Are we really happy here with this lonely game we play / looking for words to say? / Searching but not finding understanding anyway / We're lost in this masquerade" (Blue Magic 1974; Benson 1976). Wimbush's harmonic architecture transposes Leon Russell's melody and lyric from a lament about a couple's dissolution to a broader social dilemma—masks seem at once a facilitator of social life and the greatest impediment to mutual care.

John Guare dramatizes the dilemma in *Six Degrees of Separation* when Ouisa Kittridge, the jet-setting wife of a Manhattan art dealer, finds herself unable to rescue Paul, a young man who is perhaps her social opposite: a black, gay grifter with no home. Recognizing both their surprisingly sincere connection and the similarity of their façades, Ouisa agrees to be Paul's patron but finds she cannot halt state intervention that she and her social circle initiated the police apprehend a con artist who stole nothing from his marks. Spurred by regret, she seeks Paul by providing the police and courts the false surnames he gave her, but they cannot locate him. She shares the state's response in a direct address to the audience: "We weren't family. We didn't know Paul's name" (Guare 1992, 61). Ouisa Kittredge sings a variation of the blues—*nobody knows my name*, as James Baldwin would write—when she discovers a double bind: the socially outcast must misrepresent himself to enter a severely restricted circle of care, but this very misrepresentation makes it impossible for him to be known and (thus) cared for in his own person. *Are* we really happy, lost in this masquerade?

One could assume, from the consumption of antidepressants and the abuse of other pain-numbing substances, a keen awareness of being unknown and uncared for. Yet, the diagnostic tools normative socialization provides impede *striking through the mask* that Herman Melville associated with socially approved misrepresentations (Renker 1997). To the extent that masquerade stimulates substitutions and affiliations, it potentially offers the capacity to enlarge the circle of care. However, masking can also serve to impose charged social distinctions, reproducing some imagined connections while frustrating others. Think of the fraught boundaries of kin, gender, nation, faith, race, species—the conditional protections and acute vulnerabilities that attend being cast in these categories. The masquerade of culture divides the world into like and unlike so that a social group can recognize who or what is entitled to care.

The psychoanalytic philosopher Slavoj Žižek argues that a socialized person's access to reality becomes distorted by the ideological frame supplied by culture: "The function of ideology," he writes, "is not to offer us a point of escape from our reality but to offer us the social reality itself as an escape" from "'antagonism': a traumatic social division that cannot be symbolized" (see Žižek 1989, 45).[3] To the extent that capitalist modernity cuts (even those whom it also benefits), the goring, amputation, and alienation must be rendered nonexistent. In this sense, the masquerade requires epistemic injustices: unequal distribution of credibility and suppression of terminology that might prove revelatory (Fricker 2009). Injury and loss must never have occurred, must be beyond assignation, and (thus, most important) beyond redress. The limits of officially accepted discourse force many to go about in the drag of the unhurt masquerade turns malicious.

Striking through this veil would seem to require a double action: both identifying the misnaming and redressing the economy of subordination and deprivation. This project is not so easy as it might seem. For, what I am describing is not an escape from naming. In this context, a refusal to name is an evasive maneuver, designed to make it impossible to identify and assess those injuries a social order intends to leave unrepaired. Rather, I am talking about a difficult and ongoing task of inquiry and renegotiation—rewriting as an ongoing process of better approximation, given that recognition and distribution must be responsive to changes both in self-knowledge and in historical circumstance. The potential to rename and the ethics of both self-declaration and of critical listening must be rigorous. If all human declarations are provisional and temporal and all understandings asymptotes merely *approaching* total comprehension, then the conversation must be open-ended, continuous, recursive—the pursuit of a question, rather than the location of an immutable answer. As novelist Milan Kundera has it: "love is a continual interrogation." Kundera does not mean the terror of the police interrogation but a lover's endless fascination in which eager listening does not satiate but generates the desire for further elaboration—with attention to change.

INK AND THE ALCHEMY OF RACIALIZATION

Watts, Los Angeles exploded in 1965 after an all-too-common incident of police brutality. Dr. Martin Luther King responded, famously, that a riot is the language of the unheard. People racialized as black appear in Vincent Wimbush's introduction as a paradigmatic case for the unhearing that sustains epistemic injustice. For Africans dispersed into slave societies of the Atlantic world, he traces the discredited voice to a decisive shift in the context and consequences of masquerade.

In their African context, "a cult of masking" enabled sociality, including "basic communication" as well as "structuring of and orientation to the world" (6). Masking indicated a complex conception of the mediation of reality and careful selection of priests and oracles to oversee it.[4] Transshipped Africans were immersed in a world in which the forms of "African writing and graphic systems, individual signs and sign complexes, remnants of Arabic literacy and Muslim magic, . . . contexts of use and learning, and ideologies of inscription"—in short, a whole repertoire of mediations, including the written—were subordinated to the scriptural (Gundaker 1998, 33). Europeans attempted to monopolize this sphere of representation, in overseeing the selection of sacred and civic scriptures, as well as protocols of proper interpretation (Wimbush 2013, 11–13).

In the Introduction, Wimbush argues that the flesh of African persons—christened as black—becomes an object for European exegesis (4). The etymology of this blackness reveals how flesh could be translated into reading material. Modern English inherits the word black from Middle Dutch, Old Saxon, Middle Low German, and Old High German, in which *blac* or *blah* was "the colour of ink" ("Black, Adj. and n." 2022). The tie to racial blackness is not subtle. In fact, physicians of the day suspected that black Africans' color was the result of a kind of alchemy, darkening an originally lighter epidermis. They speculated that pale-skinned moors may have become negroes through an "atramentous condition," a chemical reaction of elements akin to that which produced "atramentum," that Latin word for dark writing ink ("Atramentous, Adj." 2020).

Perhaps the beginning of racial masquerade in European modernity was ink. Taking my cue from early modern English stage plays in which racial blackness is the consequence of a coating of ink, I view stage blackface as specifically *inkface*—a crucial cultural mechanism for translating tribal markings and tattoos (of indigenous Africans or Americans) into objects made for Europeans' assessments (Grier 2015).[5] The subjection of African sign systems—whether oral, gestural, or inscribed—to European hermeneutics was a momentous cultural translation. The outpouring of Eurocentric knowledges—from pens and presses and now in the digital era—comprises an avalanche we have yet to dig from underneath. But what can be done to overthrow what Wimbush calls "white men's semiosphere or epistemic regime for the mediatization of knowledge" (10)? The question is not an idle one, as that epistemic regime aims to determine economic value, justice, security, enjoyment, and future advantage.[6]

At home or in diaspora, conquered Africans have been wrenched into a signifying system not of our own making—one in which our Gods, symbols, kin systems, and memory are not exactly overthrown but translated and overwritten. In the masterpiece *Beloved*, Toni Morrison dramatizes this deep and consequential resignification. Sethe, the novel's protagonist, is tasked with making ink for the plantation's superintendent, Schoolteacher. Living as a free woman in Cincinnati, she tells the daughter she delivered while fleeing slavery in Kentucky:

> He liked the ink I made. It was [the plantation mistress's] recipe, but he preferred how I mixed it and it was important to him because at night he sat down to write in his book. It was a book about [the enslaved people on the plantation] but we didn't know that right away. We just thought it was his manner to ask us questions. (Morrison 1987, 37)

In the last decades of chattel slavery in the United States, Sethe confronts the alphabetical component of white epistemological authority in a cruel irony: the enslaved woman must make the very ink that the white Schoolteacher uses to teach his pupils to write her "human characteristics on the left [side of the page]; her animal ones on the right" (Morrison 1987, 193). Schoolteacher perversely converts her labor, knowledge, and speech—and those of the other captive Africans—into the signs of his education and civilization. Indeed, as critic Anne Goldman argues, his sense of himself as slave-master has its foundation in his writerly skill (Goldman 1990, 325).

For Morrison, the remedy for the descendants of overwritten Black captives is not simply to obtain literary skill and masterfully write our own story. She communicated as much in *Song of Solomon* (1977), when narrating how the Dead family at its center came by their unusual surname. In her hands, the Dead name is not as the Nation of Islam once preached—a slave name imposed by the white master. Rather, it results from a would-be white liberator: a drunken Union soldier who misplaces a Black *freedman*'s words on a government form. For this allegorical Black family, (white) textual imposition is inevitable, even in the midst of Jubilee. Constituted by the overwriting of inkface, New World Africans cannot return to the status of *tabula rasa*. The bearers of dead names *can* pursue and solicit continual reinventions, as at the end of *Jazz*, "say, make me, remake me. You are free to do it and I am free to let you" (Morrison 1993, 229). They can find in this surrender the possibility for transcendence, as at the end of *Song of Solomon*: "For now [the hero, Milkman] knew what Shalimar knew: If you surrendered to the air, you could *ride* it" (Morrison 1977, 337).

MAKE(-)UP THE BLACK SELF IN PRINT: MORRISON'S THEORY OF THE NOVEL

In *Song*, protagonist's Aunt Pilate is the organic theorist of this capacity to invent and reinvent the self in dialectic relationship with the world. Her birth is a mystery: she brings herself forth from her dead mother's womb without the aid of amniotic fluid or muscular exertion. This apparent self-manufacture has two signs: Pilate has no navel to indicate that she was ever dependent on another and wears no make-up (having made herself up!). Yet, she does not simply revel in the splendid, Cartesian isolation this self-creation might suggest. Instead, she forges an artificial umbilical cord that supplies her adult ear with the sound of her father's written word. He selects Pilate's name blindly from the Bible, his grieving curse against the God who failed to save his wife during childbirth:

> He chose a group of letters that seemed to him strong and handsome; saw in them a large figure that looked like a tree hanging in some princely but protective way over a row of smaller trees. He had copied the group of letters out on a piece of brown paper; copied, as illiterate people do, every curlicue, arch, and bend in the letters, and presented it to the midwife. (Morrison 1977, 18)

The literate midwife attempts to burn the name of "Christ-killing Pilate," but Macon inserts it in the Bible. When she sets off on her life's journey, Pilate takes this lone word her illiterate father ever wrote and hangs it from an earring she fashions from her mother's snuffbox.

Morrison never offers a direct exegesis of this homemade jewelry. I can attest that it has continually revealed itself to this reader over two decades. I understand it, now, as a miraculous relay system: Holy Scripture becomes paternal note. A biblical passage becomes a pinch of snuff. The mother chews the father's word and magically expresses it in the daughter's ear. In converting inscription to speech, Morrison confronts a problem as old as Greek philosophy—the written text's alleged deficiency when compared to the responsive voice of the living person (Middleton 1995, 19–20). At the same time, she also enters an intra-Protestant controversy over the dead letter of the Biblical text—a struggle at the heart of sectarian battles among early modern Britons, including those who colonized North America. Since England's monarch was also the head of the Anglican church, theological statements and legal proclamations had a similar force and purpose, especially in the far-flung provinces. As they wanted Church doctrine to have the solidity of law, Anglican priests rarely extemporized in their sermons. Textual fixity was intended to guarantee in Britain and the empire "a stable social order protected from the volatility of more immediate spiritual experience" (Gustafson 2000, 16).

Meanwhile, Puritan and subsequent dissenters "identified a minister's ceremonial reading of text . . . as a sign of spiritual deadness" preferring "a semispontaneous oral performance that permitted the preacher's [inspired and improvised] response to his immediate setting" (Gustafson 2000, 17). *Say, make me, remake me . . .* This dissident theological orientation is crucial to Morrison's vision of a repaired relationship between scriptures and society. Pilate's earring is figure for print with its voice restored—Morrison's wish that readers reincorporate a vaunted and impersonal medium into the social repertoire. There is no possibility of *un*doing a masculinist, Eurocentric overwriting—that of the King James who commissioned this authoritative English translation of the Bible and pursued both colonial settlement in North America and absolute power for the king. But, in turning the absolutist monarch's text into maternal snuff, Morrison aims for a transfiguration that would restore masculinist text's capacity for aural inspiration.[7]

I want to focus attention on the theological dimension of Morrison's literary technique. I mean to unite two conversations that often proceed on separate tracks: the one about Morrison's religious thinking; the other concerning her insistence that an oral component is essential to Black literature. The outstanding collection *Toni Morrison: Goodness and the Literary Imagination* introduces Morrison's corpus as a liturgy involving flight, pain, repentance, and endurance (Morrison 2019, 1). The authors gathered in this collection are unconcerned with the history, conventions, or material form of the novel, Morrison's primary medium. Consequently, their essays treat readers' immediate emotional engagement with Morrison's best work as more or less unmediated experience. I accept that not everyone is interested in the techniques that create this sense of present and pressing reality. Yet, Morrison was not a preacher, and public ritual was not the primary mode of interacting with her novels. Therefore, a literary scholar—or, indeed, anyone concerned with media and the production of truth—might remain curious about whether and how her stylistic choices transform a printed text typically read alone and in silence into what some readers experience as a communal ritual.

If attention to literary technique is absent from scholarship that foregrounds religion and ritual, theology and religious ceremony would seem to be the missing components in secularized literary analysis, such as Madhu Dubey's magisterial study of the motif of the "book within a book" in postmodern African American literature.[8] In *Signs and Cities: Black Literary Postmodernism*, Dubey argues that Morrison evinces a distrust of the print medium, ironic for a prolific editor and best-selling novelist. In Dubey's assessment, Morrison's novels elevate rural folks and their oral culture. Thus, she concludes that Morrison's corpus, though formally innovative, constitutes a dead-end when it comes to imagining a *future* for a largely urbanized Black population in the US.

Dubey levies this judgment after demonstrating that Morrison's early essays romanticize and essentialize (Southern) black community. Dubey then reads novels such as *Song of Solomon* and *Jazz* as examples of aesthetic principles dictated in the essays. Yet, it seems a generic error to read the fiction as exempla of a dogma set out in the essays.[9] After all, if the etymology of essay is in the French for trial, experiment, would it not be more fitting to consider Morrison's novels a test of the principles the essays articulate, an ongoing experiment with both the form and the propositions in the essays? An analysis of fleeting glances at printed objects in the novels demonstrates the fruitfulness of this method.

Consider what initially appears to be a frivolous detail about Pilate: Morrison writes that Pilate's blueberry-colored lips looked "as if she had on lipstick but blotted away the shine on a scrap on newspaper" (Morrison 1977, 30). Here is an emblem for print and orality occupying the same ground, even in dialogue with each other. Morrison imagines a woman whose mouth could leave its imprint on the supposedly impersonal and objective medium of the print newspaper, which so often serves (explicitly or implicitly) as an organ upholding the unequal commercial and sexual relations of racial capitalism. Dubey might point to this text as doubly desecrated—ripped apart and marred. I grant that, but pursue a more reparative analysis: namely, a rapprochement between media that should never have been split into a hierarchy. As with Pilate's earring, the figure of lipstick on newsprint can be seen as the products of the press and the mouth occupying the same plane.

If Morrison appears to err in some of her artistic manifestos in elevating and reifying a rural or African communal past, I think it bears remembering what she attempted to confront: a social structure in which the subordination of Black people to the magic of the Eurocentric book had not been overcome but also could not simply be wished away. In the wake of slavery, diaspora, and colonialism, the Black person could not simply retreat to an atavistic past but would have to learn to deploy the mediations of urbanized modernity without being enthralled to them.

Morrison does not object to print, mediation, masquerade. Rather, she objects to the *supremacy* of print, its elevation above other mediators. In the scriptural regime of the West, text is supreme—beyond human appeal. With his Jesuit training perhaps showing, Walter Ong describes the written—what Wimbush would call the scriptural—as transcendent, antisocial, unanswerable: "There is no way directly to refute a text. After absolutely total and devastating refutation, it says exactly the same thing as before" (Ong 1991, 79). Perhaps the most useful part of Morrison's project now is her attempt to return text (and with it, European authority over signification) to sociality.

In this sense, Morrison's quest for a speaking text is not a rejection of her medium at all but an attempt to bring this great technology back into social intercourse. Dubey is undoubtedly correct that to take print down from its perch in fiction does not redress social inequalities in the world beyond the novels. However, it might serve to make readers aware of them, to stimulate the imagination for how to bring about this equal standing in other realms than that of fiction. If Barbara and Karen Fields are correct that race comes into material existence, in part, through "rituals of deference and dominance," then Morrison's attempt to reorient preacher, congregation, speech, and text could serve as good practice for living otherwise (Fields and Fields 2012, 25).

In describing her efforts to remake her text as if it were a preacher open to changing circumstances and her readers into participants and co-creators of the text, Morrison frames the matter liturgically:

> I write in order to clear away the parts of the book that can *only* work as print. . . . Because that is one of the major characteristics of black literature as far as I'm concerned . . . it has to have . . . the participation of the *other*, that is, the audience, the reader, and that you can do with a spoken story. . . . It's a totally communal experience where I would feel unhappy if there was no controversy or no debate or no anything—no *passion* that accompanied the experience of the work. I want somebody to say amen! (Davis 1994, 231)

This ritual might aid in imagining a future for the overwritten and epistemically marginalized precisely because it accepts that an overwriting has occurred but bids the masquerade continue. Our dead names are an inheritance that perhaps cannot simply be discarded, but they can be spoken back to, brought back to an equal footing with the unanswerable text.[10]

CODA: A PERFECT SOFT-BOILED EGG

I would like to conclude with a final, miraculous image that encompasses all I've been aiming at in this essay. In another seeming digression, Pilate turns the making of a perfect soft-boiled egg into a narrative: "the egg and the water have to meet each other on a kind of equal standing. One can't get the upper hand over the other. So the temperature has to be the same for both. I knock the chill off the water first. Just the chill. I don't let it get warm because the egg is room temperature, you see" (Morrison 1977, 39). For water and egg, we are meant to read subject and medium, or content and form.[11] In this passage, we see Morrison the writer modulating the medium (the novelistic form that envelopes her subjects). Rather than rejecting the medium, she is attempting to temper its capacity to overwhelm—a historical capacity that we can see clearly in the inkface tradition, in which the white gaze overwrites the Black person and, indeed, the world.

Morrison continues with her culinary allegory of the medium and the subject. "The real secret is right here in the boiling. When the tiny bubbles come to the surface, when they as big as peas and just before they get as big as marbles. Well, right then you take the pot off the fire. You don't just put the fire out; you take the pot off" (39). Here, the surfacing bubbles figure the ink emerging from the blank white of the page. For any who doubt that Morrison is offering a recipe for cooking the books, she concludes: "Then you put a folded newspaper over the pot and do one small obligation. . . . If you do all that you got yourself a perfect soft-boiled egg" (40). According to Pilate, perfection is a paradoxical miracle of dual consistencies: "I don't like my whites to move. . . . The yolk I want soft, but not runny. Want it like wet velvet" (39).

The newspaper covering the pot is not a throwaway image but a figure for the ideal that Morrison aims to achieve aesthetically. Print is meant to surround something that was once hot, now cooling. Compared to a metal or ceramic lid, a paper covering meant can let more of the heat of orality through. A reader hopes to find enveloped in this wrapper a sublime soft-boiled egg: a miraculous achievement of structure *and* fluidity; internal cohesion *and* openness to revision—not to mention, a sensual delight that also nourishes.

The great critic Hortense Spillers writes of "the stunning alimentation of an egg"—that what it provides is not simply nourishment but a "vision of the whole world of human and property relations" (Spillers 2003, 1–2). She asks, "could we say, then, that in a very real sense, our world is an egg? The quint-essential maker of makers?" (Spillers 2003, 2). If an egg contains the theater of the world, then is there any surprise that Pilate invites Milkman across the threshold to see its soft-boiled preparation, simultaneously firm and fluid, white and colored, with an invitation so like that of the carnival-barker? "Step right in," she says. Who would have imagined—on so mundane an altar as a stove—another way of life in nascent form, wrapped in newspaper or, indeed, enfolded in a swaddling book? Blue Magic was aptly named and their call echoes in Pilate, in Wimbush, and here: *Hurry, hurry! Step right on in.*

NOTES

1. I am grateful to Vincent Wimbush and to Emory University's Pitts Theology Library for the occasion and to Cliff Mak and Ryan Black for reading and responding to this essay with great care and insight.

2. On the durable metaphor of *theatrum mundi*, or the world as a stage, see (Agnew 1988; Richards 1991). Lara Langer Cohen offers an indispensable analysis of "the underground" in US-American culture as a topographical "figure to signify [political opposition] operating secretly or from below." Cohen argues that the mysteries and revelations of sensational dime novels summon a theological hermeneutic attuned to "forms of knowledge that defy reason" (Cohen 2017, 2, 3). See also Cohen 2021.

3. I do not say "capitalism" and "modernity" out of any nostalgic desire for their precursors, to suggest that the hierarchies of the past were any less traumatizing. I mean only to draw attention to the fact that Enlightenment and the revolutions it birthed did not replace the *ancien regime* with universal liberty and equality. Rather, they maldistributed property, pleasure, and protection according to reconfigured social hierarchies. A comparative analysis to other political and economic systems is not necessary to address the harms caused by this one.

4. I do not mean to romanticize African precursors to Atlantic exile. Those respon-sible for communicating with the gods and representing the ineffable are always prone not only to error but also to self-aggrandizement or -enrichment. In invoking an African past, I want only to highlight the cultural unmooring that accompanies Atlantic dispersal.

5. See also *Inkface: Othello and White Authority in the Era of Atlantic Slavery* (forthcoming, University of Virginia Press).

6. The legal theorist Cheryl I. Harris remains essential for understanding whiteness as a form of property encompassing land, profit, enjoyment, and future gain (C. I. Harris 1993).

7. A fuller explication of this image would need to account for this ur-mother's status and function in this text—and the complex roles of Native Americans in Mor-rison's corpus. Pilate's mother is Singing Bird, an Indigenous (and Black?) woman who chooses a Black male lover when the rest of her family, apparently, denies any

African ancestry. But for Pilate's earring and the recurring imagery of birds, there is no direct trace of her in the novel. Her children are as black as their father. His ghostly form and resounding voice run throughout the novel in a way that hers do not.

Black and Indigenous offspring are also of crucial import in *Paradise*, a novel in which an Oklahoma town's eugenic dedication to the reproduction of pure blackness can proceed only because the Native American ancestry of the town's founding families, though visible in their surnames and straight hair, remains completely unspoken (Morrison 1998). Here, Morrison might be revising her own suppression of Native ancestry in *Song of Solomon*. On the complexities of Black and Native American relations in North America, see Miles and Holland 2006; Miles 2015; 2019.

8. Dubey is responding to early work on orality in Morrison's oeuvre, such as Stryz 1991; Middleton 1993. This scholarship in the 1990s was following the talking book trope so central to Gates' *The Signifying Monkey* (1989) or interest in blues, folklore, or African ritual practices. Some proceeded from secular presumptions; others were attempting to isolate Black cosmologies and practices. See T. Harris 1991; Henderson 1989b; 1989a. In founding African American literary studies, this brilliant scholarship had to establish an autonomous Black tradition in the face of accusations that African American literature is merely an imitation of a white original. In doing so, they may have emphasized Black genres and underplayed that the King James Bible is as central as these folk forms to Morrison's experience and theory of New World Black cultural life. Race, cultural hierarchy, bookishness, orality, and theology formed a clear nexus for her. For work that pursues more of these strands, see Hathaway 2019; and, especially, Christianse 2012.

9. The aim and potentiality of an essay and a novel are typically quite different. Readers usually expect an essayist to use language in a transparent way to refer to known or unknown facets of reality. The author understands that the text will be measured against readers understanding of a world beyond it. Unlike essays, novels often work as much by omission and implication as by world-making declaration; thereby soliciting desires and evoking affective responses. In short, an essayist may ignore emotive, phatic, and conative functions of language, but a novelist rarely does. On the functions of language and the differences between genres, see Jakobson 1990, chap. 7; Delany 2017. My thanks to Cliff Mak and Steven Thomas for discussion and references.

10. While Morrison used the name Dead, the dead name refers now to one left behind when people who make a gender transition also change their names. Although attempts to change one's relationship to the world take many divergent forms, those of the freedmen, the religious convert, and the person-in-transition often intersect. Black Liberation Theology will need as productive a dialogue with trans theory as it has had with Womanist Theology. See Ferguson 2004; Scott 2010; Adair 2019; Snorton 2017; Bey 2020; 2022.

11. I think Krumholz misses additional resonances in suggesting that eggs signify only "a 'white' ideological vision from which Milkman must break free" (Krumholz 1993, 560).

BIBLIOGRAPHY

Adair, Cassius. 2019. "Licensing Citizenship: Anti-Blackness, Identification Documents, and Transgender Studies." *American Quarterly* 71 (2): 569–94. https://doi.org/10.1353/aq.2019.0043.

Agnew, Jean-Christophe. 1988. *Worlds Apart: The Market and the Theater in Anglo-American Thought, 1550–1750*. New York: Cambridge University Press.

"Atramentous, Adj." 2020. In *OED Online*. Oxford University Press. http://www.oed.com/view/Entry/12637.

Benson, George. 1976. *This Masquerade*. Warner Brothers. https://www.discogs.com/master/52525-George-Benson-Breezin.

Bey, Marquis. 2020. *The Problem of the Negro as a Problem for Gender*. Minneapolis: University of Minnesota Press.

———. 2022. *Cistem Failure: Essays on Blackness and Cisgender*. Durham: Duke University Press.

"Black, Adj. and n." 2022. In *OED Online*. Oxford University Press. http://www.oed.com/view/Entry/19670.

Blue Magic. 1974. *Sideshow*. Atco.

Christianse, Yvette. 2012. *Toni Morrison: An Ethical Poetics*. New York: Fordham University Press.

Cohen, Lara Langer. 2017. "The Depths of Astonishment: City Mysteries and the Antebellum Underground." *American Literary History* 29 (1): 1–25.

———. 2021. "Going Underground: Race, Space, and the Subterranean in the Nineteenth-Century US." *American Literary History* 33 (3): 510–26.

Davis, Christina. 1994. "A Conversation with Toni Morrison." In *Conversations with Toni Morrison*, edited by Danille Taylor-Guthrie. Jackson: University Press of Mississippi.

Delany, Samuel R. 2017. "About 5,750 Words." In *The Jewel-Hinged Jaw: Notes on the Language of Science Fiction*, Revised, 1–15. Middletown, CT: Wesleyan University Press.

Ferguson, Roderick A. 2004. *Aberrations in Black: Toward a Queer of Color Critique*. Minneapolis: University of Minnesota Press.

Fields, Karen E., and Barbara J. Fields. 2012. *Racecraft: The Soul of Inequality in American Life*. New York: Verso.

Fricker, Miranda. 2009. *Epistemic Injustice: Power and the Ethics of Knowing*. Oxford: Oxford University Press.

Goldman, Anne E. 1990. "'I Made the Ink': (Literary) Production and Reproduction in 'Dessa Rose' and 'Beloved.'" *Feminist Studies* 16 (2): 313–30. https://doi.org/10.2307/3177852.

Grier, Miles P. 2015. "Inkface: The Slave Stigma in England's Early Imperial Imagination." In *Scripturalizing the Human: The Written as the Political*, edited by Vincent L. Wimbush, 193–220. New York: Routledge.

Guare, John. 1992. *Six Degrees of Separation*. New York, NY: Dramatists Play Service, Inc.

Gundaker, Grey. 1998. *Signs of Diaspora / Diaspora of Signs: Literacies, Creolization, and Vernacular Practice in African America.* Commonwealth Center Studies in American Culture Ser. New York: Oxford University Press.

Gustafson, Sandra M. 2000. *Eloquence Is Power: Oratory and Performance in Early America.* Chapel Hill: The University of North Carolina Press.

Harris, Cheryl I. 1993. "Whiteness as Property." *Harvard Law Review* 106 (8): 1707–91.

Harris, Trudier. 1991. *Fiction and Folklore: The Novels of Toni Morrison.* Knoxville: University of Tennessee Press.

Hathaway, Heather. 2019. "Rewriting Race, Gender and Religion in Toni Morrison's Song of Solomon and Paradise." *Religions* 10 (6): 345. https://doi.org/10.3390/rel10060345.

Henderson, Mae G. 1989a. "Speaking in Tongues: Dialogics, Dialectics, and the Black Woman Writer's Literary Tradition." In *Changing Our Own Words: Essays on Criticism, Theory, and Writing by Black Women*, edited by Cheryl Wall, 16–37. New Brunswick, NJ: Rutgers University Press.

———. 1989b. "(W)Riting the Work and Working the Rites." *Black American Literature Forum* 23 (4): 631–60. https://doi.org/10.2307/2904094.

Jakobson, Roman. 1990. "Linguistics and Poetics." In *Language in Literature*, edited by Krystyna Pomorska and Stephen Rudy, 62–94. Cambridge: Belknap Press.

Krumholz, Linda. 1993. "Dead Teachers: Rituals of Manhood and Rituals of Reading in Song of Solomon: Toni Morrison Double Issue." *Modern Fiction Studies* 39 (3–4): 551–74.

Middleton, Joyce Irene. 1993. "Orality, Literacy, and Memory in Toni Morrison's Song of Solomon." *College English* 55 (1): 64. https://doi.org/10.2307/378365.

———. 1995. "From Orality to Literacy: Oral Memory in Toni Morrison's Song of Solomon." In *New Essays on Song of Solomon*, edited by Valerie Smith, 19–40. Cambridge, England; New York: Cambridge University Press.

Miles, Tiya. 2015. *Ties That Bind: The Story of an Afro-Cherokee Family in Slavery and Freedom.* Oakland: University of California Press.

———. 2019. "Beyond a Boundary: Black Lives and the Settler-Native Divide." *The William and Mary Quarterly* 76 (3): 417–26.

Miles, Tiya, and Sharon Patricia Holland, eds. 2006. *Crossing Waters, Crossing Worlds: The African Diaspora in Indian Country.* New edition. Durham, NC: Duke University Press Books.

Morrison, Toni. 1977. *Song of Solomon.* First Plume Printing (1987). New York: Knopf.

———. 1987. *Beloved.* New York: Plume.

———. 1993. *Jazz.* New York: Plume Books.

———. 1998. *Paradise.* Reprint edition. New York: Vintage.

———. 2019. *Goodness and the Literary Imagination: Harvard's 95th Ingersoll Lecture with Essays on Morrison's Moral and Religious Vision.* Edited by David Carrasco, Stephanie Paulsell, and Mara Willard. Charlottesville: University of Virginia Press.

Ong, Walter J. 1991. *Orality and Literacy: The Technologizing of the Word*. New York: Routledge.

Renker, Elizabeth. 1997. *Strike through the Mask: Herman Melville and the Scene of Writing*. Baltimore: The Johns Hopkins University Press.

Richards, Jeffrey H. 1991. *Theater Enough: American Culture and the Metaphor of the World Stage, 1607–1789*. Durham, NC: Duke University Press.

Scott, Darieck. 2010. *Extravagant Abjection: Blackness, Power, and Sexuality in the African American Literary Imagination*. Sexual Cultures Series. New York: New York University Press.

Snorton, C. Riley. 2017. *Black on Both Sides: A Racial History of Trans Identity*. Minneapolis: University of Minnesota Press.

Spillers, Hortense J. 2003. "Peter's Pans: Eating in the Diaspora." In *Black, White, and in Color: Essays on American Literature and Culture*, 1–64. Chicago: University of Chicago Press.

Stryz, Jan. 1991. "Inscribing an Origin in Song of Solomon." *Studies in American Fiction* 19 (1): 31–40. https://doi.org/10.1353/saf.1991.0003.

Wimbush, Vincent L., ed. 2013. *Misreading America: Scriptures and Difference*. New York: Oxford University Press.

Žižek, Slavoj. 1989. "How Did Marx Invent the Symptom?" In *The Sublime Object of Ideology*, 11–53. London: Verso.

Chapter 9

"There Remains Only Constant Struggle"

Scholarship as Stories of Radical Black Subjectivities

Rosetta Ross

INTRODUCTION

It was my pleasure to participate in the symposium on the virtual exhibit and address by Vincent Wimbush, both entitled "Masquerade: Scripturalizing Modernities through Black Flesh," sponsored by the Pitts Theology Library at Candler School of Theology and the Institute for Signifying Scriptures.[1] Presented in five stages—I, "We [Eboes] are . . . a nation of dancers, musicians, poets"; II, "The White men had some spell or magic"; III, "The book remained silent"; IV, "The Ethiopian was willing to be saved by Jesus Christ"; V, "[T]he Scriptures became an unsealed book [of] . . . things . . . that . . . can never be told—in the exhibit and address, Wimbush identifies the exhibit as, among other things, "a wide-open window onto multiple and layered stories—onto brokenness, humiliations, degradations, chaos, slavery, violence; but also, onto flight, resistance, intentionally alternative orientations, occasional instances/islands of refreshment, joy, all short of redemption."[2] Wimbush continues, "Again, I make the point that there is from my perspective as curator and critic no redemption assumed to be on the horizon—racialization produced by scripturalization and scripturalization supercharged by racialization cannot now be unread or undone; there remains only constant struggle for and the maintenance of sharp-edged self-reflexivity."[3]

167

For purposes of organizing this response, the five stages of the exhibit and address are reinterpreted as origins, encounter, silence, conversion, and salvation. Though the address asserts the collections of stories and actions are "all short of redemption," this essay centralizes conversion and salvation and focuses on the latter part of the address that offers a conclusion and response, of sorts, to the ideas and realities explicated throughout representations and discussions of origins, encounter, and silence. Specifically, this essay centralizes the clause "there remains only constant struggle" near the beginning discussion of stage five and offers a reading of salvation not as completion or an end, but as "constant struggle." In centering this clause, the essay interprets *conversion* as the experience (akin to Wimbush's "self-reflexivity and theorizing work"[4]) that generates "constant struggle." It distinguishes conversion that generates constant struggle from conversion as attempts of the "black-fleshed person to be 'saved' within/into white men's world."[5] Further, the experience of this generative *conversion* is understood as leading to a specific salvation: being "*saved from*" the desire "to be 'saved' within/into white men's world" and *being saved for* "constant struggle." The constancy of struggle is the historic legacy of consciousness linked with action that persistently opposes the idea that "black-fleshed person[s need] to be 'saved' within/into white men's world." Through persistency, constant struggle continually yields new consciousness as well new historical realities.[6] Drawing on Charles Long's conception of encounter with the sacred, the discussion unhinges black persons' salvation from Christianity and argues that while this salvation may be described as a form of religious consciousness,[7] the consciousness is not confined to any specific religious tradition or formal conceptions of religion. Identifying interiority as the site of both "masquerade" and salvation, this essay argues that social and political activism (in this case, black women's activism) are an expressive form of the salvation that requires constancy of struggle against "masquerade."

RELIGIOUS CONSCIOUSNESS AS EXPERIENCING SACRED FORMS OF THE WORLD

The late historian of Religion Charles Long offers an interpretation of the origin of religions as the moment and a movement emerging from an encounter with what becomes understood as the sacred. Encountering the sacred occurs, Long argues, when a new form of reality breaks into human consciousness and conveys an experience of power, ultimacy, and obligation that supersedes ordinary cultural categories. Perception of the new form compels the one who recognizes it to (1) communicate the experience and (2) engage in activity aimed toward creating "an-other," qualitatively different cultural order.

Notably, for black persons, Long argues that determination to pursue another cultural order occurs "at the same time" of their self-reflective experience of "the truth of the negativity of their condition."[8]

Recognition of the sacred takes place in the inner world, within the psychic space where persons analyze experiences and engage consciousness, emotions, and self-reflection. The interior realm also cradles the grounding of individual moral life; as such it is the seat of personal sovereignty, though that sovereignty always is situated in relation to an outer world and other persons, in contrast with reigning notions of hyper-individual identity and achievement. That is, to assert the inner life as the seat of individual sovereignty does not mean that human interiority, including morality, are isolated from the social world. However, neither is it the case that inner life is entirely determined by society. Interiority is, in fact, a defense against being dominated by discourses and norms of the social order.[9] Through and within inner experience persons may create and perceive new ideas. Interiority is, in addition, the space where persons recognize congruity and incongruity between self-understanding and the way they appear to or are viewed by society. Arising through critical self-reflection and reflection on the historical world, recognition is apprehension of the sacred when it occurs as identifying an incongruity that entails reorienting one's attitudes, beliefs, principles, and practices (constant struggle) for a new congruous historical reality.[10]

In the case of black women, constant struggle against incongruity sometimes requires feigning conformity to the incongruity, including incongruous social perspectives about them.[11] Owing to the nation's collective imagination offering only a narrow space for engaging ideas and concerns about the experience and meaning of black human being in relation to white supremacy, black interiority plays a key role in sustaining ideas of embodied blackness as human, as good, and as intelligent. For black women, whose intersectional experiences include constantly negotiating patriarchy, feigning conformity functions as protection of the interior life from intrusions as the women imagine and strategize constant struggle for new realities. Legacies of the interior lives of African Americans—from the colonial era to the Jim Crow Era, to modernity, to postmodernity—are essential to personal conceptions of black freedom that emerge amid relational encounter of anti-black socio-political experience. Conceptions of freedom that derive from relational social experience arise within the inner world, where radical black subjectivity originates and is nurtured.

Because the interior life is the space of individual sovereignty, persons may choose the extent to which they perceive and ruminate upon inner experience. Persons also may choose to ignore interiority entirely. Historian of religion Sidney E. Mead characterized inhabitants of the United States in this latter way. Noting the tendency to emphasize "achievements" and "outward acts," Mead writes, "Americans have so presented to view and celebrated the external and material side of their pilgrims' progress that they have tended to conceal even from themselves the inner, spiritual pilgrimage, with its more subtle dimensions and profound depths."[12] Concealing the inner world from the self appears to be consistent with the practice that sustains what Wimbush calls "masquerade." Masking interiority also masks the relationship of empirical realities to moral life. Concealment prevents full experience of introspection and emotions such as self-reflection, regret, remorse, shame, guilt, empathy, and sorrow. Insofar as inner experience relates to and helps constitute moral life, concealment ("masquerade") skews the meaning of morality by normalizing "brokenness, humiliations, degradations, chaos, slavery, violence" and more.

While the interior life provides psychic space for developing the authenticity of black subjectivity within an anti-black culture, it also is the psychic arena that perpetuates the "masquerade." For both dispositions, the inner life is the space where relational ideas emerge, ideas such as the origin and expression of concern or neglect, determinations about the right and the good, conceiving the extent and limits of one's obligations, and resolving personal senses of responsibility and action or lack of responsibility and inaction. The emergence of these experiences joins feelings of regret, remorse, shame, guilt, penitence, and sorrow in inhabiting the interior life, as do ideas about kindness, respect, care, and celebration. While for many black women, concealing the inner experience from public view makes space to assess and access relational ideas, concealment also is the means through which these attributes of being human are not accessed or masqueraded. In the latter case, suppressing inner experience makes human brutality less objectionable and obscures or hides realities and testimonies of the world of hurt[13] that "masquerade" requires for black women.

From the Longian perspective, black encounter of the sacred may be understood as the imagining and pursuit of a cultural reality that unveils and opposes ideas and practices that organize and sustain anti-black racism as elements of the "masquerade." When seen as existential salvation, black experience of the sacred facilitates acknowledging historical experience and recognizing sources that institute and perpetuate anti-blackness, or, as Wimbush writes, persons become capable of seeing the "masquerade" more clearly. Insofar as black encounter with the sacred results in imagining and pursuing new cultural realities, the encounter may be described as conversion and an existential form of salvation. A new black subjectivity becomes the point of view from which one is oriented toward the world. Existential salvation yields specific sites of "constant struggle."[14]

MASQUERADE, THE "CULTURE OF DISSEMBLANCE," AND BLACK WOMEN'S ACTIVISM

In 1989, historian Darlene Clark Hine coined the term "culture of dissemblance" to name the inner disposition through which black women create psychic space to strategize on behalf of themselves. Because of "the interplay of racial animosity, class tensions, gender role differentiation, and regional economic variations," Hine writes,

> Black women, as a rule develop and adhered to a cult of secrecy, a culture of dissemblance, to protect the sanctity of inner aspects of their lives. The dynamics of dissemblance involved creating the appearance of disclosure, or openness about themselves and their feelings, while actually remaining an enigma. Only with secrecy, thus achieving a self-imposed invisibility, could ordinary Black women accrue the psychic space and harness the resources needed to hold their own in the often one-sided and mismatched resistance struggle.[15]

In coining the term "culture of dissemblance," Hine identifies one of black women's long-term practices of self-regard that captures both their participation in and circumvention of the "masquerade." In "creating the appearance of disclosure," black women veil their authentic selves and take part in the "masquerade." Since, as Hine indicates, Black women practice dissemblance to "harness" needed resources, their participation in the "masquerade" is both under duress and fully engaged as a stratagem. By using the appearance of disclosure to harness resources, black women exercise autonomous authority over their interiority as a resource against anti-woman and anti-black practices and as a space for maintaining and expressing self-regard.

During the Civil Rights Era, Student Nonviolent Coordinating Committee (SNCC) leader Diane Nash's description of inner experience amid segregation parallels of Wimbush's "masquerade" and black women's culture of dissemblance. Identifying the "masquerade's" artifice, Nash argued that segregation "fosters dishonesty between the races" since it "makes people lie to each other." Segregation, Nash continued, "allows white merchants to accept the customers' money, but to give them unequal service." By recognizing inequality of service for different customers as an example of the dishonesty embedded within segregation, Nash signals the centrality of economic gain to the "masquerade's" purposes. Dissemblance is one response to the "masquerade" of segregation since, as Nash notes, segregation "forces the Negro maid to tell her employer that everything is all right and that she's satisfied, but when she is among her friends she talks about the injustice of the system."[16] In this example, by creating the appearance of contentment, a black woman is able to continue the work through which she acquires resources to improve her life and live with authenticity when she is beyond the gaze of her employer and away from her immediate experience of dissatisfaction about her employment.

Through the culture of dissemblance, Hine writes, black women "create alternative self-images" and "shield from scrutiny the private, empowering definitions of self."[17] In view of black women's use of dissemblance to protect their inner lives and strategize to resist, dissemblance is a practice of radical black subjectivity. It is a means of supporting black women's persistence in (constant struggle for) uplifting themselves and their communities and changing historical reality.

THE EXAMPLE OF RUBY HURLEY

In 1951, the National Association for the Advancement of Colored People (NAACP) assigned Ruby Hurley to organize and lead work in seven states that became the NAACP's Southeast Region. Although local chapters and a few state conferences already existed in the Deep South, the NAACP had refrained from developing a nationally funded outpost in what former District of Columbia NAACP leader Archibald Grimké once labeled "enemy territory."[18] By 1951, however, the Association had more than four decades of practice establishing branches and pursuing its agenda across the nation. Hurley's Southeast work began in April 1951 when NAACP Director of Branches Gloster Current temporarily assigned her as regional coordinator. After the temporary post, Hurley was reassigned permanently to the Southeast.[19]

Prior to assignment to the Southeast, Hurley served on the NAACP national staff as Secretary for Youth work. Her engagement with the NAACP began in Washington, District of Columbia, amid the NAACP's 1939 work that presented Marian Anderson in concert at the Lincoln Memorial after the Daughters of the American Revolution rebuffed Anderson. Hurley described participating in that work as causing a type of conversion when she "started getting interested in us" and experienced the breaking apart of having been "shielded" from historical realities of black "suffering."[20] Hurley spent the rest of her career and life as an administrator within the NAACP.

When 42-year-old Hurley moved to Birmingham from New York, she already was practicing the culture of dissemblance. With intentionality, Hurley had carefully cultivated an image of herself as a proper Protestant black churchwoman. This occurred, primarily, through establishing and maintaining active relationship with congregations of the majority white Methodist Episcopal (later United Methodist) Church—from her childhood and young adulthood congregation Asbury Church in Washington, District of

Columbia, to St. Mark's Church in Harlem, New York, to St. Paul Church in Birmingham, Alabama, and, finally, to Warren Memorial Church in Atlanta, Georgia. Hurley's constructed identity reflected the politics of respectability, promoted by some black elites, in part, to ensure "respect" from whites[21] by conforming to and defending black women against constricting and exclusionary ideas about true womanhood. It also was the means through which black women created a context to work for change. Unfortunately, the politics of respectability also became an intra-communal sign about class and acceptability among African American.

Hurley took care in developing her identity not only as a Protestant church woman, but particularly as a Methodist Episcopal laywoman. This allowed her to use Methodism to legitimate work in a variety of settings including to recruit NAACP members; to organize strategy sessions, protests, NAACP meetings and activities; to engage in and interpret the NAACP's work to parachurch organizations such as the Fellowship of the Concerned and Church Women United; to quell white fears after the *Brown* decision; to organize interracial legislative training for religious leaders;[22] and to propagate and enact her own orientation against white supremacy. As did many black women peers, Hurley both engaged *and* subverted "respectability politics" to pursue a vocation and career she chose. Hurley also was unusual among many black women leaders born in the first decade of the twentieth century. Although she used a Protestant laywoman image to justify public engagement, she did not include the roles of wife and mother to help demonstrate and maintain a "respectable" identity. As a cisgendered black woman who had married and divorced twice by 1952, bore no children, and who was single for most of her career, Hurley's life had similarities to Ella Baker and Septima Clark, two other black woman Civil Rights leaders who lived most of their lives as single women without children.[23] Through speech and action as NAACP Southeastern Regional Coordinator from 1951 to 1978, Hurley joined other black women leaders in practicing the culture of dissemblance to destabilize and complexify conceptions of "acceptable" black womanhood and the meaning of African American Christianity. Through this practice, Hurley protected a self-definition that enabled her ordering, leading, and expanding southern NAACP work, including negotiating, and interpreting the Association's activity in the face of intense fears, repression, and violence. Though she used dissemblance throughout her 28-year leadership of the region, the patterns of Hurley's work discussed here is from to her first decade as regional coordinator, 1951 to 1960.

Hurley's Southeast Regional leadership emerged with intensity. She coordinated branch, state conference, and regional activity such as issuing statements and organizing opposition to violence and discrimination, including rape of black girls and women, black men being falsely charged with rape of white women, frivolous sentencing of convicted black defendants to death, muggings of black persons, assassination of southern NAACP leaders, employment discrimination, and more.[24] Hurley also began a tour of speaking engagements during which she and other staff encouraged and publicized NAACP activity.[25] Hurley raised funds through membership campaigns and received gifts supporting NAACP work.[26] She also primed constituencies for the coming groundswell of black enfranchisement by leading some of the earliest coordinated black voter registration efforts in the South.[27]

Two specific areas of immediate intensity in Hurley's Southeast Regional work related to violence and school desegregation. Beginning with the December 25, 1951, bombing that killed Florida NAACP leaders Harry and Harriette Moore, Hurley presided over or investigated a range assassinations, rapes, and other hate crime activities, including deaths of George W. Lee, Lamar Smith, Emmet Till, Medgar Evers, and more.[28] Two days after arrival in Alabama, she announced the intention to secure admission of black students to Alabama and Mississippi graduate and professional schools "'as soon as cases could be found.'"[29] By 1952, the NAACP began organizing to desegregate the nation's public schools and to respond to anticipated tension resulting from its effort to overturn the Supreme Court's *Plessy v. Ferguson* separate but equal ruling. After the 1954 *Brown* decision, Hurley's school desegregation work expanded substantially to include combatting sometimes violent backlash, pursuing and supporting plaintiffs for desegregation legal cases, addressing liberal church groups seeking to calm white fears, overseeing state and local desegregation efforts, and preparing for or making court appearances during lawsuits that challenged NAACP desegregation work.[30]

In addition to outward expressions such as demeanor and dress, Hurley practiced dissemblance through speech, evident in many speaking engagements in the period immediately following the *Brown* decision, especially during work to address fears and opposition in white communities. Hurley sometimes was triply dissembled, using conciliation, the "politics of respectability," and deflection to work within while breaking apart the logics and methods of the "masquerade." During a 1955 speech before a group of Alabama Church Women of the Fellowship of the Concerned, Hurley displayed these three distinct masks. First, as she began to speak, Hurley assumed a disposition of conciliation and collaboration:

> As a woman active in the Methodist Church and as one working in the National Association for the Advancement of Colored People, it is a pleasure to speak to other women who are concerned with the application of Christian principles in human relations. In these times it is very important and necessary that women of all races and creeds come together to consider the role that they can play today.

The opening of this avenue of communication can help create an understanding which is so necessary if we are to live together as children of God.[31]

Second, Hurley presented "acceptability" of NAACP work by identifying its conformity to Christianity, national heroes, and U.S. constitutional policies, though the NAACP sought to move far beyond the toleration and false stasis advocated by those opposing its work:

> The organization which I represent has been working for forty-six years to make it possible for American citizens who happen to be Negroes to enjoy the blessings of liberty, and rights and privileges of first-class citizenship. Contrary to the beliefs of many, we are not more radical than Jesus Christ or Thomas Jefferson or others who framed the Declaration of Independence or Constitution, particularly, the 13th, 14th, and 15th Amendments. We work through the courts, the legislative bodies, and we seek to change ideas and attitudes through the use of educational techniques. We do not expect to legislate prejudice out of the hearts and minds of people, but we do try to keep personal prejudices from becoming operative against our entire group simply because of the accident of our birth.[32]

Third, Hurley first described the diminishment of black persons to deflect her challenge of supremacist ideas within the white imagination as a preamble to arguing for quality education for African Americans:

> The NAACP is working for white and colored Americans, for as we try to remove the stigma of "inferiority" from our people, we, also, believe it important to show white Americans the error of their idea of "superiority." Segregation which has kept us so long apart has aided the growth of many erroneous ideas, which we call "stereotyped."[33]

CONCLUSION

"Masquerade" requires everyone to participate in masking, but it does not and cannot compel all meanings or functions of masks. While its framework structures modern and postmodern life, the necessity for a response that preserves and promotes black psychic well-being suggests existential salvation as a means of living within the "masquerade" while opposing its existence. Radical black subjectivity—opposition to the idea that there is no significant life or reality outside the "masquerade's" constructed logics of white supremacy—is the means through which the ongoing legacy of black social and political activism develops counter-meanings and counter-historical realities, while also always recognizing the imperative of the constancy of struggle.

NOTES

1. I am drawing on bell hooks's definition of radical black subjectivity as self-construction that is "oppositional and liberatory." Hooks argues that radical black subjectivity repudiates essentialized blackness and affirms "multiple experiences of blackness" that make "diverse cultural productions possible." See bell hooks, *Yearning: Race, Gender, and Cultural Politics* (Boston: South End, 1991), 29.

2. Vincent L. Wimbush, "'Everything about Me Was Magic': The Black-Fleshed and the Making and Management of Modernities," Opening Address, Emory-ISS Symposium, November 3, 2021, 2.

3. Wimbush, "'Everything about Me Was Magic': The Black-Fleshed and the Making and Management of Modernities," 15.

4. Wimbush, "'Everything about Me Was Magic': The Black-Fleshed and the Making and Management of Modernities," 15.

5. Wimbush, "'Everything about Me Was Magic': The Black-Fleshed and the Making and Management of Modernities," 14.

6. The meaning of the constancy of struggle I intend to communicate here relates to both the legacy of Black opposition to the erasure of "black-fleshed" persons through succumbing to "white salvation" as well as the determination of any person or persons at any moment in history to participate in that legacy through contemporary struggle against the forces and institutions that inhibit black thriving. Gordon, Menzel, Shulman, and Syedullah discuss what I am aiming toward by the idea of the constancy of struggle as a legacy of facilitation. In analysis sharing thoughts on Afropessimism, they argue that there are "numerous examples of how prior, radical so-called 'failures' transformed relationships . . . facilitated other kinds of outcome." They assert facilitation of later outcomes emerges from "a constant negotiation of ongoing efforts to build relationships with others, which means . . . establishing new situations of action and meaning," even from unsuccessful negotiation work. This "constant negotiation" is related to what I interpret as the meaning of the constant struggle. They continue, "The trail goes back to the Haitian Revolution and back to every act of resistance from Nat Turner's Rebellion in the USA, Sharpe's in Jamaica, or Tula's in Curaçao and so many other efforts for social transformation to come." See Lewis R. Gordon, Annie Menzel, George Shulman and Jasmine Syedullah "Critical Exchange: Afro Pessimism," *Contemporary Political Theory* 17, 1 (Feb 2018): 105–137, 109. Also see, William Jones's *Is God a White Racist? A Preamble to Black Theology* (Boston: Beacon, 1973).

7. By religious consciousness, I mean having a sense of the self as valuable and as an arbiter of values in the world and having self-awareness of one's concerns and values.

8. Charles H. Long, Charles, *Significations: Signs, Symbols, and Images in the Interpretation of Religion* (Colorado: The Davies Group, Publishers, 1999), 191.

9. Kevin Quashie, *The Sovereignty of Quiet: Beyond Resistance in Black Culture* (New Brunswick, NJ: Rutgers, 2012), 6.

10. Charles H. Long, *Ellipsis: The Collected Writings of Charles H. Long: Ellipsis* (London, New York: Bloomsbury, 2018), 280, 282.

11. Darlene Clark Hine, "Rape and the Inner Lives of Black Women in the Middle: Preliminary Thoughts on the Culture of Dissemblance," *Signs* Vol. 14, No. 4 (Summer 1989), 915.

12. Sidney E. Mead, *The Lively Experiment: The Shaping of Christianity in America* (New York: Harper & Row, 1963), 8.

13. Long, Charles, *Significations*, 165.

14. bell hooks, "Postmodern Blackness," 425–426. Drawing on both Long and hooks here, I am equating this experience to Wimbush's assertion of "unmasking and relating the complete story of experiences had, but also the *imperative* of doing so" and the announcement of "[T]he veil [removed]." See Wimbush, 14, italics added.

15. Darlene Clark Hine, "Rape and the Inner Lives of Black Women in the Middle: Preliminary Thoughts on the Culture of Dissemblance," *Signs* Vol. 14, No. 4 (Summer 1989), 915. Underlining added. Similarly, sociologist Patricia Hill Collins writes, "Resisting by doing something that 'is not expected' could not have occurred without Black women's long-standing rejection of mammies, matriarchs, and other controlling images," Collins writes. Their combined "individual acts of resistance suggest that a distinctive, collective Black women's consciousness exists," which is a "private, hidden space of Black women's consciousness, the 'inside' ideas that allow Black women to cope with and, in many cases, transcend the confines of intersecting oppressions of race, class, gender, and sexuality."15. Black "women simply do not define themselves as mammies, matriarchs, welfare mothers, mules, or sexually denigrated women," 15.

16. Diane Nash, "Inside the Sit-ins and Freedom Rides: Testimony of a Southern Student" in *The New Negro*, ed. Matthew H. Ahmann (Notre Dame: Fides, 1961), 47.

17. Darlene Clark Hine, "Rape and the Inner Lives of Black Women in the Middle: Preliminary Thoughts on the Culture of Dissemblance," *Signs* Vol. 14, No. 4 (Summer 1989), 916.

18. "Most Militant Negro Woman in the South," *Jet*, October 6, 1955; Patricia Sullivan, *Lift Every Voice: The NAACP in the Making of the Civil Rights Movement* (New York: The New Press, 2009), 41.

19. "Establish Temporary NAACP Headquarters inSoutheast," *Atlanta Daily World*, March 27, 1951, 3; "Roy Wilkins Address To Climate Big State Wide NAACP Rally in Alabama," *The Chicago Defender*, March 31, 1951, 3; John H. Britton, Interviewer, Transcript of a Recorded Interview with Mrs. Ruby Hurley, Director, Southeastern Regional Office of the National Association for the Advancement of Colored People, Atlanta, GA, January 26, 1968, The Civil Rights Documentation Project; Venue: 1527 New Hampshire Ave., NW, Washington, DC, 20036, The Moorland-Spingarn Research Center, Howard University, Washington, DC, 9.

20. John H. Britton, Interviewer, Recorded Interview with Mrs. Ruby Hurley Director, Southeastern Regional Office of the National Association for the Advancement of Colored People, The Civil Rights Documentation Project, Atlanta, GA, January 26, 1968, 1–2.

21. Evelyn Brooks Higginbotham coined the term "politics of respectability" to name Black women's conformity to and defense against the "cult of true womanhood" (or the "cult of domesticity"), a term scholars use to name the nineteenth

century value system that defined the meaning of womanhood for upper and middle class (White) women and which emphasized piety, purity, submission, and homemaking as women's virtues. See Evelyn Brooks Higginbotham, *Righteous Discontent: The Women's Movement in the Black Baptist Church, 1880–1920* (Cambridge: Harvard, 1993), 14, passim.

22. See, for example, "Gleanings," The Fellowship of the Concerned, Alabama Church Women Meeting Minutes, Pilgrim Congregational Church, Birmingham, AL, May 3, 1955, Southern Regional Council Files, Fellowship of the Concerned, 1955, Microfilm, Reel 196, Document 462–66, Robert W. Woodruff Library Archives, The Atlanta University Center, Atlanta, GA; Kevin M. Kruse, "The Paradox of Massive Resistance: Political Conformity and Chaos in the Aftermath of Brown v. Board of Education," *Saint Louis University Law Journal* 48, no. 3 (Spring 2004): 1009–35; North Georgia Conference of United Methodist Women, *A Story Not Yet Over—The Journey: United Methodist Women in North Georgia*, 1992, Volume II (Atlanta: North Georgia Conference of United Methodist Women, 1992).

23. Septima Clark's son was reared primarily by his paternal grandparents. For a portion of her life Ella Baker was a foster mother to her niece, as was Hurley who fostered a college-aged former NAACP youth leader.

24. "Form Florida Committee for Groveland Defense," *Negro Star*, August 17, 1951, Vol. 44, No. 16, 4; "NAACP Secures Conviction of White Man in Alabama Rape," *Negro Star*, March 21, 1952, Vol. 44, No. 49, 1; "Mississippi Muggings," *The Chicago Defender*, April 5, 1952, 19; "Warn Army of Tension at Air Base," *The Chicago Defender*, August 2, 1952, 1–2; "NAACP Asks Probe of Florida Posse Killing," *Negro Star*, September 5, 1951, Vol. 45, No. 20, 1; "Birmingham Medic Center Tests Ike's Bias Riding," *Atlanta Daily World*, August 20, 1953, 1; "Complaints Filed-With ICC Vs. 11 Railroad Companies," *Atlanta Daily World*, December 17, 1953, 3; "NAACP Opens Attack on Segregation in Travel," *Wichita Post-Observer*, December 18, 1953, Vol. 45, No. 50, 12; "Lynching in Mississippi," *The Chicago Defender*, May 21, 1955, 1; "Mississippi," *The Chicago Defender*, May 14, 1955, 18b; "Memorial Services Held for Pastor," *Atlanta Daily World*, May 31, 1955, 4; "NAACP Urges U.S. Action in M No. 'Reign of Terror,'" *Baltimore Afro-American*, September 17, 1955, 14; James Hicks, "'Forget Emmett Till,' Marshall Tells 500; Bares Plan for Action," *Baltimore Afro-American*, October 8, 1955, 15; "Lynch Case Verdict Stirs Whole Nation," *Baltimore Afro-American*, October 8, 1955, 9; Jimmy Hicks, "Unbelievable! Jimmy Hicks' Inside Story of Lynch Trial" (second in a series of four) *Baltimore Afro-American*, October 15, 1955, 1; "Cincinnati Roundup," *The Chicago Defender* October 29, 1955, 18; "Indignation Still High over Till Lynching," *Baltimore Afro-American*, November 5, 1955, 14; "'Ready for Hospital'—Says Emmett Till's Mother," *Baltimore Afro-American*, November 19, 1955, 1.

25. "Roy Wilkins Address to Climate Big State Wide NAACP Rally in Alabama," *The Chicago Defender*, March 31, 1951, 3; "Ware Urges NAACP to Push Citizenship Drive," *Atlanta Daily World*, June 12, 1951, 3; "NAACP Pushes Opposition to Red Cross' 'Blood Bank,'" *Atlanta Daily World*, September 28, 1951, 5; "NAACP State Meet Set for Dec. 7" *Atlanta Daily World*, October 14, 1951, 5; "Atlantans Ready for State NAACP Meeting at Savannah," *Atlanta Daily World*, December 9,

1951, A5; "Thurgood Marshall to Address State NAACP Meet at Savannah," *Atlanta Daily World*, Nov. 25, 1951, 1; "Harry T. Moore Slaying to Bring Southwide Protest," *Atlanta Daily World*, January 4, 1952, 4; "Birmingham Host City to Region 4 of NCNW Meet," *Atlanta Daily World*, April 25, 1952, 1.

26. "Women's Clubs Give to NAACP," *Negro Star*, August 24, 1951, Vol. 44, No. 17, 1; Hurley letter to Current, August 9, 1951, Papers of the NAACP, Part II, Box C221, Folder 4; "Teachers Give $1600 to NAACP Legal Defense" *Negro Star*, August 22, 1952, Vol. 45, No. 18, 1.

27. "Negro Vote Rejections to Be Basis for Suit," *Atlanta Daily World*, September 12, 1952, 5; "NAACP Wins Fight to Cut Poll Tax in Alabama," *Atlanta Daily World*, December 29, 1953, 1.

28. "Harry T. Moore Slaying to Bring Southwide Protest," *Atlanta Daily World*, January 4, 1952, 4; E. Jackson, "Delegates Pledge to Carry on Moore's Work at NAACP," *Atlanta Daily World*, January 22, 1952, 1; "Delegates Map Plans for Political Action at NAACP Meeting in Fla.," *Atlanta Daily World*, January 20, 1952, 1.

29. "Ala. M No. Targets of New NAACP Suits," *Atlanta Daily World*, Apr. 5, 1951, 2.

30. "NAACP Views 'No Compromise' on School Bias," *Atlanta Daily World*, May 23, 1954, 1; "Week-End Chats" by James A. Hamlett, Jr., *Plaindealer* (Kansas City, KS), July 30, 1954, Vol. 56, No. 11, 1; "Branches of M No. NAACP Threatened," *Atlanta Daily World*, September 16, 1954, p. 1, 7; "55 Delegates From 16 States at NAACP Meet," *Atlanta Daily World*, June 5, 1955; *Crisis*, June-July 1955; "Supreme Court Decision Claims Major Attention at NAACP Meet," *Atlanta Daily World*, June 23, 1955, 1; "Delegates from 30 States Attend Annual NAACP Confab at Atlantic City. NAACP Maps Civil Rights Action for Showdown," Kansas City, Kansas *Plaindealer*, June 24, 1955, vol. 57, No. 25, 1; "Integrated Unit Views Mixing," *The Chicago Defender*, July 30, 1955, 4; "Official Is Vautious on Lynch-Murder Commitment," *Atlanta Daily World*, September 9, 1955, 1; "Raps Dixie for Defying High Court Ruling," *The Chicago Defender*, November 12, 1955, 5.

31. Gleanings, "The Fellowship of the Concerned," Alabama Church Women, Pilgrim Congregational Church, Birmingham, Alabama, May 3, 1955, Southern Regional Council Files, Atlanta University Center Robert W. Woodruff Library Archives, Hurley-FOC Alabama, 1955 - reel196, doc462–466, 2.

32. Gleanings, "The Fellowship of the Concerned," 2–3.

33. Gleanings, "The Fellowship of the Concerned," 3.

BIBLIOGRAPHY

"Ala. M No. Targets of New NAACP Suits." *Atlanta Daily World*, April 5, 1951.

"Atlantans Ready for State NAACP Meeting at Savannah." *Atlanta Daily World*, December 9, 1951.

"Birmingham Host City to Region 4 of NCNW Meet." *Atlanta Daily World*, April 25, 1952.

"Birmingham Medic Center Tests Ike's Bias Riding." *Atlanta Daily World*, August 20, 1953.

"Branches of M No. NAACP Threatened." *Atlanta Daily World*, September 16, 1954.

"Cincinnati Roundup." *The Chicago Defender*, October 29, 1955.

"Complaints Filed-With ICC Vs. 11 Railroad Companies." *Atlanta Daily World*, December 17, 1953.

Crisis, June-July 1955.

"Delegates from 16 States at NAACP Meet." *Atlanta Daily World*, June 5, 1955.

"Delegates from 30 States Attend Annual NAACP Confab at Atlantic City. NAACP Maps Civil Rights Action for Showdown." Kansas *Plaindealer*, June 24, 1955.

"Delegates Map Plans for Political Action at NAACP Meeting in Fla.," *Atlanta Daily World*, January 20, 1952.

"Establish Temporary NAACP Headquarters in Southeast." *Atlanta Daily World*, March 27, 1951.

"The Fellowship of the Concerned," *Gleanings*, Alabama Church Women, Pilgrim Congregational Church, Birmingham, AL, May 3, 1955, Southern Regional Council Files, Atlanta University Center Robert W. Woodruff Library Archives, Hurley-FOC Alabama,1955 - reel196, doc462–466.

"Form Florida Committee for Groveland Defense." *Negro Star*, August 17, 1951.

Gordon, Lewis R., Annie Menzel, George Shulman, and Jasmine Syedullah. "Critical Exchange: Afro Pessimism." *Contemporary Political Theory* 17, 1 (Feb 2018): 105–37.

Hamlett, Jr., James A. "Week-End Chats." *Plaindealer* (Kansas City, Kansas), July 30, 1954.

"Harry T. Moore Slaying to Bring Southwide Protest." *Atlanta Daily World*, January 4, 1952.

Hicks, James. "'Forget Emmett Till,' Marshall Tells 500; Bares Plan for Action." *Baltimore Afro-American*, October 8, 1955.

Hicks, Jimmy. "Unbelievable! Jimmy Hicks' Inside Story of Lynch Trial." (second in a series of four) *Baltimore Afro-American*, October 15, 1955.

Higginbotham, Evelyn Brooks. *Righteous Discontent: The Women's Movement in the Black Baptist Church, 1880–1920.* Cambridge: Harvard University Press, 1993.

Hine, Darlene Clark. "Rape and the Inner Lives of Black Women in the Middle: Preliminary Thoughts on the Culture of Dissemblance" *Signs* 14, No. 4 (Summer 1989): 912–20.

hooks, bell. *Yearning: Race, Gender, and Cultural Politics*. Boston: South End, 1991.

Hurley, Ruby to Gloster Current. August 9, 1951. Papers of the NAACP, Part II, Box C221, Folder 4.

"Indignation Still High Over Till Lynching." *Baltimore Afro-American*, November 5, 1955.

"Integrated Unit Views Mixing." *The Chicago Defender*, July 30, 1955.

Jackson, E. O. "Delegates Pledge to Carry on Moore's Work at NAACP." *Atlanta Daily World*, January 22, 1952.

Jones, William. *Is God a White Racist? A Preamble to Black Theology*. Boston: Beacon, 1973.

Kruse, Kevin M. "The Paradox of Massive Resistance: Political Conformity and Chaos in the Aftermath of Brown v. Board of Education." *Saint Louis University Law Journal* 48, no. 3 (Spring 2004): 1009–35.

Long, Charles H. *Ellipsis: The Collected Writings of Charles H. Long: Ellipsis.* London, New York: Bloomsbury, 2018.

Long, Charles H. *Significations: Signs, Symbols, and Images in the Interpretation of Religion.* Colorado: The Davies Group, Publishers, 1999.

"Lynch Case Verdict Stirs Whole Nation." *Baltimore Afro-American,* October 8, 1955.

"Lynching in Mississippi." *The Chicago Defender,* May 21, 1955.

Mead, Sidney E. *The Lively Experiment: The Shaping of Christianity in America.* New York: Harper & Row, 1963.

"Memorial Services Held for Pastor." *Atlanta Daily World,* May 31, 1955.

"Mississippi." *The Chicago Defender,* May 14, 1955.

"Mississippi Muggings." *The Chicago Defender,* April 5, 1952.

"Most Militant Negro Woman in the South." *Jet,* October 6, 1955.

Mrs. Ruby Hurley, Director, Southeastern Regional Office of the National Association for the Advancement of Colored People. Recorded Interview by John H. Britton, The Civil Rights Documentation Project, Atlanta, Georgia, January 26, 1968. The Moorland-Spingarn Research Center, Howard University, Washington, District of Columbia.

"NAACP Asks Probe of Florida Posse Killing." *Negro Star,* September 5, 1951.

"NAACP Opens Attack on Segregation in Travel." *Wichita Post-Observer,* December 18, 1953.

"NAACP Pushes Opposition to Red Cross' 'Blood Bank,'" *Atlanta Daily World,* Sep 28, 1951.

"NAACP Secures Conviction of White Man in Alabama Rape." *Negro Star,* March 21, 1952.

"NAACP State Meet Set for Dec. 7." *Atlanta Daily World,* October 14, 1951.

"NAACP Urges U.S. Action in M No. 'Reign of Terror.'" *Baltimore Afro-American,* September 17, 1955.

"NAACP Views 'No Compromise' on School Bias." *Atlanta Daily World,* May 23, 1954.

"NAACP Wins Fight to Cut Poll Tax in Alabama." *Atlanta Daily World,* December 29, 1953.

Nash, Diane. "Inside the Sit-ins and Freedom Rides: Testimony of a Southern Student" in *The New Negro,* edited by Matthew H. Ahmann, 43–62. Notre Dame: Fides, 1961.

"Negro Vote Rejections to Be Basis for Suit." *Atlanta Daily World,* September 12, 1952.

North Georgia Conference of United Methodist Women, *A Story Not Yet Over—The Journey: United Methodist Women in North Georgia,* 1992, Volume II. Atlanta: North Georgia Conference of United Methodist Women, 1992.

"Official Is Vautious on Lynch-Murder Commitment." *Atlanta Daily World,* September 9, 1955.

Quashe, Kevin. *The Sovereignty of Quiet: Beyond Resistance in Black Culture*. New Brunswick, NJ: Rutgers University Press, 2012.

"Raps Dixie for Defying High Court Ruling." *The Chicago Defender*, November 12, 1955.

"'Ready for Hospital'—Says Emmett Till's Mother." *Baltimore Afro-American*, November 19, 1955.

"Roy Wilkins Address to Climate Big State Wide NAACP Rally in Alabama." *The Chicago Defender*, March 31, 1951.

Sullivan, Patricia. *Lift Every Voice: The NAACP in the Making of the Civil Rights Movement*. New York: The New Press, 2009.

"Supreme Court Decision Claims Major Attention at NAACP Meet." *Atlanta Daily World*, June 23, 1955.

"Teachers Give $1600 to NAACP Legal Defense." *Negro Star*, August 22, 1952.

"Thurgood Marshall to Address State NAACP Meet at Savannah." *Atlanta Daily World*, November 25, 1951.

"Ware Urges NAACP to Push Citizenship Drive." *Atlanta Daily World*, June 12, 1951.

"Warn Army of Tension at Air Base." *The Chicago Defender*, August 2, 1952.

Wimbush, Vincent L. "'Everything about Me Was Magic': The Black-Fleshed and the Making and Management of Modernities." Opening Address, Emory-Institute for Signifying Scriptures Symposium, November 3, 2021.

"Women's Clubs Give to NAACP." *Negro Star*, August 24, 1951.

Chapter 10

Olaudah Equiano or Gustavus Vassa and Oluale Kossola or Cudjo Lewis

History Writing and the Masquerade

Marla Frederick

"Masquerade: Scripturalizing Modernities through Black Flesh," a unique Exhibition by Vincent Wimbush, constitutes a distinct set of pieces that ask us to consider the work of masquerade in the making of the modern subject.[1] Told through the prism of *The Interesting Narrative of the Life of Olaudah Equiano, or Gustavus Vassa, The African. Written by Himself,* first published in 1789, the exhibit offers an important challenge for the reader to consider the concept of Masquerade:[2] Wimbush's five stages of the Exhibition—that move us from representations of Africa, to white men's acts of writing, to the violence that is "scripturalization," to the meaning of religious conversion and finally the need to mask and unmask as an ongoing character of the modernization process—are interesting, though troubling reminders of the long consequences of European colonialism. The Exhibition aims to "open a wide and provocative window onto the universal phenomenon of masquerade . . . with scripturalization/-izing (or hyper-signification) of black flesh/blackface as one of its most persistent and disturbing modern practices and ideologies."[3] In numerous ways this Exhibition resonates with another text about another African enslaved in the Americas, Kossola, or Cudjo Lewis, whose story is the subject of Zora Neale Hurston's *Barracoon: The Story of the Last "Black Cargo."*[4] In provocative ways these two texts speak to the problems of modernity and the subjects upon which such a concept is built.

First, their stories underscore how the writing of the narrative, or scripturalizing, stands key to the making of modern subjects, particularly those dis-
possessed of learning and for whom questions persist about their intellectual
abilities. Equiano's Narrative, written "By Himself" and Kossola's story told
to Hurston offer different points of departure, even as questions consistently
remain about the text of those whose narratives are "written by themselves."
Secondly, at the same time, the ways in which Equiano writes himself into
history and the ways in which Kossola is written into history are different.
One is a self-writing subject with a first person "I" persona while the latter is
the subject of third person analysis. Finally, the reception of both texts point
to the politics of scripturalization.

MAKING A MODERN SUBJECT

The names themselves tell a story—*Olaudah Equiano or Gustavus Vassa*
/ Oluale Kossola or Cudjo Lewis. The changes from the names related to
their homelands—first names Olaudah and Oluale—to names forced upon
them—Gustavus and Cudjo; and surnames Vassa and Lewis reflect complex
situations and identity formation. The two individuals were (re)named by
those whose pens held the power of ownership and categorization. Gustavus,
if we understand that as his birth name, had already been given two other
names, biblical references indeed, Michael and Jacob, before being renamed
Gustavus. The two men's stories are similar though different.

Wimbush points out that Equiano died in "1797 as a man of some notoriety
and wealth and influence," while Kossola, or Cudjo Lewis, as he came to
be called in the Americas, died in a homeland not of his choosing in an area
called "African Town," now named Plateau, AL.[5] He died poor, desolate and
hoping only that someone might one day recognize him and reconnect him
with his homeland or in the very least that someone like Zora Neal Hurston
might write his story into history. After the official end of the transatlantic
slave trade, Kossola was "brought to the US (illegally) aboard the Clotilda
to Mobile, AL in 1859." He was "born circa 1841, in the town of Bante, the
home to the Isha subgroup of the Yoruba people of West Africa.[6] Kossola
worked on a plantation in Alabama until Emancipation and then sharecropped
along with other freed people. Zora Neale Hurston first met him in 1927 and
interviewed him as [the last African slave in the US.] The differences and
similarities between Equiano and Kossola are in some ways stark and speak
to the power of masquerade and the modern subject.

Both captured and both enslaved, their stories are two of the few remaining
ones of the over 15 million enslaved persons whose lives were stolen during
the Transatlantic Holocaust. Captured, as he tells the story, in his homeland

in Southern Nigeria, Equiano is then shipped to the new world, with transnational migrating points between Africa, the US, the Caribbean, Europe and South America. His is a transnational story of enslavement and freedom, written into view. Published eight times before his death and twice the decade after his death, Equiano's autobiography, "combines (in unequal parts) slave narrative, sea yarn, military adventure, ethnographic reportage, historical fiction, travelogue, picaresque saga, sentimental novel, allegory, tall tale, pastoral origins myth, gothic romance, conversion tale, and abolitionist tract, with different features coming to the fore at different times, and the mood vacillating accordingly," as literary scholar Cathy Cohen writes.[7] Equiano died a man of means, known throughout Europe for his abolitionist work; Kossola died relatively unknown, but for the story that Hurston would tell. The writing of their stories, the process of scripturalization becomes central to how we understand them and the politics of the modernity their stories both help to create and illuminate.

First- and Third-Person Subjects

How one sees oneself and how another reads one can often reflect different narratives of the same person. As Wimbush explains, "such constructed-ness includes ongoing mimetic racialization practices and ideologies (scripturalization), which in turn reflect types or stages of enslavement, resistance, complex subjectivization." Equiano through autobiography has an opportunity to narrate the stories that he wants his readers to know about him, all while marking his own self as modernized. Kossola, on the other hand, is written into history by Hurston at a time when Hurston herself is under suspicion by the broader public. She has a wealthy white patron, named Charlotte Mason, who encourages Hurston to gather as much black folklore as possible. Hurston is an anthropologist and folklorist who writes subjects as they are, not as they "should be." In giving voice to Kossola, Hurston is writing against what she sees as the dominance of European voices in telling the stories of black people. "All these words from the seller, but not one word from the sold. The Kings and Captains whose words moved ships. But not one word from the cargo" her story laments.[8] Kossola's story will change that. Yet, Hurston's words prove problematic for her early mid-twentieth century audience.

In relaying Kossola's story Hurston uses his dialect and refuses to censor the details of his narrative, thumbing her nose at the presses that insist she use "language rather than dialect." This propensity toward unvarnished truth makes those who support her uncertain and it threatens the balance of Hurston's livelihood. Her candor, ultimately, renders *Barracoon* unpublishable during Hurston's lifetime. While she gathered the story in 1927 and worked diligently over the years to publish it, she could never find a publishing home for the story. It was not the neat story of black triumph that went with uplift biographies, narratives that told of the possibilities of modernity and the strength of the new modern subject. Hurston's writings were different.

She listened to Lewis and wrote the stories as told to her, without filter, a type of anti-mask. Kossola is stolen from Africa, aided by the Dahomian tribe that came one night and slaughtered and captured his entire village—placing the heads of the conquered leaders on sticks and marching out of the village with the captured. Kossola is a man of broken English, who is betwixt and between his homeland of Africa and the Americas. Upon meeting him, Hurston says that she first wants to know "how you feel today?"[9] After a muted silence, Kossola responds,

> "I thank God I on prayin' groun' and in a Bible country." "But didn't you have a God back in Africa" Hurston asks. His head drops "between his hands and the tears spring fresh. . . . 'Excusee me I cry. I can't help it when I hear de name call. Oh, Lor. I no see Afficky soil no mo!'" Another long silence, Then, "How come you astee me ain' we had no God back dere in Afficky?" "Because you said 'thank God you were on praying ground and in a Bible country.'" 'Yeah, in Afficky we always know dere was a God; he name Alahua, but po' Affickans we cain readee de Bible, so we doan know God got a Son. We ain' ignant—we jes doan know.'"[10]

For Wimbush, "the religious conversion," he explains in examining Equiano's life story, "is metonymic of the larger ongoing attempt on the part of this particular black-fleshed person to be "saved" within/into white men's world. Such attempts on the part of many if not most in the Black Atlantic worlds, Wimbush contends, constitutes a "layered and complex history—of representations, resistance, flight, accommodation, survival—all masquerade." Kossola is converted into the white man's religion in the US, but as an extension of what he has already experienced in Africa. The text, for Kossola, offers new pieces of an already existing puzzle. At the same time, his affection toward this experience and the reading of this new text append to all the ways that black-fleshed persons are "'saved' within/into white men's worlds," and exposed to the "magic" of these new "talking books." Rebuffing the assumptions of African ignorance, Kossola explains, "We ain't ignant—we jes doan know.'" As Wimbush explains in his introduction to this text, "religious conversion must no longer be taken flatly or as something obvious and simple. Because it takes place in the world that all experience in time and space the business of 'conversion' must be interpreted as part of the dynamics of negotiation of the dominant."[11] It is this "negotiation of the dominant" even in the telling of Kossola's story and in the scripturalization that attends the very writing and reading of the Bible, that raises questions about to what extent the subject possesses agency even in and through his "salvation" experience. The faith experience in the context of slavery and oppression is indeed layered to the point that one must ask how do we understand the agency or lack thereof of enslaved subjects in the conversion process? To what extent does belief reflect the earnest desire of an individual's spiritual awakening and to what extent does it serve the larger end of accommodating the expectations of a larger white world? Kudjo's simple rebuttle, "We ain't ignant," demonstrates his investment in asserting his agency, while at the same time notifying the listener (Hurston) and her would be audience that their interpretations of him are but partial truths.

RECEPTION OF SCRIPTURALIZED AFRICA

"Reading *Barracoon*, one understands immediately the problem many black people, years ago, especially black intellectuals and political leaders, had with it," writes Alice Walker in her forward to the book.[12] For black leaders in the US anxious to uphold the possibility of black assimilation into American society in the mid-century, Hurston's works were problematic at best. She advocated for a type of scripturalization that marked stories candidly and transparently, telling of slave trading Africans and head-hunting encounters with Dahomian warriors with the broken English of Kossola, and his both assimilated and unassimilated life. "It resolutely records the atrocities African peoples inflicted on each other, long before shackled Africans, traumatized, ill, disoriented, starved, arrived on ships as 'black cargo' in the hellish West."[13]

And, yet this is the type of scripturalizing for which Hurston is known. With debates between sociologists and anthropologists raging in the mid-twentieth century, the challenge was whose image of the Negro would prevail. Hurston is of the school of cultural specificity scholars, as anthropologist Lee Baker describes them, those who want to tell black history in transparent fashion, without editing.[14] They argued that cultures were different and "specific" not in hierarchical relationship to one another. It is a school of black anthropologists and folklorists like Hurston, Arthur Fauset, Irene Diggs and Katherine Dunham, those who tried to carve out an African American culture through folklore, advancing Herskovitsian notions of African cultural retentions, and finding redemption in the stories of Africa, believing that culture at its best is relative. Those whom Baker calls the "cultural legitimacy" scholars are ever concerned not only about telling the story, scripturalizing, but explaining it in a way that "assumed that a large percentage of African Americans deviated from American cultural and behavioral standards."[15]

According to sociologists such as Ira Reid, E. Franklin Frazier, Charles Johnson, Kelly Miller and George Edmond Haynes these deviations "were inevitable responses to deleterious environmental conditions, racial discrimination, and the heritage of slavery."[16] They were largely Black sociologists, trained in the Robert Park school of sociology, which strove to prove, against prevailing logics, that Blacks, though lacking in certain Western cultural norms due to slavery, could assimilate into white American society. Blacks would be known, not for their connection to Africa, but rather for their ability to assimilate into Western, European culture. It was this narration of their assimilability that made them the more desirable modern subjects. Writing the subject into being thus determined to what extent the subject gained access to the Western World. In arguing before the Supreme Court, Thurgood Marshall rejected anthropological views on culture and embraced sociological views that aimed to show that African Americans could indeed integrate into American society if given equitable access to schooling through the Brown decision.[17]

If, as Wimbush suggests in his first stage, "Knowing the World through Masquerade," Equiano's portrait of Africa affirms the images of Africa that make for a respectable modern subject, he does so by proclaiming that "We are a nation of dancers, musicians, and poets." The remaking of Africa is as a land of possibility in the writings of Equiano; but it is remade as a land of tribal warfare in the writings of Hurston. There is here a sharp contrast of views. The modern subject narrated by Equiano offers the subject an opportunity to enter modernity, not as backwards and unlearned, but as a subject of possibility, one open to a new fashioning of the self. According to Wimbush, *"The Interesting Narrative* was successful beyond other such narratives for several reasons, not least because as it was mostly directed toward abolitionist colleagues it was so much a masquerade, a bravura performance, of modern subjectivity."[18] For Cudjo Lewis, however, the story of the Dahomey's quest for blood, the raid of the village in which Cudjo lived, the placing on sticks the heads of those captured—these actions all reinforced in Hurston's era the idea of Africa as backward and uncivilized. While Equiano is able to sell his more refined narrative of Africa and the development of his human subject for money, Hurston struggled mightily to find publishers willing to purchase and distribute the story of Lewis. This reality in itself meant that Lewis, like Hurston, would die penniless and virtually unknown.

The lives of Olaudah Equiano or Gustavus Vassa and Kossola or Cudjo Lewis speak most poignantly to the making of the modern subject, with the masquerade of scripturalization as apt theory for understanding the dynamics and the results. Their performative stance for audiences of Whites as well as Blacks speak to the ongoing processes of masquerading that make for complex configurations and reconfigurations of the self. Kossola/Lewis speaks through Hurston, an interpreter presumably working against the social pressure to masquerade, as Paul Laurence Dunbar put it, to "Wear the Mask that grins and lies" all the while scripturalizing the subject at his and her own social cost.[19] Olaudah Equiano's story indeed opens up opportunities for us to read and re-read these narratives that speak loudly in their time and in ours about the power and constraints of representation.

Wimbush's invitation for us to push beyond an analysis of classic categories of race and religion to consider "a different order of and orientation to thinking; with the disruption or destabilization, if not explosion, of standing categories and social-cultural practices, including, but not limited to academic ones—all such that shape and define our world"[20] is a large and necessary task. It compels us to move into a broader, more in-depth study of the very processes that give rise to the categories that order our lives, the ones we, in the present, co-constitute. Masquerade, scripturalization—the terms which he creates for this very process are important, if not ironic, in the work of reorienting our understanding of words and their power. Even as new words give voice to processes of exclusion and domination, they also provide the means through which others may become disposed. Such ironies cause us to question not only the writing of history but the meanings attached to the writing of history and the politics of those realities. Wimbush's analysis thus raises important questions not only about the categories that have been created, but also about the potentialities extant in the ever-present question, "where do we go from here?"

NOTES

1. *Masquerade: Scripturalizing Modernities through Black Flesh*, http://digital.pitts.emory.edu/s/masquerade/page/intro.

2. Ibid. The five stages include *Stage I*—Knowing the World through/as Masquerade; *Stage II*—Transfer of Learning and Power; *Stage III*—White Violence on Black Flesh; *Stage IV*—Black Mimetic Translation of Scripturalization; and *Stage V*—Signifying on Mimetic Scripturalization of Black Flesh.

3. "Orientation to Exhibition," http://digital.pitts.emory.edu/s/masquerade/page/about.

4. Zora Neale Hurston, *Barracoon: The Story of the Last "Black Cargo."* New York: HarperCollins, 2018.

5. Ibid., 15.

6. Ibid., xv.

7. Cathy N. Davidson Source: *NOVEL: A Forum on Fiction* Vol. 40, No. 1/2, The Early American Novel (Fall 2006–Spring 2007), 18–51, 19.

8. Hurston, 6.

9. Hurston, 18.

10. Ibid.
11. Wimbush, Introduction, "Everything about Me Was Magic," 21.
12. Hurston, x.
13. Ibid.
14. Lee Baker, *From Savage to Negro: Anthropology and the Construction of Race, 1896–1954.* Berkeley: University of California Press, 1998.
15. Baker, 178.
16. Baker, 178.
17. Baker, 178.
18. https://digital.pitts.emory.edu/s/masquerade/page/about
19. Paul Laurence Dunbar, "We Wear the Mask," from *The Black Writers of America: A Comprehensive Anthology,* (New York: Macmillan Publishing Company, 1972) p. 352.
20. Wimbush, Introduction, 22.

BIBLIOGRAPHY

Davidson, Cathy N. *NOVEL: A Forum on Fiction,* Vol. 40, No. 1/2, The Early American Novel (Fall 2006–Spring 2007), pp. 18–51.

Baker, Lee. *From Savage to Negro: Anthropology and the Construction of Race, 1896–1954.* Berkeley: University of California Press, 1998.

Hurston, Zora Neale Hurston. *Barracoon: The Story of the Last "Black Cargo."* New York: HarperCollins, 2018.

Wimbush, Vincent L. "Introduction: 'Everything about Me Was Magic': The Black-Fleshed and the Making and Management of Modernities." In *Masquerade: Scripturalizing Modernities through Black Flesh.* Edited by Vincent L. Wimbush. Lanham, MD: Lexington Books/Fortress Academic, 2023.

Wimbush, Vincent. *Masquerade: Scripturalizing Modernities through Black Flesh.* http://digital.pitts.emory.edu/s/masquerade/page/intro.

Index

Page references for figures are italicized.

About the Editor and Contributors

Vincent L. Wimbush is founding director, The Institute for Signifying Scriptures.

Rachel E. C. Beckley is lecturer, Department of History, University of Kansas, Lawrence.

Cécile Coquet-Mokoko is professor of US cultural history and African American studies, Universite de Versailles Saint-Quentin-en-Yvelines, France.

Marla Frederick is Asa Candler Griggs Professor of Religion and Culture, Candler School of Theology, Emory University.

Miles P. Grier is associate professor, Department of English, Queens College, City University of New York, Flushing.

Jacqueline M. Hidalgo is professor of Latina/o/x studies and of religion, Williams College, Williamstown, MA.

P. Kimberleigh Jordan is lecturer, Department of Philosophy and Religion, Spelman College, Atlanta, GA.

Velma E. Love is associate professor of interdisciplinary studies, The Interdenominational Theological Center, Atlanta, GA.

Carolyn M. Jones Medine is the Inaugural All Shall Be Well Professor in Religion, University of Georgia, Athens, GA.

Rosetta Ross is professor of religion, Spelman College, Atlanta, GA.

Shay Welch is assistant professor of philosophy, Spelman College, Atlanta, GA.